T0198160

# Get the eBook FREE!

(PDF, ePub, Kindle, and liveBook all included)

We believe that once you buy a book from us, you should be able to read it in any format we have available. To get electronic versions of this book at no additional cost to you, purchase and then register this book at the Manning website.

Go to https://www.manning.com/freebook and follow the instructions to complete your pBook registration.

That's it!
Thanks from Manning!

*GraphQL in Action*

# GraphQL in Action

SAMER BUNA

MANNING

SHELTER ISLAND

For online information and ordering of this and other Manning books, please visit
www.manning.com. The publisher offers discounts on this book when ordered in quantity.
For more information, please contact

Special Sales Department
Manning Publications Co.
20 Baldwin Road
PO Box 761
Shelter Island, NY 11964
Email: orders@manning.com

Manning Publications Co.
20 Baldwin Road
PO Box 761
Shelter Island, NY 11964

| | |
|---|---|
| Development editor: | Karen Miller |
| Technical development editor: | Alain Couniot |
| Review editor: | Aleksandar Dragosavljević |
| Production editor: | Deirdre Hiam |
| Copy editor: | Tiffany Taylor |
| Proofreader: | Katie Tennant |
| Technical proofreader: | Valentin Crettaz |
| Typesetter: | Gordan Salinovic |
| Cover designer: | Marija Tudor |

ISBN 9781617295683
Printed in the United States of America

*To my wife, Chalena,*
*for all your unconditional, loving support*

*To my children, Odin, Ally, and Leo,*
*for inspiring me each and every day*

*To my parents, Nemeh and Sharif,*
*for teaching me the value of hard work and always pushing me to the limit*

# brief contents

# contents

*10* **Using GraphQL APIs with Apollo client 293**

# *preface*

GraphQL is a game changer. It immediately grabbed my full attention when I first heard about it back in 2015, when Facebook first announced the project. I've been a frustrated maintainer and user of multiple REST-ish APIs, and hearing how Facebook engineers were trying to solve common data API problems with this new GraphQL language was a clear sign for me to learn about it.

GraphQL has many advantages and disadvantages. It solves many technical problems beautifully; but the best thing about it, in my opinion, is that it greatly improves the communication process between frontend clients and backend services. Not only does GraphQL make communication a lot more efficient for both sides, but it also gives them both a rich, declarative language. GraphQL services can use that language to express what data they can provide, and GraphQL clients can use the language to express what data they need. GraphQL also enables frontend developers to be independent of backend developers, and that in itself is a big deal. Frontend developers get more freedom and a stronger impact on the features of the data APIs they use.

GraphQL is programming-language agnostic. You can create GraphQL services in JavaScript, Java, Ruby, Python, C#, PHP, Go, and many other languages. However, I had to pick a programming language for the project we're building in this book. I chose JavaScript because it is the most popular programming language out there. This does mean you need to be familiar with JavaScript to get the best value out of this book, including modern JavaScript (ECMAScript 2015+) and the Node.js runtime. The book's project also uses the React JavaScript library in chapters 9 and 10, but all the React code is provided and explained where needed.

There is no shortage of learning resources for GraphQL, but what I noticed while learning it is a scarcity of practical, non-abstract materials. That is why I designed this book to be a practical reference for working with a full-stack GraphQL-based project.

This book took me a long time to produce. I researched and developed the ideal flow for learning the many concepts covered in the book. I also provide many resources to make your learning experience as smooth as possible. The book features a GitHub repository, and progress milestones throughout the book have Git branches that you can check out. I hope this will help you better follow the code and allow you to restart at any point.

Learning GraphQL was one of the best time investments I have ever made. GraphQL allows me to implement ideas faster, and it makes my projects perform better. Working with GraphQL is simply a more pleasant experience overall. I hope this book will enable you to make that investment and join in on all the joy we GraphQL lovers are having in the GraphQL ecosystem of excellence.

## *Other online resources*

To keep the content of the book tightly focused on GraphQL, I provide external links to articles and other resources to help you expand on some concepts and understand them in more detail if you need to.

If you get stuck implementing this book examples, web search is your best friend. It's highly likely that someone else has experienced the problems that you might experience, asked about it on sites like Stack Overflow, and received an answer.

There are many video training courses on GraphQL on the internet. Pluralsight has many, including one of my own. I also have many video resources at jsComplete.com, many of which feature working with GraphQL. You can also join our Slack help channel at jscomplete.com/help and ask the community there any GraphQL or JavaScript questions.

# *about the author*

**SAMER BUNA** has over 20 years of practical experience in designing, implementing, and optimizing software. He has worked in several industries, including real estate, government, education, and publications.

Samer has authored several technical books and online courses about JavaScript, Node.js, React.js, GraphQL, and more. You can find his courses on Pluralsight, LinkedIn Learning, O'Reilly, Manning, and other sites. He recently created the jsComplete.com platform to offer interactive and adaptive learning strategies for code education.

You can find Samer on Twitter and other social networks under the handle @samerbuna.

# *about the cover illustration*

The figure on the cover of *GraphQL in Action* is captioned "Jardinière Française," or French farmer. The illustration is taken from a collection of dress costumes from various countries by Jacques Grasset de Saint-Sauveur (1757-1810), titled *Costumes de Différents Pays*, published in France in 1797. Each illustration is finely drawn and colored by hand. The rich variety of Grasset de Saint-Sauveur's collection reminds us vividly of how culturally apart the world's towns and regions were just 200 years ago. Isolated from each other, people spoke different dialects and languages. In the streets or in the countryside, it was easy to identify where they lived and what their trade or station in life was just by their dress.

The way we dress has changed since then, and the diversity by region, so rich at the time, has faded away. It is now hard to tell apart the inhabitants of different continents, let alone different towns, regions, or countries. Perhaps we have traded cultural diversity for a more varied personal life—certainly, for a more varied and fast-paced technological life.

At a time when it is hard to tell one computer book from another, Manning celebrates the inventiveness and initiative of the computer business with book covers based on the rich diversity of regional life of two centuries ago, brought back to life by Grasset de Saint-Sauveur's pictures.

# *Part 1*

# *Exploring GraphQL*

Do you use Yelp, Shopify, Coursera, or GitHub? If so, you have consumed a GraphQL API! These are just a few of the companies that adopted GraphQL as their data communication solution.

The first part of this book answers the why, what, and how questions about GraphQL. The word *GraphQL* can mean different things to different people, but it is fundamentally a "language" that API consumers can use to ask for data. This part will get you comfortable with the fundamentals of that language.

In chapter 1, you'll learn what exactly GraphQL is, what problems it solves, and what problems it introduces. You'll explore the design concepts behind it and how it is different from the alternatives, like REST APIs.

Chapter 2 explores GraphQL's feature-rich interactive playground. This playground takes advantage of GraphQL's introspective power, which you can use to explore what you can do with GraphQL and to write and test GraphQL requests. You'll use this playground to explore examples of GraphQL queries and mutations. You'll learn about the fundamental parts of a GraphQL request, and you'll test practical examples from the GitHub GraphQL API.

Chapter 3 introduces you to the many built-in features of the GraphQL language that let you customize and organize data requests and responses. You'll learn about fields and arguments, aliases, directives, fragments, interfaces, and unions.

# *Introduction to GraphQL*

*1*

**This chapter covers**

- Understanding GraphQL and the design concepts behind it
- How GraphQL differs from alternatives like REST APIs
- Understanding the language used by GraphQL clients and services
- Understanding the advantages and disadvantages of GraphQL

Necessity is the mother of invention. The product that inspired the creation of GraphQL was invented at Facebook because the company needed to solve many technical issues with its mobile application. However, I think GraphQL became so popular so fast not because it solves technical problems but rather because it solves communication problems.

Communication is hard. Improving our communication skills makes our lives better on many levels. Similarly, improving the communication between the different parts of a software application makes that application easier to understand, develop, maintain, and scale.

That's why I think GraphQL is a game changer. It changes the game of how the different "ends" of a software application (frontend and backend) communicate with each other. It gives them equal power, makes them independent of each other, decouples their communication process from its underlying technical transport channel, and introduces a rich new language in a place where the common previously spoken language was limited to a few words.

GraphQL powers many applications at Facebook today, including the main web application at facebook.com, the Facebook mobile application, and Instagram. Developers' interest in GraphQL is very clear, and GraphQL's adoption is growing fast. Besides Facebook, GraphQL is used in many other major web and mobile applications like GitHub, Airbnb, Yelp, Pinterest, Twitter, *New York Times*, Coursera, and Shopify. Given that GraphQL is a young technology, this is an impressive list.

In this first chapter, let's learn what GraphQL is, what problems it solves, and what problems it introduces.

## 1.1   *What is GraphQL?*

The word *graph* in GraphQL comes from the fact that the best way to represent data in the real world is with a graph-like data structure. If you analyze any data model, big or small, you'll always find it to be a graph of objects with many relations between them.

That was the first "Aha!" moment for me when I started learning about GraphQL. Why think of data in terms of resources (in URLs) or tables when you can think of it naturally as a graph?

Note that the *graph* in GraphQL does not mean that GraphQL can only be used with a "graph database." You can have a document database (like MongoDB) or a relational database (like PostgreSQL) and use GraphQL to represent your API data in a graph-like structure.

The *QL* in GraphQL might be a bit confusing, though. Yes, GraphQL is a query language for data APIs, but that's only from the perspective of the frontend consumer of those data APIs. GraphQL is also a runtime layer that needs to be implemented on the backend, and that layer is what makes the frontend consumer able to use the new language.

The GraphQL language is designed to be declarative, flexible, and efficient. Developers of data API consumers (like mobile and web applications) can use that language to request the data they need in a language close to how they think about data in their heads instead of a language related to how the data is stored or how data relations are implemented.

On the backend, a GraphQL-based stack needs a runtime. That runtime provides a structure for servers to describe the data to be exposed in their APIs. This structure is what we call a *schema* in the GraphQL world. An API consumer can then use the GraphQL language to construct a text request representing their exact data needs.

The client sends that text request to the API service through a transport channel (for example, HTTPS). The GraphQL runtime layer accepts the text request, communicates with other services in the backend stack to put together a suitable data response, and then sends that data back to the consumer in a format like JSON. Figure 1.1 summarizes the dynamics of this communication.

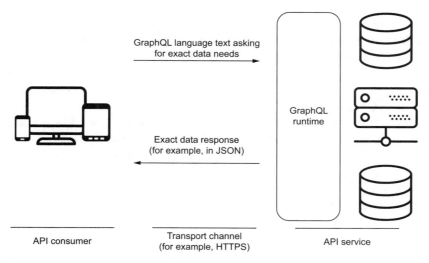

**Figure 1.1   GraphQL is a language and a runtime.**

## Using GraphQL with other libraries

GraphQL is not specific to any backend or frontend framework, technical stack, or database. It can be used in any frontend environment, on any backend platform, and with any database engine. You can use it on any transport channel and make it use any data representation format.

In frontend web or mobile applications, you can use GraphQL by making direct Ajax calls to a GraphQL server or with a client like Apollo or Relay (which will make the Ajax request on your behalf). You can use a library like React (or React Native) to manage how your views use the data coming from a GraphQL service, but you can also do that with APIs native to their UI environments (like the DOM API or native iOS components).

Although you do not need React, Apollo, or Relay to use GraphQL in your applications, these libraries add more value to how you can use GraphQL APIs without having to do complex data management tasks.

### 1.1.1   The big picture

In general, an API is an interface that enables communication between multiple components in an application. For example, an API can enable the communication that

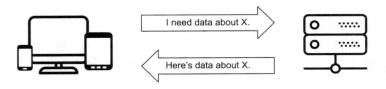

Figure 1.2   The big picture of data APIs

needs to happen between a web client and a database server. The client tells the server what data it needs, and the server fulfills the client's requirement with objects representing the data the client asked for (figure 1.2).

There are different types of APIs, and every big application needs them. For GraphQL, we are specifically talking about the API type used to read and modify data, which is usually referred to as a *data API*.

GraphQL is one option out of many that can be used to provide applications with programmable interfaces to read and modify the data the applications need from data services. Other options include REST, SOAP, XML, and even SQL itself.

SQL (Structured Query Language) might be directly compared to GraphQL because *QL* is in both names, after all. Both SQL and GraphQL provide a language to query data schemas. They can both be used to read and modify data. For example, if we have a table of data about a company's employees, the following is an example SQL statement to read data about the employees in one department.

**Listing 1.1   SQL statement for querying**

```
SELECT id, first_name, last_name, email, birth_date, hire_date
FROM employees
WHERE department = 'ENGINEERING'
```

Here is another example SQL statement that inserts data for a new employee.

**Listing 1.2   SQL statement for mutating**

```
INSERT INTO employees (first_name, last_name, email, birth_date, hire_date)
VALUES ('Jane', 'Doe', 'jane@doe.name', '01/01/1990', '01/01/2020')
```

You can use SQL to communicate data operations as we did in listings 1.1 and 1.2. The database servers to which these SQL statements are sent may support different formats for their responses. Each SQL operation type has a different response. A SELECT operation might return a single row or multiple rows. An INSERT operation might return just a confirmation, the inserted rows, or an error response.

**TIP**   Although SQL could be used directly by mobile and web applications to communicate data requirements, it would not be a good language for that purpose. SQL is simply too powerful and too flexible, and it would introduce many challenges. For example, exposing your exact database structure publicly would be a significant security problem. You can put SQL behind another service layer, but that means you need to create a parser and analyzer to perform operations on users' SQL queries before sending them to the database. That parser/analyzer is something you get out of the box with any GraphQL server implementation.

While most relational databases directly support SQL, GraphQL is its own thing. GraphQL needs a runtime service. You cannot just start querying databases using the GraphQL query language (at least, not yet). You need to use a service layer that supports GraphQL or implement one yourself.

**TIP** Some databases allow their clients to use GraphQL to query them directly. An example is Dgraph (az.dev/dgraph).

JSON is a language that can be used to communicate data. Here is a JSON object that can represent Jane's data.

**Listing 1.3   JSON object representing data**

```
{
  "data": {
    "employee":{
      "id": 42,
      "name": "Jane Doe",
      "email": "jane@doe.name",
      "birthDate": "01/01/1990",
      "hireDate": "01/01/2020"
    }
  }
}
```

**NOTE** The data communicated about Jane does not have to use the same structure the database uses to save it. I used camel-case property names, and I combined `first_name` and `last_name` into one `name` field.

JSON is a popular language for communicating data from API servers to client applications. Most of the modern data API servers use JSON to fulfill the data requirements of client applications. GraphQL servers are no exception; JSON is the popular choice to fulfill the requirements of GraphQL data requests.

JSON can also be used by client applications to communicate their data requirements to API servers. For example, here is a possible JSON object that communicates the data requirements for the employee object response in listing 1.3.

**Listing 1.4   JSON example for querying**

```
{
  "select": {
    "fields": ["name", "email", "birthDate", "hireDate"],
    "from": "employees",
    "where": {
```

```
      "id": {
        "equals": 42
      }
    }
  }
}
```

GraphQL for client applications is another language they can use to express their data requirements. The following is how the previous data requirement can be expressed with a GraphQL query.

---

**Listing 1.5   GraphQL example of querying**

```
{
  employee(id: 42) {
    name
    email
    birthDate
    hireDate
  }
}
```

The GraphQL query in listing 1.5 represents the same data need as the JSON object in listing 1.4, but as you can see, it has a different and shorter syntax. A GraphQL server can understand this syntax and translate it into something the data storage engine can understand (for example, the GraphQL server might translate the query into SQL statements for a relational database). Then, the GraphQL server can take what the storage engine responds with, translate it into something like JSON or XML, and send it back to the client application.

This is nice because no matter what storage engine(s) you have to deal with, with GraphQL, you make API servers and client applications both work with a universal language for requests and a universal language for responses.

In a nutshell, GraphQL is all about optimizing data communication between a client and a server. This includes the client asking for needed data and communicating that need to the server, and the server preparing a fulfillment for that need and communicating the fulfillment back to the client. GraphQL allows clients to ask for the exact data they need and makes it easier for servers to aggregate data from multiple data storage resources.

At the core of GraphQL is a strong type system that is used to describe data and organize APIs. This type system gives GraphQL many advantages on both the server and client sides. Types ensure that clients ask for only what is possible and provide clear and helpful errors. Clients can use types to minimize any manual parsing of data elements. The GraphQL type system allows for rich features like having an introspective API and being able to build powerful tools for both clients and servers. One of the popular GraphQL tools that relies on this concept is GraphiQL, a feature-rich browser-based editor to explore and test GraphQL requests. You will learn about GraphiQL in the next chapter.

### 1.1.2 GraphQL is a specification

Although Facebook engineers started working on GraphQL in 2012, it was 2015 when they released a public specification document. You can see the current version of this document by navigating to az.dev/graphql-spec; it is maintained by a community of companies and individuals on GitHub. GraphQL is an evolving language, but the specification document was a genius start for the project because it defined standard rules and practices that all implementers of GraphQL runtimes must adhere to. There have been many implementations of GraphQL libraries in many different programming languages, and all of them closely follow the specification document and update their implementations when that document is updated. If you work on a GraphQL project in Ruby and later switch to another project in Scala, the syntax will change, but the rules and practices will remain the same.

You can ultimately find *everything* about the GraphQL language and runtime requirements in the official specification document. It is a bit technical, but you can still learn a lot from it by reading its introductory parts and examples. This book will not cover everything in the document, so I recommend that you skim through it once you are finished reading the book.

The specification document starts by describing the syntax of the GraphQL language. Let's talk about that first.

> **GraphQL server libraries**
>
> Alongside the specification document, Facebook also released a reference implementation library for GraphQL runtimes in JavaScript. JavaScript is the most popular programming language and the one closest to mobile and web applications, which are two of the popular channels where using GraphQL can make a big difference. The reference JavaScript implementation of GraphQL is hosted at az.dev/graphql-js, and it's the one we use in this book. I'll refer to this implementation as *GraphQL.js*.
>
> To see a list of other GraphQL server libraries, check out az.dev/graphql-servers.

### 1.1.3 GraphQL is a language

Though the *Q* (for *query*) is right there in the name, and querying is associated with reading, GraphQL can be used for both reading and modifying data. When you need to read data with GraphQL, you use *queries*; and when you need to modify data, you use *mutations*. Both queries and mutations are part of the GraphQL language.

GraphQL operations are similar to how we use SQL SELECT statements to read data and INSERT, UPDATE, and DELETE statements to modify data. The SQL language has certain rules we must follow. For example, a SELECT statement requires a FROM clause and can optionally have a WHERE clause. Similarly, the GraphQL language has certain rules to follow. For example, a GraphQL query must have a name or be the only query in a request. You will learn about the rules of the GraphQL language in the next few chapters.

---

**GraphQL operations**

Queries represent `READ` operations. Mutations represent `WRITE`-then-`READ` operations. You can think of mutations as queries that have side effects.

In addition to queries and mutations, GraphQL also supports a third request type called a *subscription*, used for real-time data monitoring requests. Subscriptions represent continuous `READ` operations. Mutations usually trigger events for subscriptions.

GraphQL subscriptions require the use of a data-transport channel that supports continuous pushing of data. That's usually done with WebSockets for web applications.

---

A query language like GraphQL (or SQL) is different from programming languages like JavaScript and Python. You cannot use the GraphQL language to create user interfaces or perform complex computations. Query languages have more specific use cases, and they often require the use of programming languages to make them work. Nevertheless, I would like you to first think of the query language concept by comparing it to programming languages and even spoken languages like English. This is a very limited comparison, but I think it will help you understand and appreciate a few things about GraphQL.

In general, the evolution of programming languages is making them closer and closer to spoken human languages. Computers used to only understand imperative instructions, and that is why we have been using imperative paradigms to program them. However, computers today are starting to understand declarative paradigms, and we can program them to understand *wishes*. Declarative programming has many advantages (and disadvantages), but what makes it such a good idea is that we always prefer to reason about problems in declarative ways. Declarative thinking is easy for humans.

We can use the English language to declaratively communicate data needs and fulfillments. For example, imagine that John is the client and Jane is the server. Here is an English data communication session:

*John: "Hey Jane, how long does it take sunlight to reach planet Earth?"*

*Jane: "A bit over 8 minutes."*

*John: "How about the light from the moon?"*

*Jane: "A bit under 2 seconds."*

John can also easily ask both questions in one sentence, and Jane can easily answer them both by adding more words to her answer.

When we communicate using the English language, we understand special expressions like "a bit over" and "a bit under." Jane also understands that the incomplete second question is related to the first one. Computers, on the other hand, are not very good (yet) at understanding things from the context. They need more structure.

GraphQL is just another declarative language that John and Jane can use for their data communication session. It is not as good as the English language, but it is a structured language that computers can easily parse and use. For example, here's a hypothetical single GraphQL query that represents both of John's questions to Jane.

---

**Listing 1.6  John's questions to Jane in GraphQL**

```
{
  timeLightNeedsToTravel(toPlanet: "Earth") {
    fromTheSun: from(star: "Sun")
    fromTheMoon: from(moon: "Moon")
  }
}
```

---

The example GraphQL request in listing 1.6 uses a few of the GraphQL language parts like fields (`timeLightNeedsToTravel` and `from`), parameters (`toPlanet`, `star`, and `moon`), and aliases (`fromTheSun` and `fromTheMoon`). These are like verbs and nouns in English. You will learn about all the syntax parts that you can use in GraphQL requests in chapters 2 and 3.

### 1.1.4  GraphQL is a service

If we teach a client application to speak the GraphQL language, it will be able to communicate any data requirements to a backend data service that also speaks GraphQL. To teach a data service to speak GraphQL, you implement a runtime layer and expose that layer to the clients that want to communicate with the service. Think of this layer on the server side as simply a translator of the GraphQL language, or a GraphQL-speaking agent that represents the data service. GraphQL is not a storage engine, so it cannot be a solution on its own. This is why you cannot have a server that speaks just GraphQL; you need to implement a translating runtime layer.

A GraphQL service can be written in any programming language, and it can be conceptually split into two major parts, structure and behavior:

- The *structure* is defined with a strongly typed *schema*. A GraphQL schema is like a catalog of all the operations a GraphQL API can handle. It simply represents the capabilities of an API. GraphQL client applications use the schema to know what questions they can ask the service. The *typed* nature of the schema is a core concept in GraphQL. The schema is basically a graph of *fields* that have *types*; this graph represents all the possible data objects that can be read (or updated) through the service.
- The *behavior* is naturally implemented with functions that in the GraphQL world are called *resolver functions*. They represent most of the smart logic behind GraphQL's power and flexibility. Each field in a GraphQL schema is backed by a resolver function. A resolver function defines what data to fetch for its field.

A resolver function represents the instructions on how and where to access raw data. For example, a resolver function might issue a SQL statement to a relational database, read a file's data directly from the operating system, or update some cached data in a document database. A resolver function is directly related to a field in a GraphQL request, and it can represent a single primitive value, an object, or a list of values or objects.

---

**The GraphQL restaurant analogy**

A GraphQL schema is often compared to a restaurant menu. In that analogy, the wait-staff act like instances of the GraphQL API interface. No wonder we use the term *server*!

Table servers take your orders back to the kitchen, which is the core of the API service. You can compare items on the menu to fields in the GraphQL language. If you order a steak, you need to tell your server how you would like it cooked. That's where you can use field arguments:

```
order {
  steak(doneness: MEDIUMWELL)
}
```

Let's say this restaurant is very busy and hired a chef with the sole responsibility of cooking steaks. This chef is the resolver function for the `steak` field!

---

**TIP**  Resolver functions are why GraphQL is often compared to the remote procedure call (RPC) distributed computing concept. GraphQL is essentially a way for clients to invoke remote—resolver—functions.

### AN EXAMPLE OF A SCHEMA AND RESOLVERS

To understand how resolvers work, let's take the query in listing 1.5 (simplified) and assume a client sent it to a GraphQL service.

---

**Listing 1.7   Simplified example query text**

```
query {
  employee(id: 42) {
    name
    email
  }
}
```

The service can receive and parse any request. It then tries to validate the request against its schema. The schema has to support an `employee` field, and that field has to represent an object with an `id` argument, a `name` field, and an `email` field. Fields and arguments must have types in GraphQL. The `id` argument is an integer. The `name` and `email` fields are strings. The `employee` field is a custom type (representing that exact id/name/email structure).

Just like the client-side query language, the GraphQL community standardized a server-side language dedicated to creating GraphQL schema objects. This language is known as the *schema language*. It's often abbreviated SDL (schema definition language) or IDL (interface definition language).

Here's an example to represent the `Employee` type using GraphQL's schema language.

##### Listing 1.8 GraphQL schema language example

```
type Employee(id: Int!) {
  name: String!
  email: String!
}
```

This custom `Employee` type represents the structure of an employee "model." An object of the employee model can be looked up with an integer `id`, and it has `name` and `email` string fields.

The exclamation marks after the types mean they cannot be empty. A client cannot ask for an `employee` field without specifying an `id` argument, and a valid server response to this field must include a `name` string and an `email` string.

> **TIP** The schema language type definitions are like the database CREATE statements used to define tables and other database schema elements.

Using this type, the GraphQL service can conclude that the GraphQL query in listing 1.7 is valid because it matches the supported type structure. The next step is to prepare the data it is asking for. To do that, the GraphQL service traverses the tree of fields in that request and invokes the resolver function associated with each field. It then gathers the data returned by these resolver functions and uses it to form a single response.

This example GraphQL service needs at least three resolver functions: one for the `employee` field, one for the `name` field, and one for the `email` field.

The `employee` field's resolver function might, for example, do a query like SELECT * FROM employees WHERE id = 42. This SQL statement returns all columns available on the `employees` table. Let's say the `employees` table happens to have the following fields: id, first_name, last_name, email, birth_date, and hire_date.

Then the `employee` field's resolver function for employee #42 might return an object like the following.

##### Listing 1.9 Response from the database for employee #42

```
{
  "id": 42,
  "first_name": "Jane",
  "last_name": "Doe",
  "email": "jane@doe.name",
```

```
    "birth_date": "01/01/1990",
    "hire_date": "01/01/2020"
}
```

The GraphQL service continues to traverse the fields in the tree one by one, invoking the resolver function for each field. Each resolver function is passed the result of executing the resolver function of its parent node. So both the `name` and `email` resolver functions receive the object in listing 1.9 (as their first argument).

Let's say we have the following (JavaScript) functions representing the server resolver functions for the `name` and `email` fields:

```
// Resolver functions
const name => (source) => `${source.first_name} ${source.last_name}`;
const email => (source) => source.email;
```

Here, the `source` object is the parent node.

> **TIP**  The `email` resolver function is known as a "trivial" resolver because the `email` field name matches the `email` property name on the parent source object. Some GraphQL implementations (for example, the JavaScript implementation) have built-in trivial resolvers and use them as default resolvers if no resolver is found for a field.

The GraphQL service uses all the responses of these three resolver functions to put together the following single response for the query in listing 1.7.

**Listing 1.10   Example GraphQL response object**

```
{
  data: {
    employee: {
      name: 'Jane Doe',
      email: 'jane@doe.name'
    }
  }
}
```

We'll start to explore how to write custom resolvers in chapter 5.

> **TIP**  GraphQL does not require any specific data serialization format, but JSON is the most popular one. All the examples in this book use the JSON format.

## 1.2    *Why GraphQL?*

GraphQL is not the only—or even the first—technology to encourage creating efficient data APIs. You can use a JSON-based API with a custom query language or implement the Open Data Protocol (OData) on top of a REST API. Experienced backend developers have been creating efficient technologies for data APIs since long before

GraphQL. So why do we need a new technology? If you asked me to answer the "Why GraphQL?" question with a single word, that word would be *standards.*

GraphQL provides comprehensive standards and structures to implement API features in maintainable and scalable ways. GraphQL makes it mandatory for data API servers to publish documentation (the schema) about their capabilities. That schema enables client applications to know everything available for them on these servers. The GraphQL standard schema has to be part of every GraphQL API. Clients can ask the service about its schema using the GraphQL language. We'll see examples in chapter 3.

Other solutions can be made better by adding similar documentation. The unique thing about GraphQL here is that the documentation is part of how you create the API service. You cannot have out-of-date documentation. You cannot forget to document a use case. You cannot offer different ways to use APIs, because you have standards to work with. Most important, you do not need to maintain the documentation of your API separately from that API. GraphQL documentation is built-in, and it's first class.

The mandatory GraphQL schema represents the possibilities and the limits of what can be answered by the GraphQL service. But there is some flexibility in how to use the schema because we are talking about a graph of nodes, and graphs can be traversed using many paths. This flexibility is one of the great benefits of GraphQL because it allows backend and frontend developers to make progress in their projects without needing to constantly coordinate their progress with each other. It basically decouples clients from servers and allows both of them to evolve and scale independently. This enables faster iteration in both frontend and backend products.

I think this standard schema is among the top benefits of GraphQL—but let's talk about the technological benefits of GraphQL as well.

One of the most significant—and perhaps most popular—technological reasons to consider a GraphQL layer between clients and servers is *efficiency.* API clients often need to ask the server about multiple resources, and the API server usually knows how to answer questions about a single resource. As a result, the client ends up having to communicate with the server multiple times to gather all the data it needs (figure 1.3).

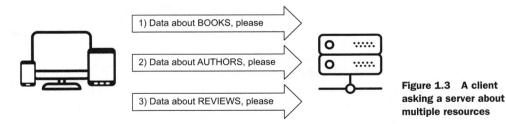

**Figure 1.3  A client asking a server about multiple resources**

1) Data about BOOKS, please

2) Data about AUTHORS, please

3) Data about REVIEWS, please

With GraphQL, you can basically shift this multirequest complexity to the backend and have your GraphQL runtime deal with it. The client asks the GraphQL service a single question and gets a single response with precisely what the client needs (figure 1.4).

**Figure 1.4    GraphQL shifts multirequest complexities to the backend side**

You can customize a REST-based API to provide one exact endpoint per view, but that's not the norm. You will have to implement it without a standard guide.

Another big technological benefit of GraphQL is communicating with multiple services. When you have multiple clients requesting data from multiple data storage services (like PostgreSQL, MongoDB, and a Redis cache), a GraphQL layer in the middle can simplify and standardize this communication. Instead of a client going directly to multiple data services, you can have that client communicate with the GraphQL service. Then the GraphQL service communicates with the different data services (figure 1.5). This is how GraphQL keeps clients from needing to communicate in multiple languages. A GraphQL service translates a single client's request into multiple requests to multiple services using different languages.

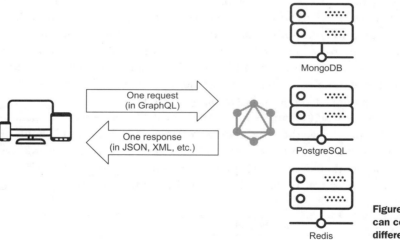

**Figure 1.5    GraphQL can communicate with different data services.**

One other benefit of GraphQL that I think is often underrated is how it improves the frontend developer experience. The GraphQL schema gives frontend developers a lot of power and control to explore, construct, validate, test, and accurately perform data-need communication without depending on backend developers. It eliminates the need for the server to hardcode the shape or size of the data, and it decouples clients from servers. This means clients and servers can be developed and maintained separately from each other, which is a significant benefit on its own.

More important, with GraphQL, developers express their UI data requirements using a declarative language. They express *what* they need, not *how* to make it available. There is a tight relationship between what data a UI needs and the way a developer can describe that data need in GraphQL.

> ### GraphQL is a translator
> Imagine three people who speak three different languages and have different types of knowledge. Then imagine that you have a question that can only be answered by combining the knowledge of all three people. If you have a translator who speaks all three languages, the task of putting together an answer to your question becomes easy. That is what a GraphQL service can do for clients. This point is valid with other data API options, but GraphQL provides standard structures that enable implementing this kind of data need in easier and more maintainable ways.

### 1.2.1 What about REST APIs?

GraphQL APIs are often compared to REST APIs because the latter have been the most popular choice for data APIs demanded by web and mobile applications. GraphQL provides a technological alternative to REST APIS. But why do we need an alternative? *What is wrong with REST APIs?*

The biggest relevant problem with REST APIs is the client's need to communicate with multiple data API endpoints. REST APIs are an example of servers that require clients to do multiple network round trips to get data. A REST API is a collection of endpoints where each endpoint represents a resource. So, when a client needs data about multiple resources, it has to perform multiple network requests to that REST API and then put together the data by combining the multiple responses it receives. This is a significant problem, especially for mobile applications, because mobile devices usually have processing, memory, and network constraints.

Furthermore, in a REST API, there is no client request language. Clients do not have control over what data the server will return because they do not have a language to communicate their exact needs. More accurately, the language available for clients of a REST API is very limited. For example, the READ REST API endpoints are either GET /ResourceName, to get a list of all the records for that resource, or GET /ResourceName/ ResourceID to get a single record identified by an ID.

In a pure REST API (not a customized one), a client cannot specify which fields to select for a record in that resource. That information is in the REST API service itself, and the REST API service always returns all the fields regardless of which ones the client actually needs. GraphQL's term for this problem is *over-fetching* of information that is not needed. It is a waste of network and memory resources for both the client and the server.

One other big problem with REST APIs is versioning. If you need to support multiple versions, that usually means new endpoints. This leads to more problems while using and maintaining these endpoints, and it might be the cause of code duplication on the server.

**NOTE**   The REST API problems mentioned here are specific to what GraphQL is trying to solve. They are certainly not all of the problems with REST APIs.

REST APIs eventually turn into a mix of regular REST endpoints plus custom ad hoc endpoints crafted for performance reasons. This is where GraphQL offers a much better alternative.

It is important to point out here that REST APIs have some advantages over GraphQL APIs. For example, caching a REST API response is easier than caching a GraphQL API response, as you will see in the last section of this chapter. Also, optimizing the code for different REST endpoints is easier than optimizing the code for a single generic endpoint. There is no single magical solution that fixes all issues without introducing new challenges. REST APIs have their place, and when used correctly, both GraphQL and REST have great applications. Also, nothing prohibits using them together in the same system.

---

### REST-ish APIs

Note that I am talking about pure REST APIs in this comparison. Some of the problems mentioned here and solved by GraphQL can also be solved by customizing REST APIs. For example, you can modify the REST API to accept an `include` query string that accepts a comma-separated list of fields to return in the response. This will avoid the over-fetching problem. You can also make a REST API include sub-resources with some query flags. There are tools out there that you can add on top of REST-based systems, and they can enable such customizations or make those systems easier to implement.

Such approaches might be okay on a small scale, and I have personally used them with some success. However, compared to what GraphQL offers, these approaches require a lot of work and cause slower iterations in projects. They are also not standardized and do not scale well for big projects.

---

### 1.2.2   *The GraphQL way*

To see the GraphQL way of solving the REST API problems we have talked about, you need to understand the concepts and design decisions behind GraphQL. Let's review the major ones.

#### THE TYPED GRAPH SCHEMA

To create a GraphQL API, you need a typed schema. A GraphQL schema contains fields that have types. Those types can be primitive or custom. Everything in the GraphQL schema requires a type. This type system is what makes a GraphQL service predictable and discoverable.

#### THE DECLARATIVE LANGUAGE

GraphQL has a declarative nature for expressing data requirements. It provides clients with a declarative language for expressing their data needs. This declarative nature enables a thinking model in the GraphQL language that is close to the way we think about data requirements in English, and it makes working with a GraphQL API a lot easier than the alternatives.

## THE SINGLE ENDPOINT AND CLIENT LANGUAGE

To solve the multiple round-trip problem, GraphQL makes the responding server work as a single endpoint. Basically, GraphQL takes the custom endpoint idea to an extreme and makes the whole server a single smart endpoint that can reply to all data requests.

The other significant concept that goes with the single smart endpoint is the rich client request language needed to work with that single endpoint. Without a client request language, a single endpoint is useless. It needs a language to process a custom request and respond with data for that custom request.

Having a client request language means clients are in control. They can ask for exactly what they need, and the server will reply with exactly what they ask for. This solves the problem of over-fetching data that is not needed.

Furthermore, having clients ask for exactly what they need enables backend developers to generate more useful analytics about what data is being used and what parts of the data are in higher demand. This is very useful information. For example, it can be used to scale and optimize data services based on usage patterns. It can also be used to detect abnormalities and client version changes.

## THE SIMPLE VERSIONING

When it comes to versioning, GraphQL has an interesting take. Versioning can be avoided altogether. Basically, you can add new fields and types without removing the old ones because you have a graph and can flexibly grow it by adding more nodes. You can leave paths on the graph for old APIs and introduce new ones. The API just grows, and no new endpoints are needed. Clients can continue to use older features, and they can also incrementally update their code to use new features. Using a single evolving version, GraphQL APIs give clients continuous access to new features and encourage cleaner, more maintainable server code.

This is especially important for mobile clients because you cannot control the version of the API they are using. Once installed, a mobile app might continue to use that same old version of the API for years. On the web, it is easy to control the API version because you can just push new code and force all users to use it. For mobile apps, this is a lot harder to do.

This simple versioning approach has some challenges. Keeping old nodes forever introduces downsides. More maintenance effort is required to make sure old nodes still work as they should. Furthermore, users of the APIs might be confused about which fields are old and which are new. GraphQL offers a way to deprecate (and hide) older nodes so that consumers of the schema only see the new ones. Once a field is deprecated, the maintainability problem becomes a question of how long old users continue to use it. The great thing here is that as a maintainer, you can confidently answer the questions "Is a field still being used?" and "How often is a field being used?" thanks to the client query language. The removal of unused, deprecated fields can even be automated.

### 1.2.3   *REST APIs and GraphQL APIs in action*

Let's go over a one-to-one comparison example between a REST API and a GraphQL API. Imagine that you are building an application to represent the *Star Wars* films and characters. The first UI you tackle is a view to show information about a single *Star Wars* character. This view should display the character's name, birth year, the name of their planet, and the titles of all the films in which they appeared. For example, for Darth Vader, along with his name, the view should display his birth year (41.9BBY), his planet name (Tatooine), and the titles of the four *Star Wars* films in which he appeared (*A New Hope*, *The Empire Strikes Back*, *Return of the Jedi*, and *Revenge of the Sith*).

As simple as this view sounds, you are actually dealing with three different resources: `Person`, `Planet`, and `Film`. The relationship between these resources is simple. We can easily guess the shape of the data needed. A `person` object has exactly one `planet` object and one or more `films` objects.

The JSON data for this view could be something like the following.

---
**Listing 1.11   JSON data example object for a UI component**

```
{
  "data": {
    "person": {
      "name": "Darth Vader",
      "birthYear": "41.9BBY",
      "planet": {
        "name": "Tatooine"
      },
      "films": [
        { "title": "A New Hope" },
        { "title": "The Empire Strikes Back" },
        { "title": "Return of the Jedi" },
        { "title": "Revenge of the Sith" }
      ]
    }
  }
}
```

Assuming that a data service can give us this exact structure, here is one possible way to represent its view with a frontend component library like React.js.

---
**Listing 1.12   UI view example in React.js**

```
// The Container Component:
<PersonProfile person={data.person}></PersonProfile>
// The PersonProfile Component:
Name: {data.person.name}
```

```
Birth Year: {data.person.birthYear}
Planet: {data.person.planet.name}
Films: {data.person.films.map(film => film.title)}
```

This is a very simple example. Our background knowledge of *Star Wars* helped us design the shape of the needed data and figure out how to use it in the UI.

Note one important thing about the UI view in listing 1.12: its relationship with the JSON data object in listing 1.11 is very clear. The UI view used all the "keys" from the JSON data object. See the values in curly brackets in listing 1.12.

Now, how can you ask a REST API service for the data in listing 1.11? You need a Star Wars character's information. Assuming that you know that character's ID, a REST API is expected to expose that information with an endpoint like this:

```
GET - /people/{id}
```

This request will give you the `name`, `birthYear`, and other information about the character. A REST API will also give you access to the ID of the character's planet and an array of IDs for all the films they appeared in.

The JSON response for this request could be something like the following:

```
{
  "name": "Darth Vader",
  "birthYear": "41.9BBY",
  "planetId": 1
  "filmIds": [1, 2, 3, 6],        Other information
  · - · - ·.           <----------  that is not needed
}                                   for this view
```

**TIP** Throughout this book, I use ·-·-· in code listings to indicate omitted content. This is to distinguish it from the three-dots syntax (...), which is part of both JavaScript and GraphQL (see az.dev/js-intro).

Then, to read the planet's name, you ask

```
GET - /planets/1
```

And to read the film titles, you ask

```
GET - /films/1
GET - /films/2
GET - /films/3
GET - /films/6
```

Once you have all *six* responses from the server, you can combine them to satisfy the view's data need.

Besides the fact that you had to do six network round trips to satisfy a simple data need for a simple UI, the whole approach here is imperative. You give instructions on how to fetch the data and how to process it to make it ready for the view. For example, you have to deal with the planet and film IDs, although the view does not really need them. You have to manually combine multiple data objects, although you are implementing a single view that naturally needs just a single data object.

Try asking for this data from a REST API yourself. The *Star Wars* data has an excellent REST API called SWAPI, which you can find at az.dev/swapi. Construct the same data object there. The names of the data elements might be a bit different, but the endpoint structure is the same. You will need to do exactly six API calls. Furthermore, you will have to over-fetch information that the view does not need.

SWAPI is just one pure implementation of a REST API for this data. There could be better custom implementations that make this view's data needs easier to fulfill. For example, if the API server implemented nested resources and understood the relationship between a person and a film, you could read the film data (along with the character data) with something like this:

```
GET - /people/{id}/films
```

However, a pure REST API would not have that out of the box. You would need to ask the backend engineers to create this custom endpoint for your view. This is the reality of scaling a REST API: you add custom endpoints to efficiently satisfy clients' growing needs. Managing custom endpoints like these is hard.

For example, if you customized your REST API endpoint to return the film data for a character, that would work great for the view you are currently implementing. However, in the future, you might need to implement a shorter or longer version of the character's profile information. Maybe you will need to show only one of their films or display the film description in addition to the title. Every new requirement will mean a change must be made to customize the endpoint further or come up with new endpoints to optimize the communication needed for the new views. This approach is simply limited.

Let's now look at the GraphQL approach. A GraphQL server is a single smart endpoint. The transport channel does not matter. If you are doing this over HTTP, the HTTP method certainly does not matter either. Let's assume that you have a single GraphQL endpoint exposed over an HTTPS transport channel at a /graphql endpoint.

Since you want to ask for data in a single network round trip, there has to be a way for you to express the complete data needs for the server to parse. You do this with a GraphQL query:

```
GET or POST - /graphql?query={ ·-·-· }
```

A GraphQL query is just a string, but it must include all the pieces of the data that you need. This is where the declarative power comes in.

Let's compare how this simple view's data requirement can be expressed with English and with GraphQL in table 1.1.

Table 1.1   How GraphQL is close to English

| In English | In GraphQL |
|---|---|
| The view needs:<br>a person's name,<br><br>birth year,<br>planet's name,<br><br><br>and the titles of all their films. | ```<br>{<br>  person(ID: ·–·–·) {<br>    name<br>    birthYear<br>    planet {<br>      name<br>    }<br>    films {<br>      title<br>    }<br>  }<br>}<br>``` |

Can you see how close the GraphQL expression is to the English version? It is as close as it can get. Furthermore, compare the GraphQL query with the original JSON data object that we started with (table 1.2).

Table 1.2   The similar structure between a GraphQL query and its response

| GraphQL query (question) | Needed JSON (answer) |
|---|---|
| ```<br>{<br>  person(ID: ·–·–·) {<br>    name<br>    birthYear<br>    planet {<br>      name<br>    }<br>    films {<br>      title<br>    }<br>  }<br>}<br>``` | ```<br>{<br>  "data": {<br>    "person": {<br>      "name": "Darth Vader",<br>      "birthYear": "41.9BBY",<br>      "planet": {<br>        "name": "Tatooine"<br>      },<br>      "films": [<br>        { "title": "A New Hope" },<br>        { "title": "The Empire Strikes Back" },<br>        { "title": "Return of the Jedi" },<br>        { "title": "Revenge of the Sith" }<br>      ]<br>    }<br>  }<br>}<br>``` |

The GraphQL query is the exact structure of the JSON data object, except without all the "value" parts (bold in table 1.2). If you think of this in terms of a question-answer relation, the question is the answer statement without the answer part.

If the answer statement is

*The name of the Star Wars character who has the ID 4 is Darth Vader.*

A good representation of the question is the same statement without the answer part:

*(What is) the name of the Star Wars character who has the ID 4?*

The same relationship applies to a GraphQL query. Take a JSON data object and remove all the "answer" parts (the values), and you end up with a GraphQL query suitable to represent a question about that JSON data object.

If you analyze the GraphQL query against the UI view that uses it, you'll find that every element of the GraphQL query is used in the UI view, and every dynamic part that is used in the UI view appears in the GraphQL query.

This obvious mapping is one of the greatest powers of GraphQL. The UI view knows the exact data it needs, and extracting that requirement from the view code is fairly easy. You simply look for what variables are used in the view.

If you think about this in terms of multiple nested UI components, every UI component can ask for the exact part of the data that it needs, and the application's complete data needs can be constructed by putting together these partial data needs from components.

> **TIP**  GraphQL provides a way for a UI component to define the partial data
> need via a feature called *fragments*. You will learn about GraphQL fragments
> in chapter 3.

Furthermore, if you invert this mapping model, you find another powerful concept. If you have a GraphQL query, you know exactly how to use its response in the UI because the query will have the same structure as the response. You do not need to inspect the response to know how to use it, and you do not need any documentation about the API. It is all built in.

*Star Wars* data has a GraphQL API (see az.dev/swapi-graphql). You can use the GraphiQL editor available there to test a GraphQL query. We'll talk about the GraphiQL editor in the next chapter, but you can go ahead and try to construct the example data `person` object. There are a few minor differences that you will learn about later in the book, but here is the official query you can use against this API to read the data requirement for the same view (with Darth Vader as an example).

---

**Listing 1.13  GraphQL query for the *Star Wars* example | az.dev/gia**

```
{
  person(personID: 4) {
    name
    birthYear
    homeworld {
      name
    }
    filmConnection {
```

```
        films {
          title
        }
      }
    }
  }
}
```

**TIP** If you are reading the print version of this book, you can copy the text of all useable code listings in the book at az.dev/gia. The query in listing 1.13 can be found there along with any listings that have the link in their caption.

Just paste this query in the editor area and click the run button. This request will give you a response structure very close to what the view used. You expressed the data need in a way that is close to how you would express it in English, and you get all the data in a single network round trip.

> **Is GraphQL a REST killer?**
>
> When I first learned about GraphQL, I tweeted that "REST APIs can REST IN PEACE!" Joking aside, I don't really think that GraphQL is a REST API "killer." I do think, however, that more people will pick GraphQL over REST for APIs used by web and mobile applications. REST APIs have their place, but I don't think that place is for web and mobile applications.
>
> I believe GraphQL will do to REST what JSON did to XML. XML is still pretty heavily used, but almost every web-based API I know of today uses the JSON format.

GraphQL offers many advantages over REST APIs, but let's also talk about the challenges GraphQL brings to the table.

## 1.3 GraphQL problems

Perfect solutions are fairy tales. The flexibility that GraphQL introduces opens a door to some clear issues and concerns.

### 1.3.1 Security

A critical threat for GraphQL APIs is resource-exhaustion attacks (aka denial-of-service attacks). A GraphQL server can be attacked with overly complex queries that consume all the server resources. It is very simple to query for deeply nested relationships (user –> friends –> friends –> friends …) or use field aliases to ask for the same field many times. Resource-exhaustion attacks are not specific to GraphQL, but when working with GraphQL, you have to be extra careful about them.

> **NOTE** This resource-exhaustion problem can also come from non-malignant client applications that have certain bugs or bad implementations. Remember that a GraphQL client is free to ask for whatever data it requires, so it might just ask for too much data at once.

There are some mitigations you can use. You can implement cost analysis on the query in advance and enforce limits on the amount of data that can be consumed. You can also implement a timeout to kill requests that take too long to resolve. In addition, since a GraphQL service is just one layer in any application stack, you can handle the rate-limit enforcement at a lower level under GraphQL.

If the GraphQL API endpoint you are trying to protect is not public and is designed for internal use by your client applications (web or mobile), you can use an *allow-list* approach and preapprove queries the server can execute. Clients can ask the server to execute preapproved queries using a unique query identifier. While this approach reintroduces some dependencies between servers and clients, automation strategies can be used to mitigate against that issue. For example, you can give the frontend engineers the freedom to modify the queries and mutations they use in development and then automatically replace them with their unique IDs during deployment to production servers. Some client-side GraphQL frameworks are already testing similar concepts.

Authentication and authorization are other concerns that you need to think about when working with GraphQL. Do you handle them before, after, or during GraphQL's fields resolving process?

To answer this question, think of GraphQL as a domain-specific language (DSL) on top of your backend data-fetching logic. It is just one layer that you could put between the clients and your actual data services. Think of authentication and authorization as another layer. GraphQL will not help with the actual implementation of the authentication or authorization logic. It is not meant for that. But if you want to put these layers behind GraphQL, you can use GraphQL to communicate the access tokens between the clients and the enforcing logic. This is very similar to the way authentication and authorization are usually implemented in REST APIs.

In chapter 8, we'll go over an example of implementing an authentication layer behind GraphQL.

### 1.3.2   *Caching and optimizing*

One task that GraphQL makes a bit more challenging is clients' caching of data. Responses from REST APIs are a lot easier to cache because of their dictionary nature. A specific URL gives certain data, so you can use the URL itself as the cache key.

With GraphQL, you can adopt a similar basic approach and use the query text as a key to cache its response. But this approach is limited, is not very efficient, and can cause problems with data consistency. The results of multiple GraphQL queries can easily overlap, and this basic caching approach will not account for the overlap.

There is a brilliant solution to this problem. A graph query means a *graph cache*. If you normalize a GraphQL query response into a flat collection of records and give each record a global unique ID, you can cache those records instead of caching the full responses.

This is not a simple process, though. There will be records referencing other records, so you will be managing a cyclic graph. Populating and reading the cache will require query traversal. You will probably have to implement a separate layer to handle this cache logic. However, this method will be a lot more efficient than response-based caching.

One of the other most famous problems you may encounter when working with GraphQL is commonly referred to as *N+1 SQL queries.* GraphQL query fields are designed to be standalone functions, and resolving those fields with data from a database might result in a new database request per resolved field. For simple REST API endpoint logic, it is easy to analyze, detect, and solve N+1 issues by enhancing the constructed SQL queries. For GraphQL dynamically resolved fields, it is not that simple.

Luckily, Facebook is pioneering one possible solution to this data-loading-optimization problem: it's called DataLoader. As the name implies, DataLoader is a utility you can use to read data from databases and make it available to GraphQL resolver functions. You can use DataLoader instead of reading the data directly from databases with SQL queries, and DataLoader will act as your agent to reduce the SQL queries you send to the database (figure 1.6).

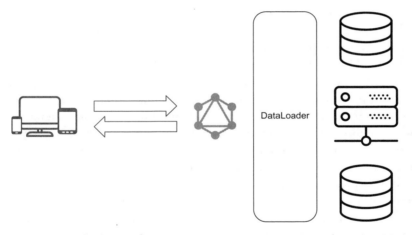

**Figure 1.6   DataLoader can optimize the requests between GraphQL and databases.**

DataLoader uses a combination of batching and caching to accomplish that. If the same client request results in a need to ask the database about multiple things, Data-Loader can consolidate these questions and batch load their answers from the database. DataLoader also caches the answers and makes them available for subsequent questions about the same resources.

We'll explore the practical benefits of DataLoader in chapter 7.

**TIP**  There are other SQL optimization strategies that you can use. For example, you can construct optimal join-based SQL queries by analyzing GraphQL requests. If you are using a relational database with native efficient capabilities to join tables of data and reuse previously parsed queries, then in many cases, a join-based strategy may be more efficient than ID-based batching. However, ID-based batching is much easier to implement.

### 1.3.3  Learning curve

Working with GraphQL requires a bigger learning curve than the alternatives. A developer writing a GraphQL-based frontend application has to learn the syntax of the GraphQL language. A developer implementing a GraphQL backend service has to learn a lot more than just the language: they have to learn the API syntax of a GraphQL implementation. They must also understand schemas and resolvers, among many other concepts specific to a GraphQL runtime.

This is less of an issue in REST APIs because they do not have a client language or require any standard implementations. You have the freedom to implement REST endpoints however you wish because you don't have to parse, validate, and execute special language text.

### Summary

- The best way to represent data in the real world is with a graph data structure. A data model is a graph of related objects. GraphQL embraces this fact.
- A GraphQL system has two primary components: the query language, which can be used by consumers of data APIs to request their exact data needs; and the runtime layer on the backend, which publishes a public schema describing the capabilities and requirements of data models. The runtime layer accepts incoming requests on a single endpoint and resolves incoming data requests with predictable data responses. Incoming requests are strings written with the GraphQL query language.
- GraphQL is all about optimizing data communication between a client and a server. GraphQL allows clients to ask for the exact data they need in a declarative way, and it enables servers to aggregate data from multiple data storage resources in a standard way.
- GraphQL has an official specification document that defines standard rules and practices that all implementers of GraphQL runtimes must adhere to.
- A GraphQL service can be written in any programming language, and it can be conceptually split into two major parts: a structure that is defined with a strongly typed schema representing the capabilities of the API, and behavior that is naturally implemented with functions known as resolvers. A GraphQL schema is a graph of fields, which have types. This graph represents all the possible data objects that can be read (or updated) through the GraphQL service. Each field in a GraphQL schema is backed by a resolver function.

- The difference between GraphQL and its previous alternatives is that it provides standards and structures to implement API features in maintainable and scalable ways. The alternatives lack such standards. GraphQL also solves many technical challenges like having to do multiple network round trips and deal with multiple data responses on the client.
- GraphQL has some challenges, especially in the areas of security and optimization. Because of the flexibility it provides, securing a GraphQL API requires thinking about more vulnerabilities. Caching a flexible GraphQL API is also a lot harder than caching fixed API endpoints (as in REST APIs). The GraphQL learning curve is also steeper than that of many of its alternatives.

# Exploring
# GraphQL APIs

2

**This chapter covers**

- Using GraphQL's in-browser IDE to test GraphQL requests
- Exploring the fundamentals of sending GraphQL data requests
- Exploring read and write example operations from the GitHub GraphQL API
- Exploring GraphQL's introspective features

The easiest way to start learning about the powerful features of the GraphQL language is to use its feature-rich interactive in-browser IDE. This IDE uses GraphQL's type system to provide features you can use to explore what you can do with GraphQL and to write and test your GraphQL requests without leaving your browser. Using this IDE, we will continue to explore examples of GraphQL queries and mutations. We'll look at the fundamental parts of a GraphQL request and test examples from the official GitHub GraphQL API.

## 2.1 The GraphiQL editor

When thinking about the requests your client applications need to make to servers, you can benefit from a graphical tool to first help you come up with these requests and then test them before committing to them in application code. Such a tool can also help you improve these requests, validate your improvements, and debug any requests that are running into problems. In the GraphQL world, this tool is called GraphiQL (with an *i* before the *QL* and pronounced "graphical"). GraphiQL is an open source web application (written with React.js and GraphQL) that can be run in a browser.

GraphiQL is one of the reasons GraphQL is popular. It is easy to learn, and it will be a very helpful tool for you. I guarantee that you will love it. It is one of my favorite tools for frontend development, and I cannot imagine working on a GraphQL-based project without it.

You can download GraphiQL and run it locally, but an easier way to get a feel for what this tool has to offer is to use it with an existing GraphQL API service like the *Star Wars* service that we previewed in chapter 1.

Head over to az.dev/swapi-graphql in your browser to find the GraphiQL editor, which works with the *Star Wars* data and is publicly available for you to test. Figure 2.1 shows what it looks like.

This editor is a simple two-pane application: the left pane is the editor, and the right pane is where the results of executing GraphQL requests appear.

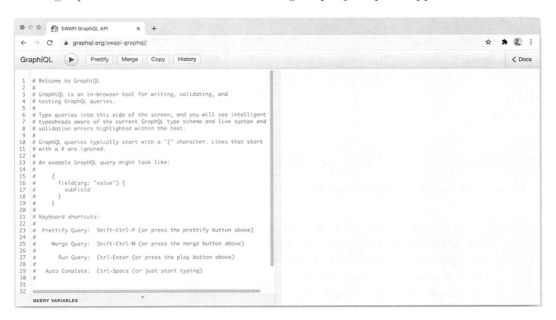

**Figure 2.1   The GraphiQL editor**

Go ahead and type the following simple GraphQL query in the editor.

**Listing 2.1    A query for the `person` field**

```
{
  person(personID: 4) {
    name
    birthYear
  }
}
```

This simple GraphQL query asks for the name and birth year of the person whose ID is 4. To execute the query, you can press Ctrl-Enter or press the run button (with the little black triangle). When you do, the result pane shows the data that the query is asking for, as shown in figure 2.2.

**Figure 2.2    Executing queries with GraphiQL**

The best thing about the GraphiQL editor is that it provides intelligent type-ahead and autocompletion features that are aware of the GraphQL type schema you are currently exploring. For the previous example, the editor is completely aware that there is a `person` object with `name` and `birthYear` fields. In addition, the editor has live syntax and validation error highlighting for any text you type.

> **NOTE**    The awesome features in GraphiQL are all possible because of the GraphQL schema. With one big query to the server, this editor can know about everything the server offers.

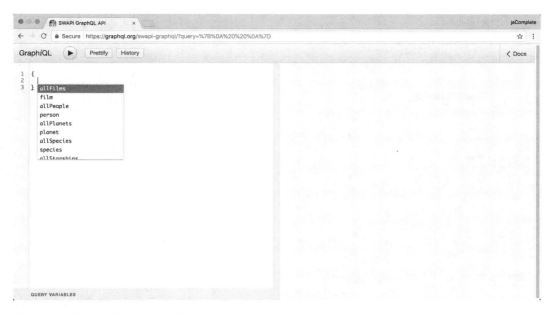

**Figure 2.3  GraphiQL's type-ahead list**

To explore these features, clear the editor pane (you can select all the text in the editor with Ctrl-A). Then, just type an empty set of curly brackets: {}. Place your cursor within this empty set, and press Ctrl-Space. You get an autocompletion list like that shown in figure 2.3.

Nice! You can very quickly start exploring what fields this GraphQL API offers right there in the editor while you are thinking about your requests. The person field we used before is one of the items in the list.

This list will also be used to autocomplete fields as you type them. Type p, and notice how the list changes to highlight what starts with p. Then, type an e and see how the list only highlights the person field. Press Enter to "pick" the currently highlighted item in the list.

The great thing about this type-ahead list is its context awareness. It shows you the fields available on the level where you are typing. For example, now that you picked the person field, type another empty set of curly brackets after the word *person*, put your cursor within this new set, and bring up the type-ahead list by pressing Ctrl-Space. You should see a new list, this time with all the fields you can ask for in the context of a person object (figure 2.4).

Context awareness is extremely helpful, and I am talking not about the "less typing" aspect but rather about the discoverability and validation aspects that enable you to work more quickly and make fewer mistakes. This is an example of the power and control I was talking about in the previous chapter. And that is how GraphQL is different.

**Figure 2.4   GraphiQL's type-ahead list is context aware.**

Before we pick the `name` and `birthYear` fields again, note that one of the closing curly brackets has a red underline. This is part of the live error highlighting you also get in this tool. Discard the type-ahead list by pressing Esc, and hover your mouse cursor over the underlined curly bracket. You should see an error complaining about unexpected syntax. This is because the text in the editor is not yet valid GraphQL syntax. Every time you start a new level of curly brackets, known as a *selection set*, it needs its own fields.

Go ahead and pick the `name` and `birthYear` fields within the `person` field. The query syntax is now valid (the red underline is gone), but the query is still missing one important piece—and this time, it is not a syntax problem.

You can always execute the query to see what the server has to say about it. If the server rejects the query, it will most likely give you a good reason why it did. For example, executing the query we have right now returns the following.

**Listing 2.2   Example GraphQL error response**

```
{
  "errors": [
    {
      "message": "must provide id or personID",
      "locations": [
        {
          "line": 2,
          "column": 3
        }
```

```
      ],
      "path": [
        "person"
      ]
    }
  ],
  "data": {
    "person": null
  }
}
```

Note that the response in listing 2.2 is a normal JSON response (200-OK) and that it gives two top-level properties: an `errors` property that is an array of error objects and a `data` property that represents an empty response. A GraphQL server response can represent partial data when that server has errors about other parts of the response. This makes the response more predictable and makes the task of handling errors a bit easier.

The error message here is helpful: the path "person" must provide id or personID. Since we are asking the server about *one* person, it needs a way to identify which person's data to return. Note again that this was not a syntax problem but rather a missing-required-value problem.

To make a path provide a value, we use syntax similar to calling functions. Place the cursor immediately after the word `person`, and type the `(` character. GraphiQL auto-completes it and shows you a new type-ahead list that, this time, knows what values can be provided as arguments for the `person` field (figure 2.5).

**Figure 2.5   Exploring field arguments with the type-ahead list**

Now you can pick the `personID` argument, give it a value of 4, and get back to the same query you started with. But this time, you discovered the elements you needed through the powerful features of the GraphiQL editor.

In addition to discovering the structure and types of elements inline while you type them, you can browse the Docs section to see full lists and more details. Click the Docs link in the top-right corner of the editor. You should see a search box that you can use to find any type in the current GraphQL schema. I typed the word `person` and picked the first result; figure 2.6 shows the schema type `Person` with its description and fields.

**Figure 2.6    GraphiQL shows the documentation schema.**

Take a moment to explore more of what the GraphiQL editor has to offer. Try more queries, and get a feeling for how easy it is to come up with them.

## 2.2    *The basics of the GraphQL language*

To ask any GraphQL server for data, we send it a *request* written in the GraphQL query language. A GraphQL request contains a tree of *fields*. Let's explore these two fundamental concepts of the language in detail.

### 2.2.1    *Requests*

At the core of a GraphQL communication is a *request* object. The source text of a GraphQL request is often referred to as a *document*. A document contains text that represents a request through operations like queries, mutations, and subscriptions. In addition to the main operations, a GraphQL document text can contain fragments that can be used to compose other operations, as we will see in the next chapter.

A GraphQL request can also contain an object representing values of variables that may be used in the request document text. The request may also include meta-information about operations (figure 2.7). For example, if the request document contains more than one operation, a GraphQL request must include information about which operation to execute. If the request document contains only one operation, the GraphQL server will just execute that. You do not even need to label the operation with a name in that case, but naming operations is a good practice to follow.

Let's look at a full GraphQL request. Here is a hypothetical example (don't worry about the new syntax just yet).

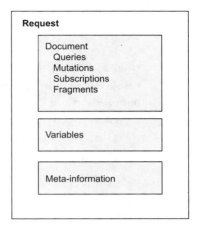

**Figure 2.7 The structure of a GraphQL request**

---

**Listing 2.3 Example GraphQL request: document**

```
query GetEmployees($active: Boolean!) {
  allEmployees(active: $active) {
    ...employeeInfo
  }
}

query FindEmployee {
  employee(id: $employeeId) {
    ...employeeInfo
  }
}

fragment employeeInfo on Employee {
  name
  email
  startDate
}
```

Since this document uses generic variables (the ones starting with the $ sign), we need a JSON object to represent values specific to a request.

---

**Listing 2.4 Example GraphQL request: variables**

```
{
  "active": true,
  "employeeId": 42
}
```

Also, since the document contains more than one operation (`GetEmployees` and `FindEmployee`), the request needs to provide the desired operation to be executed.

**Listing 2.5   Example GraphQL request: meta-information**

```
operationName="GetEmployees"
```

If we send all three elements of this request to a GraphQL server, it will parse the whole document, pick the GetEmployees query, fill the variable values, and return the data response for that query.

Three types of operations can be used in GraphQL:

- Query operations that represent a read-only fetch
- Mutation operations that represent a write followed by a fetch
- Subscription operations that represent a request for real-time data updates

The example in listing 2.3 represented a query operation. Here is a hypothetical example of a mutation operation.

**Listing 2.6   Example GraphQL mutation operation**

```
mutation RateStory {
  addRating(storyId: 123, rating: 5) {
    story {
      averageRating
    }
  }
}
```

The mutation operation in listing 2.6 adds a new five-star rating record for a story and then retrieves the new average rating of that same story. Note that this is a write followed by a read. All GraphQL mutation operations follow this concept.

Here is a hypothetical example of a subscription operation.

**Listing 2.7   Example GraphQL subscription operation**

```
subscription StoriesRating {
  allStories {
    id
    averageRating
  }
}
```

The subscription operation in listing 2.7 instructs the GraphQL server to open a socket connection with the client, send story IDs along with their average ratings, and keep doing that when the information changes on the server. This feature is a much better alternative than continuously polling data to keep a UI view up to date.

### 2.2.2   *Fields*

One of the core elements in the text of a GraphQL operation is the field. The simplest way to think about a GraphQL operation is as a way to select fields on objects.

A field always appears within a selection set (inside a pair of curly brackets), and it describes one discrete piece of information that you can retrieve about an object. It can describe a scalar value (like the name of a person or their birth year), an object (like the home planet of a *Star Wars* character), or a list of objects (like the list of films in which a *Star Wars* character appeared). For the last two cases, the fields contain another selection set to customize the information needed about the objects the fields describe.

Here is an example GraphQL query with different types of fields.

Listing 2.8  GraphQL fields

```
{
  me {
    email
    birthday {
      month
      year
    }
    friends {
      name
    }
  }
}
```

The fields `email`, `month`, `year`, and `name` are all *scalar* fields. Scalar types represent primitive leaf values. GraphQL schemas often support four major scalar types: `Int`, `String`, `Float`, and `Boolean`. The built-in custom scalar value `ID` can also be used to represent identity values. We'll see an example in chapter 4.

**TIP**  The term *leaf* comes from Graph theory. It means a vertex with no children.

You can also customize a GraphQL schema to support more scalar values with certain formats. For example, a schema can be designed to have a `Time` scalar value representing a time value in a standard and parsable format (ISO/UTC).

The `me` and `birthday` fields describe objects, so they require their own nested selection sets to represent their properties. The `friends` field describes a list of friend objects, so it also requires a nested selection set to represent the properties of the objects in that list.

All GraphQL operations must specify their selections down to fields that return scalar values (leaf values). For example, they cannot have fields that describe objects without providing further nested selection sets to specify which scalar values to fetch for these objects. The last-nested level of fields should always consist of only fields that describe scalar values. For the example in listing 2.8, if you did not specify the nested selection set for the `friends` field (the { name } part), the GraphQL query would not

be valid because in that case, not all of the last-nested-level fields would describe scalar values.

The *root fields* in an operation usually represent information that is globally accessi-
ble to your application and its current user.

> **NOTE** I use the term *root field* to refer to the first-level fields in a GraphQL
> operation.

Some typical examples of root fields include references to a currently logged-in user.
These fields are often named `viewer` or `me`. For example:

```
{
  me {
    username
    fullName
  }
}
```

Root fields are also generally used to access certain types of data referenced by a
unique identifier. For example:

```
# Ask for the user whose ID equal to 42
{
  user(id: 42) {
    fullName
  }
}
```

In this query, the `user` field represents one of many users in a graph of data. To
instruct the server to pick one user, we specify a unique ID value for the `user` field.

Note that in the previous example, the # character is used to write a comment
about the query. This is the official character to comment a single line (or the remain-
der of a line) in a GraphQL document. There is no supported way to have multiline
comments in GraphQL documents, but you can have many lines, each of which starts
with the # character. The server will just ignore all the comments. It will also ignore
any extra spaces, all line terminators, and all insignificant commas between fields.
These characters can be used to improve the legibility of source text and emphasize
the separation of tokens. They have no significance to the semantic meaning of
GraphQL documents.

## 2.3    *Examples from the GitHub API*

Now that you know about requests, documents, operations, and fields, let's put this
knowledge to use and explore some real-world examples of GraphQL requests from
the GitHub API. GitHub moved from REST APIs to GraphQL APIs in 2017. We can
use their GraphQL API explorer at az.dev/github-api; this embedded GraphiQL editor (figure 2.8) includes the proper authentication headers for the API (you need to
be logged in with a GitHub.com account).

**TIP** You can also use a standalone GraphiQL editor to explore the GitHub API (see az.dev/graphiql-app). You have to manually include an access token in that app. You can use this standalone app with any GraphQL API service.

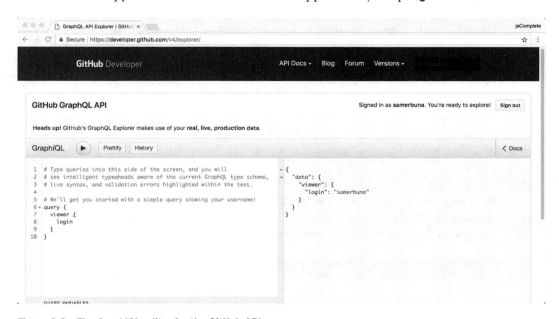

**Figure 2.8  The GraphiQL editor for the GitHub API**

Let's first look at some common queries from this API.

**WARNING** The GitHub API uses your real, live production data at GitHub.com.

### 2.3.1  Reading data from GitHub

When you first launch the GitHub GraphQL API explorer, it has a default simple query that displays your login. The currently logged-in user is represented by the `viewer` field. Under this field, you can read all the information that is available about you at GitHub.

For example, here is a query to see information about the most recent 10 repositories that you own or contribute to.

**Listing 2.9  Your most recent repos (az.dev/gia)**

```
{
  viewer {
    repositories(last: 10) {
      nodes {
        name
        description
```

```
        }
      }
    }
  }
```

Here is another query to see all the supported licenses in GitHub along with their URLs.

##### Listing 2.10   All GitHub-supported licenses (az.dev/gia)

```
{
  licenses {
    name
    url
  }
}
```

Next is a more complex query to find the first 10 issues of the facebook/graphql repository. It asks for the name of the author and the title used for the issue page, along with the date when the issue was created.

##### Listing 2.11   The first 10 issues of a repo (az.dev/gia)

```
{
  repository(owner: "facebook", name: "graphql") {
    issues(first: 10) {
      nodes {
        title
        createdAt
        author {
          login
        }
      }
    }
  }
}
```

### 2.3.2   *Updating data at GitHub*

Let's now explore some mutations we can do with the GitHub GraphQL API. The simplest mutation is to "star" a repository. If you execute the following mutation under your logged-in user, its action is equivalent to going to github.com/jscomplete/graphql-in-action and clicking the star button.

##### Listing 2.12   "Star" a repository (az.dev/gia)

```
mutation {
  addStar(input: { starrableId: "MDEwOlJlcG9zaXRvcnkxMjU2ODEwMDY=" }) {
    starrable {
      stargazers {
```

**Use listing 2.13 to find this starrableId value**

```
            totalCount
        }
      }
    }
}
```

The mutation stars the repository and then reads the new total number of stargazers after the mutation. The input for this mutation is a simple object that has a `starrableId` value, which is the node identifier for the graphql-in-action repository. I was able to find that value using this query.

**Listing 2.13    Find a repo ID (az.dev/gia)**

```
{
  repository(name: "graphql-in-action", owner: "jscomplete") {
    id
  }
}
```

Let's execute another mutation. This time, let's add a comment to an issue in a repository. I created an issue for you to test this mutation under the repository at github.com/jscomplete/graphql-in-action. You can see the details of this issue using the following query.

**Listing 2.14    The details of one issue under a repo (az.dev/gia)**

```
query GetIssueInfo {
  repository(owner: "jscomplete", name: "graphql-in-action") {
    issue(number: 1) {
      id
      title
    }
  }
}
```

This gives you the value of the `id` field needed to add a comment to the issue using a mutation. Now execute the following mutation, which uses that `id` value.

**Listing 2.15    Adding a comment to a repo issue (az.dev/gia)**

```
mutation AddCommentToIssue {
  addComment(input: {
    subjectId: "MDU6SXNzdWUzMDYyMDMwNzk=",          Tell us where you're from
    body: "Hello from California!"           ⟵⎯      in your test comment. :)
  }) {
    commentEdge {
      node {
        createdAt
      }
```

```
      }
    }
}
```

After the mutation in listing 2.15 saves your comment to the special issue, it reports the `createdAt` date for that comment. Feel free to send as many comments as you wish to this special issue, but only do so through the GitHub API explorer.

You can see the comments you added and all the other comments on this issue at github.com/jscomplete/graphql-in-action/issues/1.

### 2.3.3   *Introspective queries*

GraphQL APIs support introspective queries that can be used to answer questions about the API schema. This introspection support gives GraphQL tools powerful functionality, and it drives the features we have been using in the GraphiQL editor. For example, the awesome type-ahead list in GraphiQL is sourced with an introspective query.

Introspective queries start with a root field that's either `__type` or `__schema`, known as *meta-fields*. There is also another meta-field, `__typename`, which can be used to retrieve the name of any object type. Fields with names that begin with double underscore characters are reserved for introspection support.

**NOTE**   Meta-fields are implicit. They do not appear in the fields list of their types.

The `__schema` field can be used to read information about the API schema, such as what types and directives it supports. We will explore directives in the next chapter.

Let's ask the GitHub API schema what types it supports. Here is an introspective query to do that.

---

**Listing 2.16   Example GraphQL introspective query (az.dev/gia)**

```
{
  __schema {
    types {
      name
      description
    }
  }
}
```

This query returns all the types this schema supports, and it also includes the descriptions of these types. This is a helpful list to explore the custom types defined in the GitHub GraphQL schema. For example, you should see that the GitHub API schema defines types like `Repository`, `Commit`, `Project`, `Issue`, `PullRequest`, and many more (figure 2.9).

**Figure 2.9  Listing all the supported types under the GitHub API schema**

If you need to retrieve information about a single type, you can use the __type meta-field. For example, here is a query to find all the supported fields under the type Commit along with any arguments they accept.

---

**Listing 2.17   Supported fields under a Commit object (az.dev/gia)**

```
{
  __type(name: "Commit") {
    fields {
      name
      args {
        name
      }
    }
  }
}
```

Use the GraphiQL type-ahead feature to discover what other information you can retrieve under these introspective meta-fields.

## Summary

- GraphiQL is an in-browser IDE for writing and testing GraphQL requests. It offers many great features to write, validate, and inspect GraphQL queries and mutations. These features are made possible thanks to GraphQL's introspective nature, which comes with its mandatory schemas.
- A GraphQL request consists of a set of operations, an object for variables, and other meta-information elements as needed.
- GraphQL operations use a tree of fields. A field represents a unit of information. The GraphQL language is largely about selecting fields on objects.
- GitHub has a powerful GraphQL API that you can use to read data about repositories and users and do mutations like adding a star to a repository or commenting on an issue in a repository.
- GraphQL introspective queries offer a way for clients to get meta-information about the GraphQL API.

# 3

# *Customizing and organizing GraphQL operations*

**This chapter covers**

- Using arguments to customize what a request field returns
- Customizing response property names with aliases
- Describing runtime executions with directives
- Reducing duplicated text with fragments
- Composing queries and separating data requirement responsibilities

In any nontrivial application, you have to do many things beyond asking the server a direct, simple, single-value question. Data fetching is usually coupled with variables and meta-questions about the structure of the response. You often need to modify the data returned by the server to make it suitable for your application.

Sometimes you have to remove parts of the data or go back to the server and ask for other parts that are required based on conditions in your application. Sometimes you need a way to organize big requests and categorize them to know which part of your application is responsible for each part of your requests. Luckily, the GraphQL language offers many built-in features you can use to do all of this and much more. These customizing and organizing features are what this chapter is all about.

## 3.1   Customizing fields with arguments

The fields in a GraphQL operation are similar to functions. They map input to output. A function input is received as a list of argument values. Just like functions, we can pass any GraphQL field a list of argument values. A GraphQL schema on the backend can access these values and use them to customize the response it returns for that field.

Let's look at use cases for these field arguments and some examples used by the GitHub GraphQL API (az.dev/github-api).

### 3.1.1   Identifying a single record to return

Every API request that asks for a single record from a collection needs to specify an identifier for that record. This identifier is usually associated with a unique identifier for that record in the server's database, but it can also be anything else that can uniquely identify the record.

For example, if you ask an API for information on a single user, you usually send along with your request the ID of the user you are interested in. You can also send their email address, username, or Facebook ID connection if, for example, you are logging them in through a Facebook button.

Here is an example query that asks for information about the user whose email address is jane@doe.name.

Listing 3.1   Using field arguments

```
query UserInfo {
  user(email: "jane@doe.name") {
    firstName
    lastName
    username
  }
}
```

The `email` part inside the `user` field is called a *field argument.*

Note that for an API field representing a single record, the argument value you pass to identify that record must be a unique value on that field record in the database. For example, you cannot pass the person's full name to identify their user record because the database might list many people who have the same name.

However, you can pass multiple arguments to identify the user. For example, you can pass a full name and an address to uniquely identify a single person.

Examples of single-record fields are popular. Some GraphQL APIs even have a single-record field for every object in the system. This is commonly known in the GraphQL world as a *Node interface*: a concept popularized by the Relay framework (which also originated at Facebook). With a `Node` interface, you can look up any node in the data graph by its unique global system-wide ID. Then, based on what that node is, you can use an inline fragment to specify the properties on that node that you are interested in seeing in the response.

#### Listing 3.2  Identifying a single global node

```
query NodeInfo {
  node(id: "A-GLOBALLY-UNIQUE-ID-HERE") {
    ...on USER {
      firstName
      lastName
      username
      email
    }
  }
}
```

See section 3.4.5 later in this chapter for more details about the inline-fragment in listing 3.2.

In the GitHub API, some examples of single-record fields are `user`, `repository`, `project`, and `organization`. Here is an example to read information about the jsComplete organization, which hosts all open source resources for jsComplete.com.

#### Listing 3.3  One organization's information (az.dev/gia)

```
query OrgInfo {
  organization(login: "jscomplete") {
    name
    description
    websiteUrl
  }
}
```

### 3.1.2  *Limiting the number of records returned by a list field*

When you ask for a list of records from a collection, a good API will always ask you to provide a limit. How many records are you interested in?

It is usually a bad idea to leave a general API capability for listing records in a collection without a limit. You do not want a client to be able to fetch more than a few hundred records at a time, because that would put your API server at risk of resource exhaustion and does not scale well. This is exactly why the GitHub API requires the use of an argument like `first` (or `last`) when you ask it for a list of records. Go ahead and try to ask for all the repositories under the jsComplete organization. You can use the `repositories` field within the `organization` field in the `OrgInfo` query in listing 3.3. You should see that GitHub asks for a `first` or `last` value, as shown in figure 3.1.

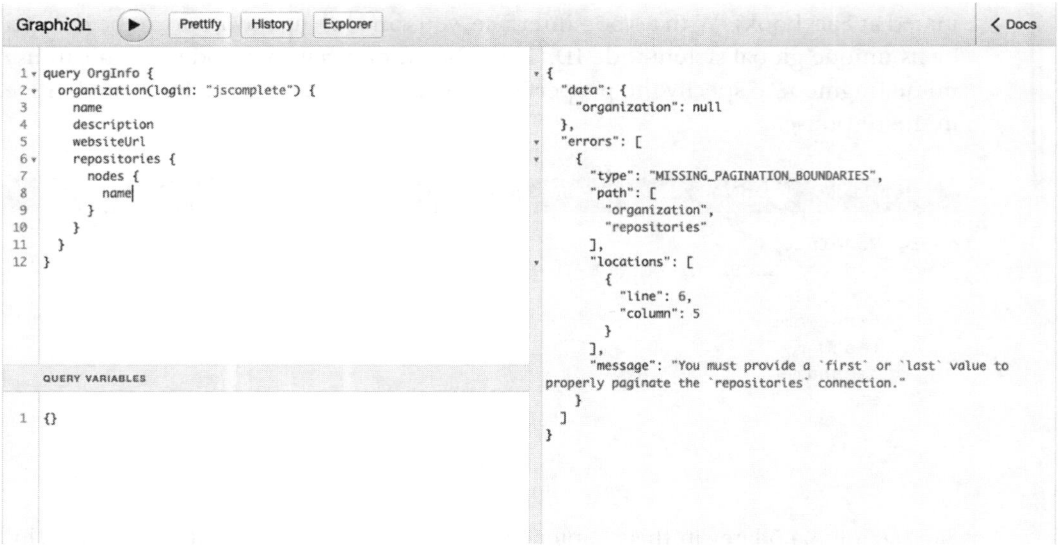

**Figure 3.1   The repositories field requires a `first` or `last` argument.**

Since any list of records in a database has a certain order, you can limit your request results using either end of that order. If you are interested in 10 records, you can get the first 10 records or the last 10 records using these arguments.

Here is the query you can use to retrieve the first 10 repositories under the jsComplete organization.

**Listing 3.4   First 10 repos under the organization (az.dev/gia)**

```
query First10Repos {
  organization(login: "jscomplete") {
    name
    description
    websiteUrl
    repositories(first: 10) {
      nodes {
        name
      }
    }
  }
}
```

By default, the GitHub API orders the repositories in ascending order by date of creation. You can customize that ordering logic with another field argument.

### 3.1.3  *Ordering records returned by a list field*

In the previous example, the GitHub API ordered the list of repositories under the jsComplete organization by the CREATED_AT repository field, which is the default order field. The API supports many other order fields, including UPDATED_AT, PUSHED_AT, NAME, and STARGAZERS.

Here is a query to retrieve the first 10 repositories when they are ordered alphabetically by name.

> **Listing 3.5  First 10 repos under an organization (az.dev/gia)**

```
query orgReposByName {
  organization(login: "jscomplete") {
    repositories(first: 10, orderBy: { field: NAME, direction: ASC }) {
      nodes {
        name
      }
    }
  }
}
```

Can you use the GitHub field arguments you learned about to find the top-10 most popular repositories under the jsComplete organization? Base a repository's popularity on the number of stars it has.

Here is one query you can use to do that.

> **Listing 3.6  10 most popular repos under an organization (az.dev/gia)**

```
query OrgPopularRepos {
  organization(login: "jscomplete") {
    repositories(first: 10, orderBy: { field: STARGAZERS, direction: DESC }) {
      nodes {
        name
      }
    }
  }
}
```

### 3.1.4  *Paginating through a list of records*

When you need to retrieve a page of records, in addition to specifying a limit, you need to specify an offset. In the GitHub API, you can use the field arguments after and before to offset the results returned by the arguments first and last, respectively.

To use these arguments, you need to work with *node identifiers*, which are different than database record identifiers. The pagination interface that the GitHub API uses is called the Connection interface (which originated from the Relay framework as well).

In that interface, every record is identified by a `node` field (similar to the `Node` interface) using a `cursor` field. The cursor is basically the ID field for each node, and it is the field we use with the `before` and `after` arguments.

To work with every node's cursor next to that node's data, the `Connection` interface adds a new parent to the node concept called an *edge*. The `edges` field represents a list of paginated records.

Here is a query that includes cursor values through the `edges` field.

**Listing 3.7  Working with cursors under edges (az.dev/gia)**

```
query OrgRepoConnectionExample {
  organization(login: "jscomplete") {
    repositories(first: 10, orderBy: { field: CREATED_AT, direction: ASC }) {
      edges {
        cursor
        node {
          name
        }
      }
    }
  }
}
```

Note that within an `edges` field, we now ask about a single `node` field because the list is no longer a list of nodes but rather a list of edges where each edge is a node plus a cursor.

Now that you can see the string values of these cursors, you can use them as the `after` and `before` arguments to fetch extra pages of data. For example, to fetch the second page of the repositories under the jsComplete organization, you need to identify the cursor of the last repository on the first page and use that cursor value as the `after` value.

**Listing 3.8  Fetching the second page of repos (az.dev/gia)**

```
query OrgRepoConnectionExample2 {
  organization(login: "jscomplete") {
    repositories(
      first: 10,
      after: "Y3Vyc29yOnYyOpK5MjAxNy0wMS0yMVQwODo1NTo0My0wODowMM4Ev4A3",
      orderBy: { field: CREATED_AT, direction: ASC }
    ) {
      edges {
        cursor
        node {
          name
        }
      }
    }
  }
}
```

The introduction of the `edges` field also allows the addition of metadata about the list. For example, on the same level where we ask for a list of edges, we can also ask how many records in total this relation has and whether there are more records to fetch after the current page. Here is the previous query modified to show some metadata about the relation.

**Listing 3.9 Meta-pagination information (az.dev/gia)**

```
query OrgReposMetaInfoExample {
  organization(login: "jscomplete") {
    repositories(
      first: 10,
      after: "Y3Vyc29yOnYyOpK5MjAxNy0wMS0yMVQwODo1NTo0My0wODowMM4Ev4A3",
      orderBy: { field: STARGAZERS, direction: DESC }
    ) {
      totalCount
      pageInfo {
        hasNextPage
      }
      edges {
        cursor
        node {
          name
        }
      }
    }
  }
}
```

Since the jsComplete organization has more than 20 repositories (two pages, in this example), the hasNextPage field is `true`. When you fetch the very last page, `hasNext-Page` will return `false`, indicating that there is no more data to fetch. This is much better than having to do an extra empty page fetch to conclude that you have reached the end of the paginated data.

### 3.1.5 Searching and filtering

A field argument in GraphQL can be used to provide filtering criteria or search terms to limit the results returned by a list. Let's see examples for both features.

In GitHub, a repository can have a list of projects to manage any work related to that repository. For example, the Twitter Bootstrap repository at GitHub uses a project per release to manage all the issues related to a single release. Here is a query that uses a search term within the `projects` relation to return the Twitter Bootstrap projects that start with `v4.1`.

**Listing 3.10 Using field arguments to search (az.dev/gia)**

```
query SearchExample {
  repository(owner: "twbs", name: "bootstrap") {
    projects(search: "v4.1", first: 10) {
```

```
      nodes {
        name
      }
    }
  }
}
```

Note that the `projects` field also implements the `Connection` interface.

Some fields allow you to filter the returned list by certain properties of that field. For example, by default, the list of your repositories under the `viewer` field includes all the repositories that you own or can contribute to. To list only the repositories that you own, you can use the `affiliations` field argument.

**Listing 3.11   Using field arguments to filter (az.dev/gia)**

```
query FilterExample {
  viewer {
    repositories(first: 10, affiliations: OWNER) {
      totalCount
      nodes {
        name
      }
    }
  }
}
```

### 3.1.6   *Providing input for mutations*

The field arguments concept is what GraphQL mutations use to accept the mutation operation's input. In the previous chapter, we used the following mutation example to add a star to the graphql-in-action repository under the jsComplete organization.

**Listing 3.12   Arguments to provide mutation input (az.dev/gia)**

```
mutation StarARepo {
  addStar(input: { starrableId: "MDEwOlJlcG9zaXRvcnkxMjU2ODEwMDY=" }) {
    starrable {
      stargazers {
        totalCount
      }
    }
  }
}
```

The `input` value in that mutation is also a field argument. It is a required argument. You cannot perform a GitHub mutation operation without an `input` object. All GitHub API mutations use this single required `input` field argument that represents an object. To perform a mutation, you pass the various input values as key/value pairs on that `input` object.

**NOTE**  Not all arguments are required. A GraphQL API can control which arguments are required and which are optional.

There are many more cases where a field argument can be useful. Explore the GitHub API and other publicly available GraphQL APIs for more useful patterns for field arguments.

## 3.2 Renaming fields with aliases

The alias feature in a GraphQL operation is very simple but powerful because it allows you to customize a response coming from the server through the request itself. By using aliases, you can minimize any post-response processing on the data.

Let me explain this with an example. Let's say you are developing the profile page in GitHub. Here is a query to retrieve partial profile information for a GitHub user.

> **Listing 3.13  Profile information query (az.dev/gia)**

```
query ProfileInfo {
  user(login: "samerbuna") {
    name
    company
    bio
  }
}
```

You get a simple user object in the response (see figure 3.2).

**Figure 3.2  The `ProfileInfo` query asking for a `company` field**

Now an application UI can use this user object in the query's response to substitute for the values in a UI template. However, suppose you have just discovered a mismatch between the structure of your response and the structure the application UI is using for the user object. The application UI was developed to expect a companyName field on a user instead of a company field (as found in the API response). What do you do? Assume that changing the application UI code itself is not an option.

If you do not have the option to use an alias (I will show you how in a bit), you can process the response every time you need to use the response object. You'll have to transform the user object from the response into a new object with the right structure. This can be costly if the structure you are working with is deep and has multiple levels.

Luckily, in GraphQL, the awesome alias feature lets us declaratively instruct the API server to return fields using different names. All you need to do is specify an alias for that field, which you can do using this syntax:

```
aliasName: fieldName
```

Just prefix any field name with an alias, and the server will return that field renamed using your alias. There is no need to process the response object. For the example in listing 3.13, all you need to do is specify a companyName alias.

**Listing 3.14   Profile information query with an alias (az.dev/gia)**

```
query ProfileInfoWithAlias {
  user(login: "samerbuna") {
    name
    companyName: company
    bio
  }
}
```

This gives a response that is ready for you to plug into the application UI (see figure 3.3).

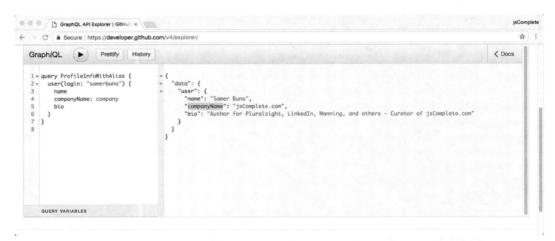

**Figure 3.3   Using the GraphQL alias feature to get a companyName field from the server**

## 3.3    *Customizing responses with directives*

Sometimes, the customization you need on a server response goes beyond the simple renaming of fields. You may need to conditionally include (or exclude) branches of data in your responses. This is where the directives feature of GraphQL can be helpful.

A *directive* in a GraphQL request is a way to provide a GraphQL server with additional information about the execution and type validation behavior of a GraphQL document. It is essentially a more powerful version of field arguments: you can use directives to conditionally include or exclude an entire field. In addition to fields, directives can be used with fragments and top-level operations.

A directive is any string in a GraphQL document that begins with the @ character. Every GraphQL schema has three built-in directives: @include, @skip, and @deprecated. Some schemas have more directives. You can use this introspective query to see the list of directives supported by a schema.

##### Listing 3.15    All the supported directives in a schema (az.dev/gia)

```
query AllDirectives {
  __schema {
    directives {
      name
      description
      locations
      args {
        name
        description
        defaultValue
      }
    }
  }
}
```

This query shows the name and description of each directive and includes an array of all possible locations where that directive can be used (figure 3.4). In addition, it lists all arguments supported by that directive. Each directive can optionally receive a list of arguments, and just like field arguments, some argument values may be required by the API server. The response to the previous query should show that in any GraphQL schema, both the @include and @skip directives have the argument if. The @deprecated directive has the argument reason.

The list of locations in the previous query's response is also important. Directives can be used only in the locations they are declared to belong to. For example, the @include and @skip directives can only be used after fields or fragments. You cannot use them at the top level of an operation. Similarly, the @deprecated directive can only be used after field definitions or ENUM values when defining a GraphQL service schema.

**NOTE**    An ENUM (enumerated) type represents a set of possible unique values. We'll see an example in the next chapter.

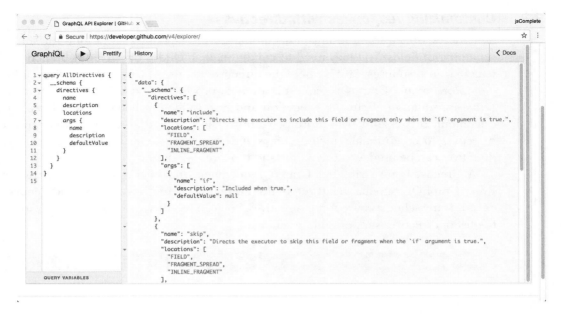

**Figure 3.4   List of all directives supported by a schema**

Since directives are usually used with arguments, they are often paired with query variables to have them sent with a dynamic value. We saw some examples of variables in the previous chapter, but let me remind you about them.

### 3.3.1   *Variables and input values*

A *variable* is simply any name in the GraphQL document that begins with a $ sign: for example, $login or $showRepositories. The name after the $ sign can be anything. We use variables to make GraphQL operations generically reusable and avoid having to hardcode values and concatenate strings.

To use a variable in a GraphQL operation, you first need to define its type. You do that by providing arguments to any named operation. For example, let's take the query example that we used to read information about the jsComplete organization at GitHub. Instead of hardcoding the login value (as we did before), let's now use a variable. The operation must have a name, and then we can use that name's arguments to define any variables. Let's call the variable $orgLogin. It should be a required string. You can see the type of the arguments using the Docs explorer. Look up the organization field to see the type of its login argument. You can also click the organization field in the query while holding the Command key (Ctrl in Windows).

As you can see in figure 3.5, the login argument has a type of String!. The trailing exclamation mark on that type is GraphQL's way of labeling the argument value as required. A value for this login argument must be specified—it cannot be null.

**Figure 3.5   Looking up one field's documentation in a schema**

Now we can use the same syntax to define the new variable. The type for `$orgLogin` should match the type of the argument where it is going to be used. Here is the `OrgInfo` query written with this new `$orgLogin` variable.

---

**Listing 3.16   Using variables for argument values (az.dev/gia)**

```
query OrgInfo($orgLogin: String!) {
  organization(login: $orgLogin) {
    name
    description
    websiteUrl
  }
}
```

Note that on the first line, the query specifies that `$orgLogin` is a `String!`.

You cannot execute the query in listing 3.16 as is. If you try, the GraphQL server will return an error. Since we used a variable, we must give the executor on the server the value that we wish to use for that variable. In GraphiQL, we do that using the variables editor, which is in the lower-left corner. In that editor, you write a JSON object that represents all variables you want to send to the executor along with the operation.

Since we used only one variable, the JSON object for that is

```
{
  "orgLogin": "jscomplete"
}
```

Now you can execute the query with different JSON objects, making it reusable for different organizations (see figure 3.6).

**Figure 3.6   Variables make a GraphQL query reusable.**

A variable like $orgLogin can also have a default value, in which case it does not need the trailing exclamation mark. You specify the default value using an equals sign after the type of the variable. For example, the previous query can have the value "jscomplete" as the default value of $orgLogin using this syntax.

---

**Listing 3.17   Using default values for variables (az.dev/gia)**

```
query OrgInfoWithDefault($orgLogin: String = "jscomplete") {
  organization(login: $orgLogin) {
    name
    description
    websiteUrl
  }
}
```

You can execute this OrgInfoWithDefault query without passing a JSON object for variables. The query will use the default value in that case. If you pass a JSON object with a value for orgLogin, that value will override the default value.

Variables can be used in fields and directives to make them accept input values of various literal primitives. An input value can be scalar, like Int, Float, String, Boolean, or Null. It can also be an ENUM value, a list, or an object. The $orgLogin variable represents a scalar string input value for the login argument within the organization field. Read the various GraphQL operation examples we have seen so far and try to identify more input values. For example, try to find where we used an object as an input value.

Now that we know how to define and use variables and values, let's use them with directives.

### 3.3.2 The @include directive

The `@include` directive can be used after fields (or fragments) to provide a condition (using its `if` argument). That condition controls whether the field (or fragment) should be included in the response. The use of the `@include` directive looks like this:

```
fieldName @include(if: $someTest)
```

This says to include the field when the query is executed with `$someTest` set to `true` and not to include the field when `$someTest` is set to `false`. Let's look at an example from the GitHub API.

Building on the previous `OrgInfo` query example, let's assume that we want to conditionally include an organization's `websiteUrl` based on whether we are showing full or partial details in the UI. Let's design a Boolean variable to represent this flag and call it `$fullDetails`.

This new `$fullDetails` variable will be required because we are about to use it with a directive. The first line of the `OrgInfo` query needs to be changed to add the type of `$fullDetails`:

```
query OrgInfo($orgLogin: String!, $fullDetails: Boolean!) {
```

Now we want to include the `websiteUrl` only when we execute the `OrgInfo` query with `$fullDetails` set to `true`. A simple use of the `@include` directive can do that. The `if` argument value in this case will be the `$fullDetails` variable. Here is the full query.

Listing 3.18   The `@include` directive (az.dev/gia)

```
query OrgInfo($orgLogin: String!, $fullDetails: Boolean!) {
  organization(login: $orgLogin) {
    name
    description
    websiteUrl @include(if: $fullDetails)
  }
}
```

Go ahead and test this query by executing it with `$fullDetails` set to `true` and then to `false`. You will see that the response honors that Boolean value and uses it to include or exclude `websiteUrl` from the response object (see figure 3.7).

**Figure 3.7   Using the @include directive with a variable**

### 3.3.3   *The @skip directive*

This directive is simply the inverse of the @include directive. Just like the @include directive, it can be used after fields (or fragments) to provide a condition (using its if argument). The condition controls whether the field (or fragment) should be excluded in the response. The use of the @skip directive looks like this:

```
fieldName @skip(if: $someTest)
```

This means to exclude the field when the query is executed with $someTest set to true and include the field when $someTest is set to false. This directive is useful to avoid negating a variable value, especially if that variable has a negative name already.

Suppose that instead of designing the Boolean variable to be $fullDetails, we decide to name it $partialDetails. Instead of inverting that variable value in the JSON values object, we can use the @skip directive to use the $partialDetails value directly. The OrgInfo query becomes the following.

**Listing 3.19   The @skip directive (az.dev/gia)**

```
query OrgInfo($orgLogin: String!, $partialDetails: Boolean!) {
  organization(login: $orgLogin) {
    name
    description
    websiteUrl @skip(if: $partialDetails)
  }
}
```

Note that a field (or fragment) can be followed by multiple directives. You can repeat `@include` multiple times or even use both `@include` and `@skip` together. All directive conditions must be met for the field (or fragment) to be included or excluded.

Neither `@include` nor `@skip` has precedence over the other. When used together, a field is included only when the include condition is true *and* the skip condition is false; it is excluded when either the include condition is false *or* the skip condition is true. The following query will never include `websiteUrl` no matter what value you use for `$partialDetails`.

**Listing 3.20  Using `@include` and `@skip` together (az.dev/gia)**

```
query OrgInfo($orgLogin: String!, $partialDetails: Boolean!) {
  organization(login: $orgLogin) {
    name
    description
    websiteUrl @skip(if: $partialDetails) @include(if: false)
  }
}
```

### 3.3.4  The @deprecated directive

This special directive can be used in GraphQL servers to indicate deprecated portions of a GraphQL service's schema, such as deprecated fields on a type or deprecated ENUM values.

When deprecating a field in a GraphQL schema, the `@deprecated` directive supports a `reason` argument to provide the reason behind the deprecation. The following is the GraphQL's schema language representation of a type that has a deprecated field.

**Listing 3.21  The `@deprecated` directive**

```
type User {
  emailAddress: String
  email: String @deprecated(reason: "Use 'emailAddress'.")
}
```

## 3.4  GraphQL fragments

When we explored directives, I kept adding "(or fragment)" whenever I mentioned the use of a directive. It is now time to discuss my favorite feature of the GraphQL language: fragments!

### 3.4.1  Why fragments?

To build anything complicated, the truly helpful strategy is to split what needs to be built into smaller parts and then focus on one part at a time. Ideally, the smaller parts should be designed in a way that does not couple them with each other. They should be testable on their own, and they should also be reusable. A big system should be the result of putting these parts together and having them communicate with each other to form features. For example, in the UI domain, React.js (and other libraries) popularized the idea of using small components to build a full UI.

In GraphQL, fragments are the composition units of the language. They provide a way to split big GraphQL operations into smaller parts. A fragment in GraphQL is simply a reusable piece of any GraphQL operation.

I like to compare GraphQL fragments to UI components. Fragments, if you will, are the components of a GraphQL operation.

Splitting a big GraphQL document into smaller parts is the main advantage of GraphQL fragments. However, fragments can also be used to avoid duplicating a group of fields in a GraphQL operation. We will explore both benefits, but let's first understand the syntax for defining and using fragments.

### 3.4.2  *Defining and using fragments*

To define a GraphQL fragment, you can use the `fragment` top-level keyword in any GraphQL document. You give the fragment a name and specify the type on which that fragment can be used. Then, you write a partial query to represent the fragment.

For example, let's take the simple GitHub organization information query example:

```
query OrgInfo {
  organization(login: "jscomplete") {
    name
    description
    websiteUrl
  }
}
```

To make this query use a fragment, you first need to define the fragment.

**Listing 3.22  Defining a fragment in GraphQL**

```
fragment orgFields on Organization {
  name
  description
  websiteUrl
}
```

This defines an `orgFields` fragment that can be used within a selection set that expands an `organization` field. The `on Organization` part of the definition is called the *type condition* of the fragment. Since a fragment is essentially a selection set, you can only define fragments on object types. You cannot define a fragment on a scalar value.

To use the fragment, you "spread" its name where the fields were originally used in the query.

**Listing 3.23   Using a fragment in GraphQL**

```
query OrgInfoWithFragment {
  organization(login: "jscomplete") {
    ...orgFields
  }
}
```

The three dots before `orgFields` are what you use to spread that fragment. The concept of spreading a fragment is similar to the concept of spreading an object in JavaScript. The same three-dots operator can be used in JavaScript to spread an object inside another object, effectively cloning that object.

The three-dotted fragment name (`...orgFields`) is called a *fragment spread*. You can use a fragment spread anywhere you use a regular field in any GraphQL operation.

A fragment spread can only be used when the type condition of that fragment matches the type of the object under which you want to use that fragment. There are no generic fragments in GraphQL. Also, when a fragment is defined in a GraphQL document, that fragment must be used somewhere. You cannot send a GraphQL server a document that defines fragments but does not use them.

### 3.4.3   *Fragments and DRY*

Fragments can be used to reduce any duplicated text in a GraphQL document. Consider this example query from the GitHub API.

**Listing 3.24   Example query with repeated sections (az.dev/gia)**

```
query MyRepos {
  viewer {
    ownedRepos: repositories(affiliations: OWNER, first: 10) {
      nodes {
        nameWithOwner
        description
        forkCount
      }
    }
    orgsRepos: repositories(affiliations: ORGANIZATION_MEMBER, first: 10) {
      nodes {
        nameWithOwner
        description
        forkCount
      }
    }
  }
}
```

This query uses a simple alias with field arguments to have two lists with an identical structure: one list for the repositories owned by the current authenticated user and a second list of the repositories under organizations of which the current authenticated user is a member.

This is a simple query, but there is room for improvement. The fields under a repository connection are repeated. We can use a fragment to define these fields just once and then use that fragment in the two places where the `nodes` field is repeated. The `nodes` field is defined on the special `RepositoryConnection` in GitHub (it is the connection between a user and a list of repositories).

Here is the same GraphQL operation modified to use a fragment to remove the duplicated parts.

Listing 3.25  Using fragments to minimize repetition (az.dev/gia)

```
query MyRepos {
  viewer {
    ownedRepos: repositories(affiliations: OWNER, first: 10) {
      ...repoInfo
    }
    orgsRepos: repositories(affiliations: ORGANIZATION_MEMBER, first: 10) {
      ...repoInfo
    }
  }
}
fragment repoInfo on RepositoryConnection {
  nodes {
    nameWithOwner
    description
    forkCount
  }
}
```

Pretty neat, right? But as I mentioned, the DRY benefit of fragments is less important. The big advantage of fragments is that they can be matched with other units of composition (like UI components). Let's talk about that!

### 3.4.4  Fragments and UI components

The word *component* can mean different things to different people. In the UI domain, a component can be an abstract input text box or Twitter's full 280-character tweet form with its buttons and counter display. You can pick any part of an application and call it a component. Components can be small or big. They can be functional on their own, or they can be parts that have to be put together to make something functional.

Bigger components can be composed of smaller ones. For example, Twitter's `TweetForm` component may consist of a `TextArea` component with a `TweetButton` component and a few others to attach an image, add a location, and count the number of characters typed in the text area.

All HTML elements can be considered simple components. They have properties and behaviors, but they are limited because they cannot represent dynamic data. The story of UI components gets interesting when we make a component represent data. We can do that with modern libraries and frameworks like React.js, Angular.js, and Polymer.js. These data components can then be reused for any data that matches the shape they have been designed to work with. The data components do not care about what that data is; they are only concerned about the shape of that data.

> **TIP** Data components are making their way into browsers with what are commonly called *web components*. Many browsers support most of the features needed to define and use web components. The Polymer.js project is designed to provide polyfills to support using web components in any browser and then to enhance the features offered by these components.

Let's assume we are building an app like Twitter by using rich data components, and let's take one example page from that app and analyze it in terms of components and their data requirements. I picked the user's profile page for this example.

The user's profile page is simple: it displays public information about a user, some stats, and a list of their tweets. For example, if you navigate to twitter.com/ManningBooks, you will see something like figure 3.8.

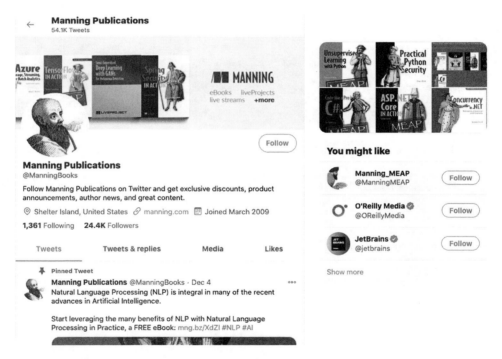

**Figure 3.8  The @ManningBooks profile page at Twitter**

I can see at least 12 components on this page:

- The `Header` component, which can include the following components: `Tweet-Count`, `ProfileImage`, `UserInfo`, `FollowingCount`, and `FollowersCount`

- The Sidebar component, which can include the following components: User-Media, MediaItem, and SuggestedFollowing
- The TweetList component, which is simply a list of Tweet components

This is just one choice of components. The page can be built with many more components, and it can also be built with just two components. No matter how small or big the components you design are, they share a simple characteristic: they all depend on data that has a certain shape.

For example, the Header component in this UI needs a data object to represent a profile. The shape of that data object might look like this.

**Listing 3.26   Possible shape of a data object for Twitter's profile page**

```
const profileData = {
  tweetsCount: ·-·-·,
  profileImageUrl: ·-·-·,
  backgroundImageUrl: ·-·-·,
  name: ·-·-·,
  handle: ·-·-·,
  bio: ·-·-·,
  location: ·-·-·,
  url: ·-·-·,
  createdAt: ·-·-·,
  followingCount: ·-·-·,
  followersCount: ·-·-·,
};
```

The TweetList component needs a data object that might look like this.

**Listing 3.27   Possible shape of a data object to represent a list of tweets**

```
const tweetList = [
  { id: ·-·-·,
    name: ·-·-·,
    handle: ·-·-·,
    date: ·-·-·,
    body: ·-·-·,
    repliesCount: ·-·-·,
    tweetsCount: ·-·-·,
    likes: ·-·-·,
  },
  { id: ·-·-·,
    name: ·-·-·,
    handle: ·-·-·,
    date: ·-·-·,
    body: ·-·-·,
    repliesCount: ·-·-·,
    tweetsCount: ·-·-·,
    likesCount: ·-·-·,
  },
  ·-·-·,
];
```

These components can be used to render information about any profile and any list of tweets. The same `TweetList` component can be used on Twitter's main page, a user's list page, or the search page.

As long as we feed these components the exact shape of data they need, they will work. This is where GraphQL comes into the picture: we can use it to describe the data shape that an application requires.

A GraphQL query can be used to describe an application data requirement. The data required by an application is the sum of the data required by that application's individual components, and GraphQL fragments offer a way to split a big query into smaller ones. This makes a GraphQL fragment the perfect match for a component! We can use a GraphQL fragment to represent the data requirements for a single component and then put these fragments together to compose the data requirements for the entire application.

To simplify the Twitter example, we will build the profile page with just these four primary components: `Header`, `Sidebar`, `TweetList`, and `Tweet`. Let's come up with the data required by the Twitter profile page example using a single GraphQL query for each of these components. The data required by the `Header` component can be declared using this GraphQL fragment.

##### Listing 3.28 Fragment for the `Header` UI component

```
fragment headerData on User {
  tweetsCount
  profileImageUrl
  backgroundImageUrl
  name
  handle
  bio
  location
  url
  createdAt
  followingCount
  followersCount
}
```

The data required by the `Sidebar` component can be declared using this fragment.

##### Listing 3.29 Fragment for the `Sidebar` UI component

```
fragment sidebarData on User {
  SuggestedFollowing {
    profileImageUrl
  }
  media {
    mediaUrl
  }
}
```

Note that the suggestedFollowing part and the media part can also come from the subcomponents we identified earlier in the Sidebar component.

The data required by a single Tweet component can be declared as follows.

**Listing 3.30    Fragment for the Tweet UI component**

```
fragment tweetData on Tweet {
  user {
    name
    handle
  }
  createdAt
  body
  repliesCount
  retweetsCount
  likesCount
}
```

Finally, the data required by the TweetList component is an array of the exact data required by a single Tweet component. So, we can use the tweetData fragment here.

**Listing 3.31    Fragment for the TweetList UI component**

```
fragment tweetListData on TweetList {
  tweets: {
    ...tweetData
  }
}
```

To come up with the data required by the entire page, all we need to do is put these fragments together and form one GraphQL query using fragment spreads.

**Listing 3.32    Combining fragments to form one query for a UI view**

```
query ProfilePageData {
  user(handle: "ManningBooks") {
    ...headerData
    ...sidebarData
    ...tweetListData
  }
}
```

Now we can send this single ProfilePageData query to the GraphQL server and get back all the data needed for all the components on the profile page.

When the data comes back, we can identify which component requested which parts of the response and make those parts available to only the components that requested them. This helps isolate a component from any data it does not need.

But this is not the coolest thing about this approach. By making every component responsible for declaring the data it needs, these components have the power to change their data requirements when necessary without having to depend on any of their parent components in the tree.

For example, let's assume Twitter decided to show the number of views each tweet has received next to the `likesCount`. All we need to do to satisfy the new data requirements for this UI change is to modify the `tweetData` fragment.

**Listing 3.33 Modifying one fragment to match its UI component's needs**

```
fragment tweetData on Tweet {
  user {
    name
    handle
  }
  createdAt
  body
  repliesCount
  retweetsCount
  likesCount
  viewsCount
}
```

None of the other application components need to worry about this change or even be aware of it. For example, the direct parent of a `Tweet` component, the `TweetList` component, does not have to be modified to make this change happen. That component always constructs its own data requirements by using the `Tweet` component's data requirement, no matter what that `Tweet` component asked for. This is great. It makes maintaining and extending this app a much easier task.

Fragments are to queries what UI components are to a full application. By matching every UI component in the application to a GraphQL fragment, we give these components the power of independence. Each component can declare its own data requirement using a GraphQL fragment, and we can compose the data required by the full application by putting together these GraphQL fragments.

### 3.4.5 Inline fragments for interfaces and unions

Earlier in this chapter, we saw an example of an inline fragment when we talked about the `Node` interface. Inline fragments are, in a way, similar to anonymous functions that you can use without a name. They are just fragments without names, and you can spread them inline where you define them.

Here is an inline fragment use case from the GitHub API.

**Listing 3.34 Inline fragment example (az.dev/gia)**

```
query InlineFragmentExample {
  repository(owner: "facebook", name: "graphql") {
    ref(qualifiedName: "master") {
      target {
        ... on Commit {
```

```
        message
      }
    }
  }
  }
}
```

Inline fragments can be used as a type condition when querying against an interface or a union. The bolded part in the query in listing 3.34 is an inline fragment on the Commit type within the target object interface; so, to understand the value of inline fragments, you first need to understand the concepts of unions and interfaces in GraphQL.

Interfaces and unions are abstract types in GraphQL. An interface defines a list of "shared" fields, and a union defines a list of possible object types. Object types in a GraphQL schema can implement an interface that guarantees that the implementing object type will have the list of fields defined by the implemented interface. Object types defined as unions guarantee that what they return will be one of the possible types of that union.

In the previous example query, the target field is an interface that represents a Git object. Since a Git object can be a commit, tag, blob, or tree, all these object types in the GitHub API implement the GitObject interface; because of that, they all get a guarantee that they implement all the fields a GitObject implements (like repository, since a Git object belongs to a single repository).

Within a repository, the GitHub API has the option to read information about a Git reference using the ref field. Every Git reference points to an object, which the GitHub API named target. Now, since that target can be one of four different object types that implement the GitObject interface, within a target field, you can expand the selection set with the interface fields; but you can also conditionally expand its selection set based on the type of that object. If the object that this ref points to happens to be a Commit, what information from that commit are you interested in? What if that object is a Tag?

This is where inline fragments are useful because they basically represent a type condition. The inline fragment in the previous query essentially means this exact condition: if the object pointed to by the reference is a commit, then return the message of that commit. Otherwise, the target will return nothing. You can use another inline fragment to add more cases for the condition.

The union concept is probably a bit easier to understand. It is basically OR logic. A type can be this or that. In fact, some union types are named xOrY. In the GitHub API, you can see an example under a repository field, where you can ask for issueOrPull-Request. Within this union type, the only field you can ask for is the special __typename meta-field, which can be used to answer the question, "Is this an issue or a pull request?"

Here is an example from the facebook/graphql repository.

Listing 3.35   Example GraphQL union type (az.dev/gia)

```
query RepoUnionExample {
  repository(owner: "facebook", name: "graphql") {
    issueOrPullRequest(number: 3) {
      __typename
    }
  }
}
```

The `issueOrPullRequest` with number 3 on this repository happens to be an issue. If you try the query with number 5 instead of 3, you should see a pull request. An inline fragment is useful here to conditionally pick fields within an `issueOrPullRequest` based on the type. For example, maybe we are interested in the merge information of a pull request and the closing information of an issue. Here is a query to pick these different fields based on the type of the `issueOrPullRequest` whose number is 5.

```
query RepoUnionExampleFull {
  repository(owner: "facebook", name: "graphql") {
    issueOrPullRequest(number: 5) {
      ... on PullRequest {
        merged
        mergedAt
      }
      ... on Issue {
        closed
        closedAt
      }
    }
  }
}
```

Since number 5 (in this repository) is a pull request, the `merged` and `mergedAt` fields will be used for this query.

Another common use of union types is to implement a search field to search among multiple types. For example, a GitHub user search might return a user object or an organization object. Here is a query to search GitHub users for the term `"graphql"`.

Listing 3.37   The union-type search field (az.dev/gia)

```
query TestSearch {
  search(first: 100, query: "graphql", type: USER) {
    nodes {
      ... on User {
```

```
      name
      bio
    }
    ... on Organization {
      login
      description
    }
  }
}
}
```

You should see users who have the term "graphql" somewhere in their profile and organizations with that term in their name or description. When the matching returned item is a User object, the fields name and bio are returned; and when the item is an Organization object, the fields login and description are returned.

## Summary

- You can pass arguments to GraphQL fields when sending requests. GraphQL servers can use these arguments to support features like identifying a single record, limiting the number of records returned by a list field, ordering records and paginating through them, searching and filtering, and providing input values for mutations.
- You can give any GraphQL field an alias name. This enables you to customize a server response using the client's request text.
- You can use GraphQL directives to customize the structure of a GraphQL server response based on conditions in your applications.
- Directives and field arguments are often used with request variables. These variables make your GraphQL requests reusable with dynamic values without needing to resort to string concatenation.
- You can use fragments, which are the composition units of GraphQL, to reuse common parts of a GraphQL query and compose a full query by putting together multiple fragments. This is a winning strategy when paired with UI components and their data needs. GraphQL also supports inline fragments that can be used to conditionally pick information out of union object types or object types that implement an interface.

# Part 2

# *Building GraphQL APIs*

In part 1 of this book, you learned the fundamentals of the GraphQL "language" that API consumers can use to ask GraphQL services for data and instruct them to do mutations. It is now time to learn how to create GraphQL services that can understand that language. In this part of the book, we'll do exactly that by building a real data API for a real web application.

In chapter 4, you'll learn about mapping planned UI features to API operations. You'll start the practical process of coming up with the structure of a GraphQL schema and understand it in the context of database models.

Chapter 5 will walk you through making a simple GraphQL schema executable using Node.js database drivers and the GraphQL.js implementation. You'll learn about resolver functions and GraphQL built-in types.

In chapter 6, you'll learn how to resolve fields from databases to implement the API queries of the book's project. Chapter 7 builds on that and explores some optimizations for GraphQL queries. And in chapter 8, you'll learn how to resolve API mutation operations to create, update, and delete database entities.

# Designing
# a GraphQL schema

**This chapter covers**

- Planning UI features and mapping them to API operations
- Coming up with schema language text based on planned operations
- Mapping API features to sources of data

In this chapter, we are going to build a real data API for a real web application. I picked the name AZdev for it, which is short for "A to Z" of developer resources. AZdev will be a searchable library of practical micro-documentation, errors and solutions, and general tips for software developers.

I am not a fan of useless abstract examples that are removed from practical realities. Let's build something real (and useful).

## 4.1 Why AZdev?

When software developers are performing their day-to-day tasks, they often need to look up one particular thing, such as how to compute the sum of an array of numbers in JavaScript. They are not really interested in scanning pages of documentation to find the simple code example they need. This is why at AZdev, they will find an entry on "Calculate the sum of numbers in a JavaScript array" featuring multiple approaches on just that particular code-development need.

AZdev is not a question-answer site. It is a library of what developers usually look up. It's a quick way for them to find concise approaches to handle exactly what they need at the moment.

Here are some examples of entries I would imagine finding on AZdev:

- Get rid of only the unstaged changes since the last Git commit
- Create a secure one-way hash for a text value (like a password) in Node
- A Linux command to lowercase names of all files in a directory

You can certainly find approaches to these needs by reading documentation and Stack Overflow questions, but wouldn't it be nice to have a site that features specific tasks like these with their approaches right there, without all the noise?

AZdev is something I have wished existed for as long as I can remember. Let's take the first step into making it happen. Let's build an API for it!

## 4.2 The API requirements for AZdev

A great way to start thinking about a GraphQL schema is to look at it from the point of view of the UIs you'll be building and what data operations they will require. However, before we do that, let's first figure out the sources of data the API service is going to use. GraphQL is not a data storage service; it's an interface to one or many (figure 4.1).

To make things interesting for the AZdev GraphQL API, we will have it work with two different data services. We'll use a relational database service to store transactional data and a document database service to store dynamic data. A GraphQL schema can resolve data from many services, even in the same query!

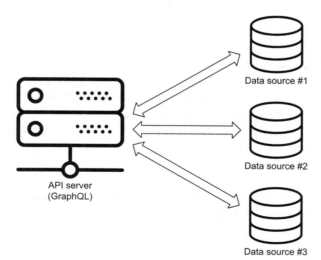

Figure 4.1  An API server interfaces data-storage services.

It's not at all unusual to have many sources of data in the same project. They don't all have to be database services. A project can use a key-value cache service, get some data from other APIs, or even read data directly from files in the filesystem. A GraphQL schema can interface as many services as needed.

For the API vocabulary, let's use the word *Task* to represent a single micro-documentation entry at AZdev and the word *Approach* for a single way or method to do that Task. A Task can have multiple Approaches. An Approach belongs to a Task.

> **NOTE** From now on, I will use the capitalized version of the words *task* and *approach* to refer to the database/API entities: for example, "Our first task is to create a Tasks table, and we will approach the Approaches table with some constraints in mind."

### Naming entities in a GraphQL schema

I am using simple names for the entities of this small API, but when you're designing a big GraphQL API with entities that are related to multiple other entities, you should invest a little time when it comes to naming things.

This is general programming advice; but for GraphQL schemas, try to use specific names for your types when possible. For example, if you have a lesson that belongs to a course, name that type `CourseLesson` instead of just `Lesson`, even if the database model is named `lessons`. This is especially important if your GraphQL service is public. Your database schemas will evolve, and the types you use to describe their entities will need to evolve as well. You'll need to deprecate types and introduce new ones. Specificity makes all that easier.

Anyone can browse AZdev and find Tasks and Approaches. Logged-in users can add new Tasks and Approaches, and they can also up-vote or down-vote Approaches.

AZdev's main entries for both Tasks and Approaches will be stored in a relational database. I picked PostgreSQL for that. We'll also store the User records in PostgreSQL. A relational database like PostgreSQL is great for, well, relations! A Task has many Approaches and is defined by a User.

> **NOTE** Why PostgreSQL? PostgreSQL is a scalable, open source, object-relational database that's free to use and easy to set up. It offers an impressive set of advanced features that will be handy when you need them. It is one of the most popular choices among open source relational databases.

Extra data elements on Approaches like explanations, warnings, or general notes will be stored in a document database. I picked MongoDB for that. A document database like MongoDB is "schemaless," which makes it a good fit for this type of dynamic data. An Approach might have a warning or an explanation associated with it, and it might have other data elements that we're not aware of at the moment. Maybe at some point we will decide to add some performance metrics on Approaches or include a list of related links. We don't need to modify a database schema for that; we can just instruct MongoDB to store these new data elements.

> **NOTE**   Why MongoDB? MongoDB is the most popular open source document (NoSQL) database. The company behind it (MongoDB, Inc.) offers a community edition that is free to use and available on the three major operating systems.

> **TIP**   This book will not be a proper source for you to learn these database services. However, the concepts we use in these services will be briefly explained, and all the commands and queries related to them will be provided as we progress through the API. I'll also provide some sample data to help test the API features we add.

### 4.2.1   *The core types*

The main entities in the API I'm envisioning for AZdev are User, Task, and Approach. These will be represented by database tables in PostgreSQL. Let's make each table have a unique *identity* column and an automated *creation* date-time column.

In a GraphQL schema, tables are usually mapped to *object types*, and table columns are mapped to *fields* under these object types. I'll use the term *model* to represent an entity in the API (a table represented by a GraphQL type), and I'll use the term *field* to represent a property on an object under that model. Models are usually defined with upper camel-case (Pascal case), while fields are defined with lower camel-case (Dromedary case).

The User model will have fields to represent the information for a user. Let's start with name and username.

Both the Task and Approach models will have a content field to hold their main text content. Here's a schema language definition (SDL) that can be used to define the three core models in this API with their fields so far.

**Listing 4.1   SDL for the three core output object types**

```
type User {
  id: ID!
  createdAt: String!
  username: String!
  name: String

  # More fields for a User object
}

type Task {
  id: ID!
  createdAt: String!
  content: String!

  # More fields for a Task object
}
```

```
type Approach {
  id: ID!
  createdAt: String!
  content: String!

  # More fields for an Approach object
}
```

> **TIP** Open your code editor, type in the initial schema text in listing 4.1, and modify it as we progress through the analysis of the AZdev API. The rest of the SDL listings in this chapter will omit some existing parts of the schema for clarity.

Note that I defined the id field using the ID type. The ID type is special and means a unique identifier; it gets serialized as a String (even if the resolved values for it are integers). Using strings for IDs (instead of integers) is usually a good practice in JavaScript applications. The integer representation in JavaScript is limited.

Also note that I defined the createdAt "date" field as a String. GraphQL does not have a built-in format for date-time fields. The easiest way to work with these fields is to serialize them as strings in a standard format (like ISO/UTC).

Remember that the exclamation mark after the ID and String types indicates that these fields cannot have null values. Each record in the database will always have an id value and a createdAt value.

---

### GraphQL type modifiers

The trailing exclamation mark is known as a type modifier because it modifies a type to be not null. Another type modifier is a pair of square brackets around the type (for example, [String]) to indicate that a type is a list of items of another type. These modifiers can also be combined. For example, [String!]! means a non-null list consisting of non-null string items. We'll see an example of that shortly.

Note that if a field is defined with the type [String!]!, that does not mean the response of that field cannot be an empty array. It means it cannot be null.

If you want a field to always have a non-empty array, you can add that validation in its resolver's logic or define a custom GraphQL type for it.

---

The id and createdAt fields are examples of how GraphQL schema types don't have to exactly match the column types in your database. GraphQL gives you flexibility for casting one type from the database into a more useful type for the client. Try to spot other examples of this as we progress through the API.

> **NOTE** The object types in listing 4.1 are known as *output types* as they are used as output to operations, and also to distinguish them from *input types*, which are often used as input to mutation operations. We'll see examples of input types later in this chapter.

> ## Where is the password field?
>
> Why is there no `password` field in the `User` type?
>
> It's important to remember here that we are not designing a database schema (yet); we are designing an API schema. Some GraphQL tools let you generate a database schema from a GraphQL API schema, but that limits the important differences between these two.
>
> The `password` field should not be a readable part of the API schema. However, it will be part of the database schema (which we build in the next chapter).
>
> Note that the `password` field will be part of the mutations to create or authenticate a user, as we will see later in this chapter.

This is a good start for the three core object types. We'll add more fields to them as we discuss their relation to UI features. Let's do that next.

## 4.3    Queries

I like to come up with pseudo-code-style operations (queries, mutations, and subscriptions) that are based on the envisioned UI context and then design the schema types and fields to support these operations.

Let's start with the queries.

### 4.3.1    Listing the latest Task records

On the main page of AZdev, I would like to list the latest Task records. The GraphQL API has to provide a query root field to do that. This list will be limited to just the last 100 records, and it will always be sorted by the creation timestamp (newer first). Let's name this field `taskMainList`.

Listing 4.2    Pseudo query #1: `taskMainList`

```
query {
  taskMainList {
    id
    content

    # Fields on a Task object
  }
}
```

Note that I named the root field `taskMainList` instead of a more natural name like `mainTaskList`. This is just a style preference, but it has an advantage: by putting the subject of the action (`task`, in this case) first, all actions on that subject will naturally be grouped alphabetically in file trees and API explorers. This is helpful in many places, but you can think about the autocomplete list in GraphiQL as an example. If you're looking for what you can do on a Task model, you just type `task`, and all relevant actions will be presented in order in the autocomplete list. I'll follow this practice for all queries, mutations, and subscriptions of every entity of this API.

A query root field is one that is defined directly under the `Query` type. Every GraphQL schema starts with its root fields. They are the entry points with which API consumers will always start their data queries.

To support the simple `taskMainList` query root field, here's a possible schema design.

**Listing 4.3 Incremental UI-driven schema design**

```
type Query {
  taskMainList: [Task!]

  # More query root fields
}
```

The type for the new `taskMainList` is `[Task!]`. The square brackets modify the type to indicate that this field is a list of objects from the Task model. The resolver of this field will have to resolve it with an array. The exclamation mark after the `Task` type inside the square brackets indicates that all items in this array should have a value and that they cannot be null.

> **Root field nullability**
>
> A general good practice in GraphQL schemas is to make the types of fields non-null, unless you have a reason to distinguish between null and empty. A non-null type can still hold an empty value. For example, a non-null string can be empty, a non-null list can be an empty array, and a non-null object can be one with no properties.
>
> Only use nullable fields if you want to associate an actual semantic meaning with the absence of their values. However, root fields are special because making them nullable has an important consequence. In GraphQL.js implementations, when an error is thrown in any field's resolver, the built-in executor resolves that field with null. When an error is thrown in a resolver for a field that is defined as non-null, the executor propagates the nullability to the field's parent instead. If that parent field is also non-null, the executor continues up the tree until it finds a nullable field.
>
> This means if the root `taskMainList` field were to be made non-null, then when an error is thrown in its resolver, the nullability will propagate to the `Query` type (its parent). So the entire data response for a query asking for this field would be null, even if the query had other root fields.
>
> This is not ideal. One bad root field should not block the data response of other root fields. When we start implementing this GraphQL API in the next chapter, we will see an example.
>
> This is why I made the `taskMainList` nullable, and it's why I will make *all* root fields nullable. The semantic meaning of this nullability is, in this case, "Something went wrong in the resolver of this root field, and we're allowing it so that a response can still have partial data for other root fields."

Another way to implement the main Tasks list is to have a generic `taskList` root field and make that field support arguments to indicate any desired sorting and what limit to use. This is actually a more flexible option as it can be made to support many specific lists. However, flexibility comes with a cost. When designing a public API, it's safer to implement the exact features of the currently envisioned UI and then optimize and extend the API according to the changing demands of the UI. Specificity helps in making better changes going forward.

### 4.3.2    Search and the union/interface types

The main feature of the AZdev UI is its search form (figure 4.2). Users will use it to find both Task and Approach objects.

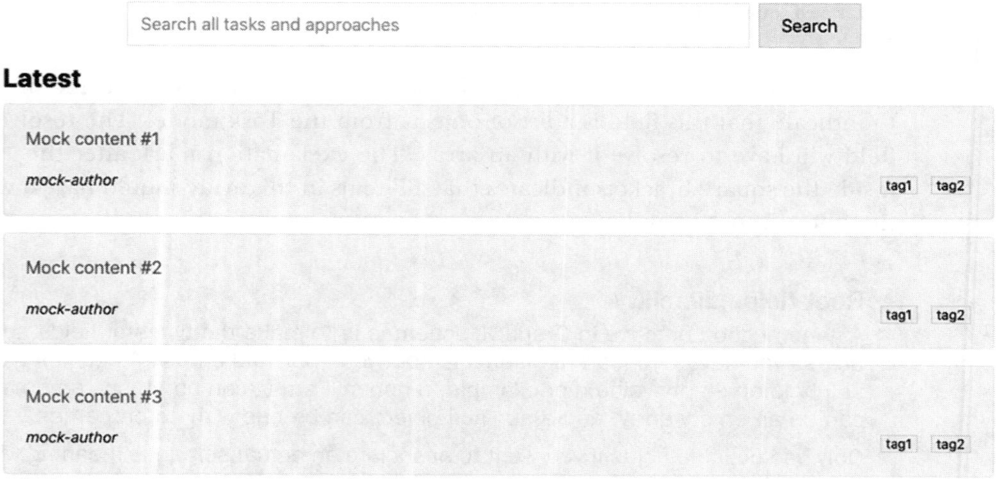

**Figure 4.2    Mock-up of the AZdev main landing page**

To support a search form, the GraphQL API should provide a query root field for it. Let's name that field `search`.

The GraphQL type of this `search` root field is interesting. It has to perform a full-text SQL query to find records and sort them by relevance. Furthermore, that SQL query must work with two models and return a mixed list of matching Task and Approach objects, which may have different fields!

For example, in the UI, when the search result item is a Task record, let's make it display how many Approach records it has; and when the search result item is an Approach record, let's make it display the Task information for that Approach record.

To support that, we can simply add these new fields to the Task and Approach types.

**Listing 4.4  The `approachCount` and `task` fields**

```
type Task {
  # · - · - ·
  approachCount: Int!
}

type Approach {
  # · - · - ·
  task: Task!
}
```

However, the search root field cannot be a list of Task records or a list of Approach records. It has to group these two models under a new type. In GraphQL, you can model this grouping with either a union type or an interface type. I'll tell you how to implement both of these types; but first, let's understand *why* we need to group the two models in one list. Why not design the API to support a query like this?

**Listing 4.5  A simple query for the search field**

```
query {
  search(term: "something") {
    taskList {
      id
      content
      approachCount
    }
    approachList {
      id
      content
      task {
        id
        content
      }
    }
  }
}
```

This design works okay, but it has one major problem: it returns two different lists for search results. That means we cannot have an accurate rank of search results based on relevance. We can only rank them per set.

To improve this design, we have to return one list of all the objects matching the search term so that we can rank them based on relevance. However, since these objects can have different fields, we need to come up with a new type that combines them.

One approach to do that is to make the `search` root field represent an array of objects that can have nullable fields based on what model they belong to: for example, something like the following.

**Listing 4.6   A better query for the search field**

```
search(term: "something") {
  id
  content

  approachCount // when result is a Task

  task {          // when result is an Approach
    id
    content
  }
}
```

This is better, and it solves the rank problem. However, it's a bit messy, as the API consumer will have to rely on knowing what fields are null to determine how to render search results.

GraphQL offers better solutions for this challenge. We can group search result items under either a union type or an interface type.

### USING A UNION TYPE

Remember that a union type represents OR logic (as discussed in chapter 3). A search result can be either a Task or an Approach. We can use the introspective __typename to ask the server what type a search result item is, and we can use inline fragments to conditionally pick the exact fields our UI requires based on the type of the returned item (just like we did for GitHub's issueOrPullRequest example in chapter 3).

With a union implementation, this is the query a consumer can use to implement the search feature.

**Listing 4.7   The union-type search field**

```
query {
  search(term: "something") {
    type: __typename
    ... on Task {
      id
      content
      approachCount
    }
    ... on Approach {
      id
      content
      task {
        id
        content
      }
    }
  }
}
```

Note that this query is just a more structured version of the query in listing 4.6. The "when x is y" comment we had there is now an official part of the query, thanks to inline fragments, and the consumer knows exactly what type an item is thanks to the __typename introspective field.

In the GraphQL schema language, to implement this union type for the search root field, we use the union keyword with the pipe character (|) to form a new object type.

##### Listing 4.8 Implementing search with a union type

```
union TaskOrApproach = Task | Approach

type Query {
  # . . . .
  search(term: String!): [TaskOrApproach!]
}
```

Note that I added parentheses after the search field to indicate that this field will receive an argument (the search term). Also note that a search result will always be an array, and any items in that array cannot be null. However, the array can be empty (when there are no matches).

### 4.3.3 Using an interface type

The query in listing 4.7 has a bit of duplication. Both the id and content fields are shared between the Task and Approach models. In chapter 3, we saw how shared fields can be implemented using an interface type.

Basically, we can think of a search item as an object that has three main properties (type, id, and content). This is its main interface. It can also have either an approachCount or a task field (depending on its type).

This means we can write a query to consume the search root fields, as follows.

##### Listing 4.9 The interface-type search field

```
query {
  search(term: "something") {
    type: __typename
    id
    content
    ... on Task {
      approachCount
    }
    ... on Approach {
      task {
        id
        content
      }
    }
  }
}
```

There are no duplicated fields in this version, and that's certainly a bit better. But how do we decide when to pick an interface over a union or the other way around?

I ask this question: "Are the models (to be grouped) similar but with a few different fields, or are they completely different with no shared fields?"

If they have shared fields, then an interface is a better fit. Only use unions when the grouped models have no shared fields.

In the GraphQL schema language, to implement an interface type for the search root field, we use the `interface` keyword to define a new object type that defines the shared fields. Then we make all the models (to be grouped) implement the new interface type (using the `implements` keyword).

---

**Listing 4.10  Implementing search with an interface type**

```
interface SearchResultItem {
    id: ID!                          Replaces the union
    content: String!                TaskOrApproach type
}

type Task implements SearchResultItem {
    # ·-·-·
    approachCount: Int!
}

type Approach implements SearchResultItem {
    # ·-·-·
    task: Task!
}

type Query {
    # ·-·-·
    search(term: String!): [SearchResultItem!]
}
```

Besides the fact that the consumer query is simpler with an interface, there is a subtle reason why I prefer the interface type here. With the interface type, looking at the implementation of the Task/Approach types, you can easily tell they are part of another type. With unions, you cannot; you have to find what other types use them by looking at code elsewhere.

> **TIP**  A GraphQL type can also implement multiple interface types. In SDL, you can just use a comma-separated list of interface types to implement.

### 4.3.4  *The page for one Task record*

Users of the AZdev UI can select a Task entry on the home page (or from search results) to navigate to a page that represents a single Task record. That page will have the record's full information, including its list of Approaches.

The GraphQL API must provide a query root field to enable consumers to get data about one Task object. Let's name this root field `taskInfo`.

**Listing 4.11    Pseudo query #2: `taskInfo`**

```
query {
  taskInfo (
    # Arguments to identify a Task record
  ) {
    # Fields under a Task record
  }
}
```

To identify a single Task record, we can make this field accept an `id` argument. Here is what we need to add in the schema text to support this new root field.

**Listing 4.12    Incremental UI-driven schema design**

```
type Query {
  # . - . - .
  taskInfo(id: ID!): Task
}
```

Great. This enables API users to fetch full information about a Task object, but how about the information of the Approach objects that are defined under that Task object? How do we enable users to fetch these?

Also, because users of the AZdev application will be able to vote on Approaches, we should probably make the API return the list of Approaches sorted by their number of votes. The simplest way to account for the number of votes on Approaches is to add a field to track how many current votes each Approach object has. Let's do that.

**Listing 4.13    The `voteCount` field**

```
type Approach implements SearchResultItem {
  # . - . - .
  voteCount: Int!
}
```

Now, to return the list of Approaches related to a Task object, we need to talk about entity relationships.

> **TIP**  Remember to always think of a GraphQL type in terms of what will be needed by the UI that's going to use that type. It's easy to add features when you need them. It's a lot harder to remove them when you don't.

### 4.3.5    *Entity relationships*

The list of Approaches under a Task object represents a relationship. A Task object can have many Approach objects.

There are a few other relationships that we have to support as well:

- When displaying a Task record in the UI, we should display the name of the user who created it. The same applies to Approach objects.
- For each Approach, the application will display its list of extra detail data elements. It's probably a good idea to have a new Approach Detail object type to represent that relation.

We need to represent four relationships in this API:

- A Task has many Approaches.
- A Task belongs to a User.
- An Approach belongs to a User.
- An Approach has many Approach Detail records.

In the database, these relationships are usually represented with integers in identity columns (primary keys and foreign keys). The clients of this API are really interested in the data these IDs represent: for example, the name of the person who authored a Task record or the content of the Approaches defined on it. That's why a client is expected to supply a list of leaf fields when they include these relation fields in a GraphQL query.

**Listing 4.14    Relation fields under `taskInfo`**

```
query {
  taskInfo (
    # Arguments to identify a Task record
  ) {
    # Fields under a Task record

    author {
      # Fields under a User record
    }

    approachList {
      # Fields under an Approach record

      author {
        # Fields under a User record
      }

      detailList {
        # Fields under an Approach Detail record
      }
    }
  }
}
```

**NOTE** I named the field representing the User relationship `author`. I've also named the list of detail records `detailList` instead of `approachDetailList`. The name of a field does not have to match the name of its type or database source.

To support these relationships in the schema, we add references to their core types.

**Listing 4.15  Incremental UI-driven schema design**

```
type ApproachDetail {
  content: String!

  # More fields for an Approach Detail record
}
```
New core type to represent Approach Detail objects

```
type Approach implements SearchResultItem {
  # .-.-.
  author: User!
  detailList: [ApproachDetail!]!
}

type Task implements SearchResultItem {
  # .-.-.
  author: User!
  approachList: [Approach!]!
}
```

Note that I used the `User` type for the `author` field. We've also planned to use the same `User` type under the `me` field scope. This introduces a problem because of the `taskList` field that we need to define under the `User` type (see section 4.3.8). When a user is asking for their own Task records, that will work fine. However, when the API reports the `author` details of a public Task record, these details should not include the `taskList` of that author. We'll figure out the solution to this problem as we implement the `me` field scope (in chapter 7).

### 4.3.6  *The ENUM type*

An Approach Detail record is just a text field (which I named `content`), but it is special because it will be under a particular category. We would like the API to support the initial set of categories `NOTE`, `EXPLANATION`, and `WARNING`. Since these three categories will be the only accepted values in an Approach Detail's categories, we can use GraphQL's special `ENUM` type to represent them. Here is how to do that (in SDL).

**Listing 4.16  The `ApproachDetailCategory` ENUM type**

```
enum ApproachDetailCategory {
  NOTE
  EXPLANATION
  WARNING
}
```

The special ENUM type allows us to enumerate all the possible values for a field. Doing so adds a layer of validation around that field, making the enumerated values the only possible ones. This is especially helpful if you're accepting input from the user for an enumerated field, but it's also a good way to communicate through the type system that a field will always be one of a fixed set of values.

Now we can modify the ApproachDetail GraphQL type to use this new ENUM type.

**Listing 4.17   GraphQL type for an Approach Detail**

```
type ApproachDetail {
  content: String!
  category: ApproachDetailCategory!
}
```

This is a good start for the GraphQL types we need to support the queries we are planning for the UI. It is, however, just a start. There are more fields to think about for the core types, and we may need to introduce more types as we make progress on the API.

> **NOTE**  You should make API consumers paginate through list-type fields like taskMainList, search, approachList and detailList (under taskInfo), and taskList (under me). Never have the API return all records under a list. Check the official AZdev API source code for examples.

### 4.3.7   *List of scalar values*

To make Task objects more discoverable, let's enable API users to supply a list of tags when they create a Task object. A tag can be something like git, javascript, command, code, and so on. Let's also make these tags part of the data response for each field that returns Task objects. It can simply be an array of strings.

**Listing 4.18   The `tags` field**

```
type Task implements SearchResultItem {
  # ------
  tags: [String!]!
}
```

### 4.3.8   *The page for a user's Task records*

Let's give logged-in users the ability to see the list of their Task records. We will name the field to support that taskList.

However, making taskList a root field might be confusing. It could be interpreted as a field to return a list of all Task records in the database!

We can name it differently to clear up that confusion, but another useful practice can also solve this issue. We can introduce a query root field representing the scope of the currently logged-in user and put the taskList field under it.

This field is commonly named me in GraphQL APIs, but that name is not a requirement. You can name it anything.

---

**Listing 4.19  Pseudo query #3: list of Task records for an authenticated user**

```
query {
  me (
    # Arguments to validate user access
  ) {
    taskList {
      # Fields under a Task record
    }
  }
}
```

Any fields under the me field will be filtered for the currently logged-in user. In the future, we might add more fields under that scope. The me field is a good way to organize multiple fields related to the current user.

To support the me { taskList } feature, we will have to introduce two fields in the schema: a root me field that returns a User type and a taskList field on the User type.

---

**Listing 4.20  Incremental UI-driven schema design**

```
type User {
  # · - · - ·
  taskList: [Task!]!
}

type Query {
  # · - · - ·
  me: User
}
```

> **NOTE**  Once again, I made the me field nullable. A session might time out on the backend, but instead of returning a completely null response for a query that has a me field, we can return null for the timed-out me field and still include partial data in other parts of the query.

Great! A logged-in user can now ask for their own Task records. But how exactly will a user log in to the API, and how do we determine if a query request is from a logged-in user? This is a good place to talk about the concept of authentication (and authorization) in GraphQL.

### 4.3.9  *Authentication and authorization*

The me field will require an access token. In this project, we're going to use a simple string access token for authentication. I'll refer to that token as authToken from now on. This string value will be stored in the database with a user record, and we can use it for personal query fields like me and search and some mutations as well.

**TIP**    A simple string value token is known as a *bearer* token. That label is often used in request headers to identify an authentication token.

When an `authToken` is included with a request, the API server will use it to identify the user who is making that request. This token is similar in concept to a session cookie. It will be remembered per user session and sent with GraphQL requests made by that session. It should be renewed when users log in to the AZdev application.

---

**What about authorization?**

Authorization is the business logic that determines whether a user has permission to read a piece of data or perform an action. For example, an authorization rule in the AZdev API could be, "Only the owner of a Task record can delete that record."

The AZdev `authToken` value will make the server determine the API consumer's identity, and that identity can then be used to enforce authorization rules.

---

We can include the `authToken` value in the GraphQL request text. For example, it can be a simple field argument. However, it's a common practice to keep access tokens separate. For web APIs, request headers can be used to include such tokens.

It's also a common practice to not do any authentication or authorization logic directly in field resolvers in a GraphQL API service and instead delegate those tasks to a higher layer, which should be the single source of truth for these concerns. For the AZdev API, that single source of truth can be the database. I'll provide the SQL statements and point out any logic in them that's crafted for authentication or authorization.

The `authToken` value is like a temporary password: it must be kept confidential in transit and in storage. Web applications should only send it over HTTPS connections, and it should not be stored in plain text in the database.

**TIP**    The string value token concept is the simplest thing we can do for authentication. If you're interested in learning about more in-depth approaches to authentication and authorization, take a look at JSON Web Tokens (JWT). JWT uses JSON to carry certain common fields such as subject, issuer, expiration time, and so on. Along with related specs like JSON Web Signature (JWS) and JSON Web Encryption (JWE), JWT can be used to secure and validate token values. You can read more about JWT at az.dev/jwt.

## 4.4    *Mutations*

To add content to AZdev (Tasks, Approaches, Details, Votes), a guest must create an account and log in to the application. This will require the API to host a `users` database table to store users' credentials. The GraphQL API will need to provide mutations to create a user and allow them to obtain an authorization token.

---

**Listing 4.21   Pseudo mutation #1: `userCreate`**

```
mutation {
  userCreate (
    # Input for a new User record
  ) {
    # Fail/Success response
  }
}
```

**Listing 4.22   Pseudo mutation #2: `userLogin`**

```
mutation {
  userLogin (
    # Input to identify a User record
  ) {
    # Fail/Success response
  }
}
```

The `userCreate` mutation will enable users to create an account for the AZdev application, and the `userLogin` mutation will enable them to perform future queries and mutations that are specific to them.

Note that for each mutation, I plan for handling a fail response as well as the normal success response. Mutations typically rely on valid user input to succeed. It's a good idea to represent errors caused by invalid uses of mutations differently from other root errors a GraphQL API consumer can cause. For example, trying to request a nonexistent field is a root error. However, trying to create a user with a username that's already in the system is a user error that we should handle differently.

---

**Payload errors**

The root `errors` field is used for server problems (like 5xx HTTP codes), but it is also used for some client issues: for example, hitting the limit on a rate-limited API or accessing something without the proper authorization. GraphQL also uses that field if the client sends a bad request that fails the schema validation. The payload errors concept is suitable for user-friendly messages when users supply bad input.

Using user-friendly errors in payloads acts as an error boundary for the operation. Some developers even use payloads with errors in query fields. You can use them to hide implementation details and not expose server errors to the API consumer.

---

We can implement this fail/success response with either a union type or a special output payload type for each entity in the system. I'll use the payload concept for the AZdev API mutations.

A mutation output payload can include user errors, the entity on which that mutation operates, and any other values that might be useful for that mutation's consumer. For example, the `userLogin` mutation can include the generated `authToken` value as part of its output payload. Here's an example of how that can be done.

**Listing 4.23   Incremental UI-driven schema design**

```
type UserError {
  message: String!
}

type UserPayload {
  errors: [UserError!]!
  user: User
  authToken: String
}
# More entity payloads

type Mutation {
  userCreate(
    # Mutation Input
  ): UserPayload!

  userLogin(
    # Mutation Input
  ): UserPayload!

  # More mutations
}
```

Note that I kept the `authToken` field separate from the `user` field in the `UserPayload` type. I think this makes any use of the API cleaner. The `authToken` value is not really part of a User record; it's just a temporary value for users to authenticate themselves for future operations. They will need to renew it at some point.

This takes care of the output of these two mutation operations. We still need to figure out the structure of their input.

> **TIP**  I kept the `UserError` type simple, with just one required `message` field. This matches the structure of the GraphQL root errors array. I think it's a good idea to also support the optional `path` and `locations` fields in this type to give API consumers more power to figure out what to do with these errors.

### 4.4.1  *Mutation input*

Mutations always have some kind of input that usually has multiple elements. To better represent and validate the structure of a multifield input, GraphQL supports a special `input` type that can be used to group scalar input values into one object.

For example, for the `userCreate` mutation, let's allow the mutation consumer to specify a first name, last name, username, and password. All of these fields are strings.

Instead of defining four scalar arguments for the userCreate mutation, we can group these input values as one input object argument. We use the input keyword to do that.

```
Listing 4.24  Incremental UI-driven schema design

# Define an input type:
input UserInput {
  username: String!
  password: String!
  firstName: String
  lastName: String
}

# Then use it as the only argument to the mutation:
type Mutation {
  userCreate(input: UserInput!): UserPayload!

  # More mutations
}
```

A couple of things to note about this new type:

- You can use any name for the input object type and the mutation argument. However, the names <Model>Input and input are the common conventions. I'll use these conventions in the AZdev schema.
- Making firstName and lastName optional allows a user to register an account with just their username (and password).

The UserInput type is similar to the core User type we designed for the queries for this API. So, why introduce a new input object type when we already have the core object type for a user?

Input object types are basically a simplified version of output object types. Their fields cannot reference output object types (or interface/union types). They can only use scalar input types or other input object types.

Input object types are often smaller and closer to the database schema, while object types are likely to introduce more fields to represent relations or other custom logic. For example, the id field is a required part of the User type, but we do not need it in the UserInput type because it's a value that will be generated by the database. Some fields will appear in input object types but should not be in their corresponding output object types. An example is the password field. We need it to create a user account (or log in), but we should never expose it in any readable capacity.

While you can pass the username, firstName, and lastName values directly to the mutation, the input object type structure is preferable because it allows passing an object to the mutation. This often reduces the complexity of the code using that mutation and enhances code readability in general. Having an input object also adds a reusability benefit to your code.

**TIP**  Although the benefit of using an input object type relates to when you have multiple scalar input values, it's a good practice to use the same pattern across all mutations, even those with a single scalar input value.

For the `userLogin` mutation, we need the consumer to send over their username and password. Let's create an `AuthInput` type for that.

Listing 4.25   Incremental UI-driven schema design

```
input AuthInput {
  username: String!
  password: String!
}

type Mutation {
  # ......
  userLogin(input: AuthInput!): UserPayload!
}
```

### 4.4.2   *Deleting a user record*

Let's also offer AZdev API consumers a way to delete their user profile. We will plan for a `userDelete` mutation to do that.

Listing 4.26   Pseudo mutation #3: `userDelete`

```
mutation {
  userDelete {
    # Fail/Success payload
  }
}
```

Note that this mutation does not have input. The user will be identified through their `authToken` value, which needs to be part of that request's headers.

For a payload, we can just return the ID of the deleted user if the operation was a success. Here's the SDL text that represents this plan:

```
type UserDeletePayload {
  errors: [UserError!]!
  deletedUserId: ID
}

type Mutation {
  # ......
  userDelete: UserDeletePayload!
}
```

### 4.4.3   *Creating a Task object*

To create a new Task record in the AZdev application, let's make the API support a `taskCreate` mutation. Here's what that mutation operation will look like.

**Listing 4.27  Pseudo mutation #4: `taskCreate`**

```
mutation {
  taskCreate (
    # Input for a new Task record
  ) {
    # Fail/Success Task payload
  }
}
```

To support this mutation, we need to define the Task input and payload types and create a new mutation field that uses them.

The input object's main field is the simple text field for the content field on a Task record. There is also the tags field, which is an array of string values. Let's also enable users to create private Tasks that are not to be included in the search (unless the user who is searching owns them).

> **TIP** Private Task entries will be handy for users to keep a reference of things they need in their private projects. Keep in mind that these entries will make things a bit more challenging since we need to exclude them, unless the API consumer is the user who owns them.

Here's the SDL text that represents what we planned for the Task entity mutations.

**Listing 4.28  Incremental UI-driven schema design**

```
input TaskInput {
  content: String!
  tags: [String!]!
  isPrivate: Boolean!
}

type TaskPayload {
  errors: [UserError!]!
  task: Task
}

type Mutation {
  # . . . . . .
  taskCreate(input: TaskInput!): TaskPayload!
}
```

### 4.4.4  *Creating and voting on Approach entries*

To create a new Approach record on an existing Task record, let's make the API support an approachCreate mutation.

**Listing 4.29  Pseudo mutation #4: `approachCreate`**

```
mutation {
  approachCreate (
```

```
    # Input to identify a Task record
    # Input for a new Approach record (with ApproachDetail)
  ) {
    # Fail/Success Approach payload
  }
}
```

A logged-in user viewing a Task record page along with the list of its mutations can up-vote or down-vote a single Approach record. Let's make the API support an approachVote mutation for that. This mutation needs to return the new votes count for the voted-on approach. We'll make that part of the Approach payload.

**Listing 4.30    Pseudo mutation #5: `approachVote`**

```
mutation  {
  approachVote (
    # Input to identify an Approach record
    # Input for "Vote"
  ) {
    # Fail/Success Approach payload
  }
}
```

Here are the schema text changes needed to support these two new mutations.

**Listing 4.31    Incremental UI-driven schema design**

```
input ApproachDetailInput {
  content: String!
  category: ApproachDetailCategory!          ◁── The ENUM type here will validate
}                                                 the accepted categories.

input ApproachInput {
  content: String!
  detailList: [ApproachDetailInput!]!
}

input ApproachVoteInput {
  up: Boolean!
}

type ApproachPayload {
  errors: [UserError!]!
  approach: Approach
}

type Mutation {
  # - - - -
```

```
approachCreate(
  taskId: ID!
  input: ApproachInput!
): ApproachPayload!

approachVote(
  approachId: ID!
  input: ApproachVoteInput!
): ApproachPayload!
}
```

Note that I opted to represent up-votes and down-votes with a simple Boolean field and not an ENUM of two values. That's an option when there are exactly two accepted values. It's probably better to use an ENUM for this, but let's keep it as a Boolean and add a comment to clarify it. We just put the comment text on the line before the field that needs it and surround that text with triple quotes ("""").

**Listing 4.32    Adding description text**

```
input ApproachVoteInput {
  """true for up-vote and false for down-vote"""
  up: Boolean!
}
```

The clarifying text is known as a *description* in a GraphQL schema, and it is part of the structure of that schema. It's not really a comment but rather a property of this type. Tools like GraphiQL expect it and display it in autocomplete lists and documentation explorers. You should consider adding a description property to any field that could use an explanation.

> **TIP** We should probably also support userUpdate and approachUpdate mutations. I'll leave that as a multichapter exercise for you. In this chapter, you need to plan for how these mutations will be called and come up with the SDL text for them.

Note again that I am naming all the mutations using the form <model>Action (e.g., taskCreate) rather than the more natural action<Model> (e.g., createTask). Now all actions on a Task record are alphabetically grouped together. We'll find the task-MainList, taskInfo, taskCreate, and taskUpdate operations next to each other.

> **TIP** The ApproachDetailInput type (listing 4.31) is identical to the ApproachDetail type (listing 4.17). However, don't be tempted to reuse output object types as input object types. In the future, we might upgrade the Approach Detail concept to also have unique IDs and creation timestamps. There is also great value in keeping everything consistent.

## 4.5    *Subscriptions*

On Twitter and other social media apps, while you're looking at a post, its counters for replies, shares, and likes are autoupdated. Let's plan for a similar feature for the vote counts. While looking at the list of Approaches on the Task page, let's make the votes autoupdate!

We can use a subscription operation to do that. This operation will have to accept a taskId input so that a user can subscribe to the vote changes on Approaches under a single Task object (rather than all Approaches in the system). Let's name this subscription operation voteChanged.

Listing 4.33  **Pseudo subscription #1: voteChanged**

```
subscription {
  voteChanged (
    # Input to identify a Task record
  ) {
    # Fields under an Approach record
  }
}
```

On the AZdev home page, which shows the list of all the latest Tasks, another subscription-based feature that will add value is to show an indicator telling the user that new Task records are available. They can click that indicator to show the new Tasks. Let's name this subscription operation taskMainListChanged.

Listing 4.34  **Pseudo subscription #2: taskMainListChanged**

```
subscription {
  taskMainListChanged {
    # Fields under a Task record
  }
}
```

To support these subscriptions, we define a new Subscription type with the new fields under it, like this:

```
type Subscription {
  voteChanged(taskId: ID!): Approach!
  taskMainListChanged: [Task!]
}
```

How does all that sound to you? Let's make it happen!

> **NOTE**  I will be adding more features to the AZdev API outside of this book, but we need to keep things simple and manageable here. You can explore the AZdev current production GraphQL API at az.dev/api and see what other queries, mutations, and subscriptions I have added.

## 4.6    *Full schema text*

Did you notice that I came up with the entire schema description so far just by think-ing in terms of the UI? How cool is that? You can give this simple schema language text to the frontend developers on your team, and they can start building the front-end app right away! They don't need to wait for your server implementation. They can even use some of the great tools out there to make a mock GraphQL server that resolves these types with random test data.

> **TIP** The schema is often compared to a contract. You always start with a contract.

The full schema text representing this book's version of the AZdev GraphQL API can be found at az.dev/gia-schema.

> **TIP** I'll repeat relevant sections of this schema text when we work through the tasks of implementing them.

With the GraphQL schema ready, let's design a database schema to support it.

## 4.7    *Designing database models*

We have four database models in this project so far:

- `User`, `Task`, and `Approach` in PostgreSQL
- `ApproachDetail` in MongoDB

Let's start with the `User` model in PostgreSQL. But before we do, it's a good idea to create a schema in a PostgreSQL database to host an application's tables rather than have them in the default public schema. This way, you will have the option to use the same PostgreSQL database to host data for many applications.

> **NOTE** A PostgreSQL schema has nothing to do with a GraphQL schema. It's just a way to organize tables and views (and other objects) in a PostgreSQL database.

To create a PostgreSQL schema, you can use this command:

```
CREATE SCHEMA azdev;
```

> **NOTE** You don't have to execute any of the code listings in this section. In chapter 5, we will start with a project template that has all the SQL and NoSQL statements that you need for the entire AZdev project. I have also pre-pared database service containers that are ready with the models we're going to design here. You can just download them and run them to prepare your environment with all database-related entities. However, I strongly recom-mend that you go over this section to be sure you understand all the database design decisions we are going to make.

### 4.7.1 The User model

The `users` database table will have a record for each registered user. Besides the unique ID and creation-time fields we're adding under each model, a user record will have a unique `username` field and a hashed `password` field. These fields are required.

We've designed the GraphQL User type to have a `name` field. However, let's design the database tables to have separate first- and last-name fields.

We need a mechanism to authenticate requests to the GraphQL API after a user logs in without having them send over their password each time. We'll manage that with a column to store temporary `authToken` values (which should be hashed as well).

Here's a SQL statement to create a table for the `User` model.

##### Listing 4.35 The `azdev.users` table

```
CREATE TABLE azdev.users (
  id serial PRIMARY KEY,
  username text NOT NULL UNIQUE,
  hashed_password text NOT NULL,
  first_name text,
  last_name text,
  hashed_auth_token text,
  created_at timestamp without time zone NOT NULL
    DEFAULT (now() at time zone 'utc'),

  CHECK (lower(username) = username)
);
```

I gave the `id` field the `serial` type and the `PRIMARY KEY` constraint. The `serial` type will automatically fill this field using a sequence of integers (which is automatically created and managed for this table). The `PRIMARY KEY` constraint will make sure that values in this column are unique and not null. We'll need the same `id` column definition in all tables as this column will be used for referential integrity constraints (making sure records reference existing records).

> **TIP** The `username` field is also unique and not null, making it practically another primary key. If you want to use the username as a primary key (and that's not a bad idea), you just need to make sure any referential integrity constraints are updated correctly if the user decides to change their username. PostgreSQL has some advanced features to help with that.

The `created_at` field will be automatically populated by PostgreSQL, through the `DEFAULT` keyword. It will store the time each record was created in the UTC time zone. Neither the `id` nor the `created_at` field will be mutated by the GraphQL API; consumers can read them if they need to.

> **TIP** Keep it simple! I find it a lot easier to store date-time values without time zone information and always store UTC values. Life is too short to deal with time-zoned date-time values and their conversions.

The CHECK constraint on the username field validates that usernames are always stored in lowercase form. This is a good practice for fields that are unique regardless of their case. I've learned that the hard way.

The hashed_auth_token field is needed to authenticate requests to the GraphQL API after a user logs in. Because HTTP APIs are stateless, instead of having the user send over their password with every GraphQL operation, once they log in successfully, we will give them a temporary random string value to use in subsequent GraphQL requests, and the server will use that value to identify them. The hashed_auth_token value should be renewed per session, and we can come up with a way to invalidate it after a time.

> **TIP** There will always be more things you can do to make an API more secure, but for the purposes of this book, we will keep things simple while going with the practical minimum. For example, don't ever store plain-text passwords or access tokens in your database! Even encrypting them is not secure enough. You should one-way hash them. That's why I named these fields using the hashed_ prefix.

Note that I used snake-case (underscore separator) for PostgreSQL column names and not camel-case like GraphQL fields. PostgreSQL column names are case insensitive (unless you use quotes). So if we named the column createdAt, it would be converted to createdat. The snake-case style is the common convention in PostgreSQL, and it will add some challenges for us down the road when we need to map these columns to GraphQL camel-case fields.

### 4.7.2 The Task/Approach models

The tasks table will have a record for each Task object that's submitted to the AZdev application. We designed a Task object to have a content text field, a list of tags, and an approachCount integer field. We'll also need to add a field to support the isPrivate property, which we planned for in the mutation to create a new Task object.

A Task object can have many tags. We could come up with a new tags database table and introduce a new many-to-many relation to it, but let's just store these tags as a comma-separated value for each Task record. Remember that GraphQL types don't need to match their data source, so we can still make the GraphQL tags field be resolved as an array of strings.

> **TIP** PostgreSQL has an advanced feature to manage a list of items for a single row. A PostgreSQL column can have an array data type! I am using the comma-separated value to keep things simple, but feel free to experiment with that array data type and see how to deal with it once we start mapping PostgreSQL columns to GraphQL fields.

A Task (or Approach) record has to belong to a User record because only logged-in users can submit new entries. For that, we can use a FOREIGN KEY constraint to validate the map between a Task and a User. We'll need to do the same for Approaches.

Here's a SQL statement to create a table for the Task model.

##### Listing 4.36   The `Tasks` table

```
CREATE TABLE azdev.tasks (
  id serial PRIMARY KEY,
  content text NOT NULL,
  tags text,
  user_id integer NOT NULL,
  is_private boolean NOT NULL DEFAULT FALSE,
  approach_count integer NOT NULL DEFAULT 0,
  created_at timestamp without time zone NOT NULL
    DEFAULT (now() at time zone 'utc'),

  FOREIGN KEY (user_id) REFERENCES azdev.users
);
```

The approaches table will have a record for each `Approach` object submitted on a Task entry. We designed an `Approach` object to have a `content` text field and a `voteCount` integer field. Each `Approach` object must be stored under a valid `User` record and mapped to a `Task` record. This table will have two `FOREIGN KEY` constraint columns: `user_id` and `task_id`.

Here's a SQL statement to create a table for the Approach model.

##### Listing 4.37   The `approaches` table

```
CREATE TABLE azdev.approaches (
  id serial PRIMARY KEY,
  content text NOT NULL,
  user_id integer NOT NULL,
  task_id integer NOT NULL,
  vote_count integer NOT NULL DEFAULT 0,
  created_at timestamp without time zone NOT NULL
    DEFAULT (now() at time zone 'utc'),

  FOREIGN KEY (user_id) REFERENCES azdev.users,
  FOREIGN KEY (task_id) REFERENCES azdev.tasks
);
```

Figure 4.3 summarizes these three tables and how they are related to each other.

Did you notice that I've used many database constraints like PRIMARY KEY, NOT NULL, UNIQUE, CHECK, and FOREIGN KEY? These database constraints will help future developers understand the design decisions we're making today, and they will be the last-standing guard if a client tries to insert invalid data into the database. When it comes to data integrity, spare no layers! The least you can do is have the database validate it. Don't skip that. You should also add more layers to give users of your API more meaningful error messages when they attempt to insert invalid data. We'll do some data validation in the GraphQL layer as well.

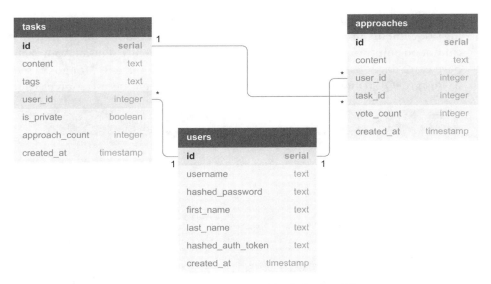

**Figure 4.3    The relationship diagram for the three tables in PostgreSQL**

### 4.7.3    *The Approach Details model*

Since this is the first (and only) data model that we have in MongoDB, we first need to create a new MongoDB database for AZdev.

In MongoDB, there is no schema concept to group related database entities. You just create a database for that purpose. You actually don't need to "create a database"; you just use it, and MongoDB automatically creates the currently used database the first time you insert any data into it.

You can run the following command to use a new database in a MongoDB client:

```
use azdev
```

A `Model` in MongoDB is represented with a `Collection` object, and—just like the database itself—you don't need to create a collection. MongoDB will accept requests to store any data in any form or shape, regardless of whether a collection for it existed before. For new types of documents, MongoDB automatically creates new collections.

> **TIP**    The flexibility in document databases is great, but it can also be a source of big problems. A simple typo might lead to having a brand-new (wrong) collection in the database. Be careful: with flexibility comes great responsibility!

You can create empty collections in MongoDB if you want, and you can also restrict the privileges of a database user to only perform certain actions on certain collections in certain databases! I think that's a great way to validate that data will be stored in its intended locations. I'll skip the privileges part here, but let's plan the collection for the extra dynamic data elements that we want to support on Approaches.

MongoDB supports performing some data validation when inserting (or updating) documents in collections. This is useful when certain fields in your documents cannot be empty or must have a particular type or structure. For an Approach entry to have extra data elements in MongoDB, we need to associate its MongoDB record with its PostgreSQL ID to be able to do the mapping between the two sources (figure 4.4).

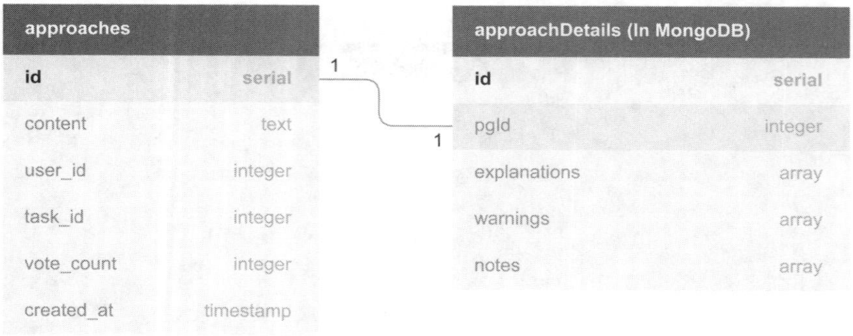

**Figure 4.4    The relationship diagram for the Approaches collection**

Let's use MongoDB schema validation to make sure we have that mapping for each Approach document. Here's the MongoDB command you can use to create the `approachDetails` collection and define its `validator` that checks for the existence of a numeric `pgId` field.

**Listing 4.38    The `approachDetails` collection**

```
db.createCollection("approachDetails", {
  validator: {
    $jsonSchema: {
      bsonType: "object",
      required: ["pgId"],
      properties: {
        pgId: {
          bsonType: "int",
          description: "must be an integer and is required"
        },
      }
    }
  }
});
```

This command creates an `approachDetails` collection. And because this is the first thing we're creating in the currently used `azdev` database, the command also creates the database. You can verify that with the `show dbs` command. The `show collections` command should report back `approachDetails`.

Each Approach record will have a single record in the `approachDetails` collection. The Approach Detail record will have fields like `explanations`, `warnings`, `notes`, and other categories in the future. Each of these fields will have an array of text items. We'll have to transform this special storage schema when resolving a GraphQL API request that asks for Approach Details.

> **TIP** Think of adding more tables and collections to the `azdev` database. For example, maybe store vote records and track who voted what and when. I'll leave that as an exercise for you if you want to expand the scope of this API and make it more challenging.

## Summary

- An API server is an interface to one or many data sources. GraphQL is not a storage engine; it's just a runtime that can power an API server.
- An API server can talk to many types of data services. Data can be queried from databases, cache services, other APIs, files, and so on.
- A good first step when designing a GraphQL API is to draft a list of operations that will theoretically satisfy the needs of the application you're designing. Operations include queries, mutations, and subscriptions.
- Relational databases (like PostgreSQL) are a good fit to store relations and well-defined, constrained data. Document databases (like MongoDB) are great for dynamic data structures.
- Draft GraphQL operations can be used to design the tables and collections in databases and to come up with the initial GraphQL schema language text.
- You should utilize the powerful data-integrity constraints and schema validators that are natively offered by database services.

# Implementing
# schema resolvers

In the previous chapter, we designed the structure of the GraphQL API schema and came up with its full SDL text. In chapters 5–8, we are going to make that schema executable. We'll use Node.js database drivers and the GraphQL.js implementation to expose the entities in the databases by using resolver functions.

## 5.1 Running the development environment

To let you focus on the GraphQL skills in this book's project, I prepared a Git repository that contains all the non-GraphQL things that you need to follow up with the project. We will use this repository in chapters 5–10. It has the skeleton for both the API server (which we're going to build in chapters 5–8) and the skeleton for the web server (which we'll build in chapters 9 and 10). Clone that repo.

---

**Listing 5.1    Command to clone the book's repo**

```
git clone https://az.dev/gia-repo graphql-in-action
```

---

### Node.js and Linux

You need a modern version of Node.js installed in your OS to follow along from this point. If you don't have Node, or if you have an old version (anything less than 12), download the latest from nodejs.org and use that.

Some familiarity with the Node.js runtime is required. You don't need to be an expert in Node, but if you have never worked with it before, it would help if you learn its basics before proceeding with this chapter. I wrote a short introductory book on Node, which you can get at az.dev/node-intro.

All the commands in this book are for Linux. They will also work on a Mac machine because macOS is Linux-based. On Microsoft Windows, you'll have to find the native equivalent of these commands, or you can spare yourself a lot of trouble and use the Windows Subsystem for Linux (see az.dev/wsl). If that is not an option, you can also run a Linux machine in a virtual hardware environment like VirtualBox.

If developing natively on Microsoft Windows is your only option, I recommend using PowerShell instead of the CMD command. Most Linux Bash shell commands work with PowerShell.

Microsoft Windows is not the best option when it comes to working with Node-based applications. Node was originally designed for Linux, and many of its internal optimizations depend on Linux native APIs. Windows support for Node started a few years after Node was first released, and there are active efforts to make it "better," but it will never be as good as Node for Linux. Running Node on Windows natively is an option, but it will give you trouble. Only develop natively on Windows if you plan to host your production Node applications on Windows servers.

---

Cloning the repo creates the graphql-in-action directory under your current working directory. There, the first step is to install the initial packages that are used by the repo.

---

**Listing 5.2    Command: installing repo dependencies**

```
$ cd graphql-in-action
$ npm install
```

Take a look at the package.json file to see the initial packages I added. These packages are used by the API server (and by the web server later). Note that I provided the scripts we will need to run these two servers.

**Listing 5.3   Run scripts in package.json**

**Command to run the provided Docker images (used in chapter 6)**

```
{
  "name": "az.dev",
  "version": "0.0.1",                              Command to run the API
  "private": true,                                 server (which we need in
  "scripts": {                                     this chapter)
  "scripts": {
    "start-dbs": "docker-compose -f dev-dbs/docker.yml up",
    "api-server": "(cd api && nodemon -r esm src/server.js)",
    "web-server": "(cd web/src && rimraf .cache dist && parcel index.html)",
    "start-blank-dbs": "docker-compose -f dev-dbs/docker-blank.yml up"
  },
  },
  .-.--.
}
```

**Command to run the web server (used in chapter 9)**

**TIP** You can add as many npm run scripts as you need, and you should use them for any tasks you wish to introduce to the project. With npm run scripts, all developers on the team can run these tasks in a standard, consistent way.

Explore the repo, and notice its three directories:

- The api directory is the focus of chapters 5–8. It's where we will put the logic of the API server implementation. It has a bare-bone Express.js server configured with an example endpoint. I've also provided all the database configurations and SQL statements used throughout the book. Take a look around.

- The web directory is the focus of chapters 9–10. It's where we will put the logic of using the API server in a web application. It has a bare-bone React app configured with some mock data.

- The dev-dbs directory has everything related to running dev database servers for development. You can use the files there to create your own database services and load them with sample data or to run the provided ready Docker images. We'll do that in the next chapter.

**TIP** Given the fast-changing ecosystem of GraphQL and other libraries used in the book, configurations and code samples may not work for you as is. Check out az.dev/gia-updates to see any updates that you may need to work through the book's code examples.

### 5.1.1   Node.js packages

For the GraphQL runtime service to communicate with databases like PostgreSQL and MongoDB, it needs a driver. We'll use Node's `pg` and `mongodb` packages for that purpose. These are not the only packages that can be used as drivers, but they are the most popular in Node's ecosystem. These packages expose JavaScript APIs to execute operations for PostgreSQL and MongoDB. We'll need to configure them to connect to these database services.

For a web server to host the project's API endpoint, we will use Express.js. There are a few other Express-related packages that we need. All these packages are already installed in the repo's starting point.

To implement the GraphQL API server, we need two new packages.

Listing 5.4   Command: installing new dependencies

```
$ npm install graphql express-graphql
```

The `graphql` package is for GraphQL.js, the JavaScript implementation of GraphQL. It takes care of things like validating and executing GraphQL operations.

To work with a GraphQL runtime, we need an interface. This is where the `express-graphql` package comes in handy. It has an HTTP(S) listener function that is designed to be used with a middleware-based web framework like Express and acts as an interface to a GraphQL schema.

> **TIP**   Although it's named `express-graphql`, this package can work with any HTTP web framework that supports connect-style middleware (Hapi, Fastify, and many others).

### 5.1.2   Environment variables

Under the api directory is a .env file that contains the default environment variables we need in this project. If you do not plan to use any of the project's defaults, you'll need to change these variables. This file is automatically loaded, and its variables are exported in api/src/config.js.

> **TIP**   Environment files like .env usually are not part of the source code as they will need to be different on different machines and environments. I've included a .env file in the repo to keep things simple.

## 5.2   Setting up the GraphQL runtime

We can now start the implementation of the project's GraphQL runtime layer. Let's first work through a very simple example so that we can focus on testing the runtime layer setup and understanding its core dynamics.

Suppose we are creating a web application that needs to know the exact current time the server is using (and not rely on the client's time). We would like to be able to send a query request to the API server as follows.

**Listing 5.5    Querying the server for the current time**

```
{
  currentTime
}
```

To respond to this query, let's make the server use an ISO UTC time string in the HH:MM:SS format.

**Listing 5.6    Format for the `currentTime` response**

```
{
  currentTime: "20:32:55"
}
```

This is a simple GraphQL request with a single operation (a query operation). GraphQL requests can also have multiple operations and include other information related to these operations (for example, variables).

For the server to accomplish this current time communication, it needs to

1   Have an interface for a requester to supply a GraphQL request.
2   Parse the supplied request and make sure it has valid syntax according to the GraphQL language rules.
3   Validate the request using a *schema*. You cannot run just any request on a GraphQL server: you can only run the ones allowed by its schema. The server also needs to validate that all the required parts of the request are supplied. For example, if a query uses variables, then the server needs to validate their existence and make sure they have the right types. If a request has more than one operation the server needs to validate that the request also includes the name of the operation that should be executed for the response.
4   *Resolve* all fields in the request into scalar data elements. If the request is for a mutation operation, the server must perform the side effects of that mutation. If the request is for a subscription operation, the server must open a channel to communicate data changes when they happen.
5   Gather all the data for the response, and serialize it into a format like JSON. The serialized response needs to include the request structure and its resolved data (and any errors the server encountered).
6   Have an interface for the requester to receive the response text generated for their request text.

All of these tasks are shared among all GraphQL requests the server has to deal with. In fact, except for the tasks where I used the italicized words (*schema* and *resolve*), all other tasks are shared among *all* GraphQL services. This means they can be abstracted and reused. We don't have to do them for each service.

Luckily, this has been done already! We don't have to reimplement any of the previous steps except dealing with schemas and resolvers. The rest is where a GraphQL implementation (like GraphQL.js) comes into the picture.

What exactly is a *GraphQL implementation*? It's basically code written in a certain language to do the bulk of the work described in the previous six steps. It exposes its own code APIs, which your code can use to perform the generic behaviors expected of a GraphQL server. Another example of a GraphQL implementation in JavaScript is Apollo Server, which wraps GraphQL.js and enhances it with many features like SDL-first implementation and a subscription-ready transport channel. We'll see an example of using Apollo Server in chapter 10.

As a GraphQL service developer, you can use your GraphQL implementation of choice to do most of the heavy lifting like parsing, validating, and executing GraphQL requests. This enables you to focus on your application logic details. You need to write a schema and come up with how the parts in that schema should be resolved (as data and side effects). We designed the AZdev schema in the previous chapter, and we will start implementing its resolvers in this chapter. However, before we do that, let's work through the simple `currentTime` field example.

### 5.2.1 Creating the schema object

For the very first GraphQL.js example, we need to use two of the functions exported by the `graphql` package:

- The `buildSchema` function that builds a schema from a schema language text.
- The `graphql` function to execute a GraphQL query against that generated schema. To avoid confusion, I'll refer to it as the `graphql` *executor function*.

Let's create two files: one to host the schema and resolver definitions and the other to execute the schema using query text supplied by the user. To keep this example simple, I'll use a command-line interface to read the query text from the user instead of introducing a more featured user interface (like an HTTP server).

Create a schema directory under api/src, and put the following index.js file in it.

> **Listing 5.7  New file: api/src/schema/index.js**

```
import { buildSchema } from 'graphql';
```

The `buildSchema` function takes a string written in the GraphQL schema language, which represents a set of *types*. Every object in a GraphQL schema must have an explicit type. This starts with the root of what the schema is offering. For example, to make the schema accept queries in general, you need to define the special `Query` type. To make the schema accept a `currentTime` field in a query operation, you need to add it within the `Query` type and mark it as a `String`.

Here's the schema text for the simple example schema we're building.

Listing 5.8    Changes in api/src/schema/index.js

```
export const schema = buildSchema(`
  type Query {
    currentTime: String!
  }
`);
```

The string in listing 5.8 is the schema language text. Note the use of backticks to allow for having the text on multiple lines.

The result of executing `buildSchema` is a JavaScript object designed to work with the `graphql` executor function.

### 5.2.2   *Creating resolver functions*

We have a schema, and we can validate any request against it if we need to, but we have not told the GraphQL service what data to associate with the `currentTime` field in that schema. If a client asks for that field, what should the server response be?

This is the job of a resolver function. Each field defined in the schema needs to be associated with a resolver function. When it is time for the server to reply with data for that field, it will just execute that field's resolver function and use the function's return value as the data response for the field.

Let's create an object to hold the many resolver functions we will eventually have. Here's one way to implement the `currentTime` resolver logic.

Listing 5.9    Changes in api/src/schema/index.js

```
export const rootValue = {
  currentTime: () => {
    const isoString = new Date().toISOString();      The ISO format is fixed. The
    return isoString.slice(11, 19);         ◁——————  11-19 slice is the time part.
  },
};
```

This `rootValue` object will have more functions as we add more features to the API. It's named `rootValue` because GraphQL.js uses it as the root of the graph. Functions within the `rootValue` object are the resolvers for the top-level nodes in your graph.

You can do anything you wish within a resolver function! For example, you can query a database for data (which is what we need to do for the AZdev API).

> **NOTE**  I exported the `schema` and `rootValue` objects. Other modules in the server will need to import and use these objects.

## 5.2.3   *Executing requests*

The schema and rootValue objects are the core elements in any GraphQL service. You can pass them to the graphql executor function along with the text of a query or mutation, and the executor will be able to parse, validate, execute, and return data based on them. This is what we need to do next to test the currentTime field.

The graphql executor function can be used for this purpose. We can test that in api/src/server.js. Add the following import line.

> **NOTE**   The api/src/server.js file has some commented-out code to start a bare-bone express web server. You can ignore these comments for now.

**Listing 5.10   Changes in api/src/server.js**

```
import { graphql } from 'graphql';
```

This graphql executor function accepts a list of arguments: the first is a schema object, the second is a source request (the operation text), and the third is a rootValue object of resolvers. Here's an example of how you call it.

**Listing 5.11   Example: signature of the graphql executor function**

```
graphql(schema, request, rootValue);
```

> **TIP**   The graphql executor function has more positional arguments that can be used for advanced cases. However, we will soon use an HTTP(S) wrapper to run this function instead of calling it directly, and we will use named arguments when we do.

The graphql executor function returns a promise. In JavaScript, we can access the resolved value of this promise by putting the keyword await in front of it and wrapping the code with a function labeled with the async keyword.

**Listing 5.12   Example: the async/await pattern**

```
async () => {
  const resp = await graphql(schema, request, rootValue);
};
```

> **NOTE**   You don't need to add listings with captions prefixed with "Example:" anywhere.

The promise resolves to the GraphQL response in JSON. Each GraphQL response has a data attribute that holds any successfully resolved data elements (and an error attribute if errors are encountered). Let's just print the resp.data attribute.

For the three arguments of the `graphql` executor function, we can import the schema and `rootValue` objects from the previous file we worked on, but where do we get the `request` text?

The `request` text is something the clients of this API server will supply. They'll do that eventually over an HTTP(S) channel, but for now, we can read it directly from the command line as an argument. We'll test the server.js file this way.

---

**Listing 5.13   Command: testing a query operation from the command line**

```
$ node -r esm api/src/server.js "{ currentTime }"
```

**This command will work after you implement the next code change. The -r esm part enables working with ECMAScript modules on older versions of Node.js.**

For this test, the request text is the third argument in the command line (for the npm run script). You can capture that in any Node script with `process.argv[2]`.

---

### The process.argv array

In Node, `process.argv` is a simple array with an item for each positional token in the command line (that ran the process), starting with the command itself. For the command in listing 5.13, `process.argv` is

```
["path/to/node/command", "api/src/server.js", "{ currentTime }"]
```

---

Here's the full code snippet in api/src/server.js that we can use to carry out this test.

---

**Listing 5.14   Changes in api/src/server.js**

```
import { graphql } from 'graphql';
import { schema, rootValue } from './schema';

const executeGraphQLRequest = async request => {
  const resp = await graphql(schema, request, rootValue);
  console.log(resp.data);
};


executeGraphQLRequest(process.argv[2]);
// -----
```

---

We simply import the `schema` and `rootValue` that we prepared, wrap the `graphql` executor function in an async function, and use `process.argv[2]` to read the GraphQL request text from the user.

This example is complete! You can test it with the command in listing 5.13, and you should see the server report the time in UTC:

```
$ node -r esm api/src/server.js "{ currentTime }"
[Object: null prototype] { currentTime: '18:35:10' }
```

**TIP** The GraphQL.js implementation uses null-prototyped objects for data responses. This is why [Object: null prototype] is part of the response. The console.log function in Node reports that when it sees it. Null-prototyped objects are generally better for maps/lists because they start empty and do not inherit any default properties. For example, you can do ({}).toString(), but you cannot do Object.create(null).toString().

**Current code**

You can use the command git checkout 5.1 to synchronize your local repo with the current progress in the code (after the currentTime test).

The 5.1 part of this command is the name of a Git *branch*. The branch you start with when you clone the repo is named main. You can always go back to any branch using the checkout command. You can also make your own commits on a branch until we check out the next branch. This will enable you to use the git diff command to compare your work with mine if you want to.

If you've made any local changes so far, you need to either commit them or get rid of them before you check out a new branch. You can also stash them with the command git add . && git stash.

## 5.3 *Communicating over HTTP*

Before adding more fields to this API, let's use a better interface than the simple command line. Let's communicate with the GraphQL service via HTTP. To do that, we need an HTTP server.

**TIP** You should host your GraphQL services behind an HTTPS service. You can use Node to create an HTTPS server, but a better option is to use a web server like NGINX (or a web service like Cloudflare) to protect your HTTP service and make it available only over HTTPS.

We're going to use the express package to create an HTTP server and the express-graphql package to wire that server to work with the GraphQL service that we have so far.

**TIP** For reference, the code to run a bare-bone Express server is commented out in api/src/server.js.

Remove the executeGraphQLRequest function and the graphql executor function (in api/src/server.js). Instead, import the graphqlHTTP named export from the express-graphql package.

**Listing 5.15   Changes in api/src/server.js**

```
import { graphqlHTTP } from 'express-graphql';
import { schema, rootValue } from './schema';

// Uncomment the code to run a bare-bone Express server

import express from 'express';
import bodyParser from 'body-parser';
import cors from 'cors';
import morgan from 'morgan';

import * as config from './config';

async function main() {
  // -----
}

main();
```

The default export in the express package is a function. To create an Express server, you just invoke that function. Then you can use the listen method on the created server to make the server listen to incoming connections on a certain port. That part is already done in the main function.

When you run this code, an HTTP server will listen on port 4321. To make the server accept incoming connections for a certain HTTP URL/VERB combination (like GET /), we need to add a server.get method (or .post, .put, or .delete) or the generic server.use method that makes the server accept all HTTP VERBs for a certain URL.

The provided main function has an example of a server.get call. Here is the signature of the server.VERB methods and an example of what you can do within it.

**Listing 5.16   Example: Express.js API to define a route and its handler**

```
server.use('/', (req, res, next) => {
  // Read something from req
  // Write something to res
  // Either end things here or call the next function
});
```

The first argument for the .use method is the URL for which the server will start accepting connections. The second argument is the function that will be invoked every time the server accepts a connection on that URL. This function is usually called the *listener* function.

The listener function exposes two important objects as arguments, req and res (the next object is not usually used for response handlers):

- The req object is how the service can read information from the HTTP request. For example, we need to read the text of the query/mutation (and other related objects) from a client that is using this API. We can do that using req.

- The `res` object is how the service can reply with data to the client that is requesting it. This is how the API server responds with the data it generates for incoming GraphQL requests.

Between reading from the request and writing to the response, we will need to execute the `graphql` executor function just as we did for the command-line test. This will happen for each GraphQL request, and it's another general process that can be abstracted and reused.

The `graphqlHTTP` function we imported from `express-graphql` is a listener function that does exactly that. It will parse the HTTP request, run the `graphql` executor function, await its response, and send its resolved data back to the requester. We just need to tell it what `schema` and `rootValue` objects to use.

Here's the `.use` method wired to work with the `graphqlHTTP` function. Put this in api/src/server.js, replacing the provided example `server.use('/')` call.

---

**Listing 5.17   Changes in api/src/server.js**

```
// .-.-.

async function main() {
  // .-.-.

  // Replace the example server.use call with:
  server.use(
    '/',
    graphqlHTTP({
      schema,
      rootValue,
      graphiql: true,
    })
  );

  server.listen(config.port, () => {
    console.log(`Server URL: http://localhost:${config.port}/`);
  });
}

main();
```

This will allow us to communicate with the schema over HTTP. Not only that, but by using `graphiql: true` in the configuration object, we will also get the mighty GraphiQL editor mounted on that URL, and it will work with our schema!

**TIP**  The `graphqlHTTP` function call returns a handler function that expects `req`/`res` arguments. That matches the signature needed for the `use` method's handler function (its second argument).

Let's test. Start the API server with the following command.

**Listing 5.18   Command: running the API server**

```
$ npm run api-server
```

You should see this message:

```
Server URL: http://localhost:4321/
```

Then head over to http://localhost:4321/. You should see the GraphiQL editor, and you should be able to test the currentTime field query in it, as shown in figure 5.1.

```
1   {
2       currentTime
3   }
```

```
▼ {
    "data": {
        "currentTime": "16:26:40"
    }
}
```

**Figure 5.1   express-graphql has the GraphiQL editor built in.**

**NOTE**   The API server is configured to run with the nodemon command instead of the node command. nodemon runs a node process while monitoring files for changes and automatically restarts that node process when it detects changes to the files. That makes the API server auto-restart whenever you save any file in the api directory.

Note that the entire HTTP channel to communicate with the server has nothing to do with the GraphQL service. It's just another service layer offering a convenient way to communicate with the GraphQL service layer. A web application can now use Ajax requests to retrieve data from the GraphQL service. In a large-scale GraphQL API service, this HTTP communication layer would be a separate entity that can be managed and scaled independently.

**TIP**   You can turn off the GraphiQL editor in production (if you want to) and use .post instead of .use for the graphqlHTTP handler. That way, the service will only work for Ajax post requests.

**Current code**

Use git checkout 5.2 to reset your local repo to the current progress in the code.

## 5.4    *Building a schema using constructor objects*

The GraphQL schema language is a great programming-language-agnostic way to describe a GraphQL schema. It's a human-readable format that's easy to work with, and it is the popular, preferable format for describing your GraphQL schemas. However, it has some limitations.

GraphQL.js has another format that can be used to create a GraphQL schema and its various types. Instead of text written with the schema language, you can use JavaScript objects instantiated from calls to various constructor classes. For example, you can use the `GraphQLSchema` constructor to create a schema object, the `GraphQLObjectType` constructor to create an object type, the `GraphQLUnionType` to create a union type, and many more classes just like these.

This format is useful if you need to construct a schema programmatically. It's more flexible and easier to test, manage, and extend.

> **NOTE**   The method of using objects to create a GraphQL schema does not have a universally agreed-on name. I've heard "code-first" and "resolvers-first," but I don't think these names fairly represent the method. I'll refer to it in this book as the *object-based method*.

Let's start exploring this object-based method by converting the schema we have so far (which only supports a `currentTime` field).

### 5.4.1    *The Query type*

Since we are now going to use the object-based method to build the schema, you can delete everything you have so far in api/src/schema/index.js.

To create a GraphQL schema using this method, we need to import a few objects from the `graphql` package, as follows.

**Listing 5.19   New code replacing what's in api/src/schema/index.js**

```
import {
  GraphQLSchema,
  GraphQLObjectType,
  GraphQLString,
  GraphQLInt,
  GraphQLNonNull,
} from 'graphql';
```

These type-based objects are designed to work together to help us create a schema. For example, to instantiate a schema object, you just do something like this.

**Listing 5.20   Example: creating a schema object**

```
const schema = new GraphQLSchema({
  query: new GraphQLObjectType({
    name: 'Query',
```

```
    fields: {
      // Root query fields are defined here
    }
  }),
});
```

These calls to `GraphQLSchema` and `GraphQLObjectType` return special objects designed to work with the `graphql` executor function.

Instead of inlining the call to `GraphQLObjectType`, let's extract it into its own variable. I'll name it `QueryType`. In this type's `fields` property, we need to add the `currentTime` field, specify its type, and include its resolver function. Here's the code.

##### Listing 5.21   Changes in api/src/schema/index.js

```
const QueryType = new GraphQLObjectType({
  name: 'Query',
  fields: {
    currentTime: {
      type: GraphQLString,
      resolve: () => {
        const isoString = new Date().toISOString();
        return isoString.slice(11, 19);
      },
    },
  },
});

export const schema = new GraphQLSchema({
  query: QueryType,
});
```

**TIP**  Don't memorize the ways to use these constructor and type helpers. Just understand and retain their capabilities and what they enable you to do.

An object type has a `name` and a list of `fields` (represented with an object). Each field has a `type` property and a `resolve` function.

This code maps to the schema-language version we had before. We're just doing it with objects instead of strings. Instead of `currentTime: String`, this method requires defining a property `currentTime` and giving it a configuration object with a `type` of `GraphQLString`. Instead of a `rootValue` object, we define a `resolve` function.

The `resolve` function is the same one we had under the `rootValue` object, but now it's part of the schema object. Using the object-based method, we don't need a `rootValue` object because all resolvers are included where they're needed alongside their fields. The schema object created with `GraphQLSchema` is executable on its own.

I used the `GraphQLString` scalar type for `currentTime`. The GraphQL.js implementation offers a few similar scalar types, including `GraphQLInt`, `GraphQLBoolean`, and `GraphQLFloat`.

To test this code, we need to remove the `rootValue` concept from api/src/server.js.

**Listing 5.22  Changes in api/src/server.js**

```
// .-.-.
import { schema } from './schema';
// .-.-.

async function main() {
  // .-.-.
  server.use(
    '/',
    graphqlHTTP({
      schema,                          Remove the
      graphiql: true,                  rootValue object
    }),
  );
  server.listen(config.port, () => {
    console.log(`Server URL: http://localhost:${config.port}/`);
  });
}

main();
```

That's it. You can test in GraphiQL that the service supports the currentTime field, but now using the object-based method.

**Current code**

Use git checkout 5.3 to reset your local repo to the current progress in the code.

### 5.4.2  Field arguments

To explore the GraphQL.js API further, let's look at an example with a bigger scope. Let's make the API support a sumNumbersInRange field that accepts two arguments (begin and end) representing a range of numbers and returns the sum of all whole numbers in that range (inclusive to its edges). Figure 5.2 shows the desired end result.

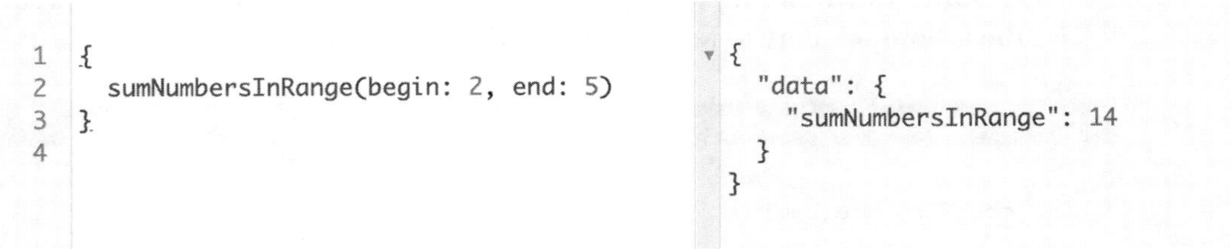

```
1  {
2    sumNumbersInRange(begin: 2, end: 5)
3  }
4
```

```
▼ {
    "data": {
      "sumNumbersInRange": 14
    }
  }
```

**Figure 5.2  The sumNumbersInRange field**

Here's a simple implementation of the sumNumbersInRange field. Add this to the fields property for QueryType.

**Listing 5.23  Changes in api/src/schema/index.js**

```
fields: {
  // ......

  sumNumbersInRange: {
    type: new GraphQLNonNull(GraphQLInt),
    args: {
      begin: { type: new GraphQLNonNull(GraphQLInt) },
      end: { type: new GraphQLNonNull(GraphQLInt) },
    },
    resolve: function (source, { begin, end }) {
      let sum = 0;
      for (let i = begin; i <= end; i++) {
        sum += i;
      }
      return sum;
    },
  },
},
```

The sumNumbersInRange field has a type of new GraphQLNonNull(GraphQLInt). The GraphQLNonNull wrapper around this integer type indicates that this field will always have a value. The response of a sumNumbersInRange field in a query will never be null.

The definition of sumNumbersInRange included an args property to define the structure of the arguments it accepts and their types (which I defined using new GraphQLNonNull(GraphQLInt) as well). Both of these arguments are required. A client cannot ask for the sumNumbersInRange field without specifying the begin and end numbers for that range. The GraphQL service will throw an error if that happens.

The resolver function for sumNumbersInRange makes use of its arguments. The first argument is always the source parent object of that resolved level. For sumNumbersInRange, there is no parent object because it is a root field. The second argument for the resolve function exposes the field argument values as defined by the API consumer. I destructured begin and end from that argument as both of these values are required.

The resolver function simply loops over the range, computes the sum, and returns it. Use the following query to test the new field this API now supports.

**Listing 5.24  The sumNumbersInRange leaf field**

```
{
  sumNumbersInRange(begin: 2, end: 5)
}
```

Note that the sumNumbersInRange field has no sub-selection set because it's a leaf field that resolves to a scalar value. However, to learn about custom object types, next we will change it to a non-leaf field that requires a sub-selection set.

**NOTE** The GraphQLNonNull helper is the GraphQL.js way to specify a type modifier, and it's equivalent to the exclamation mark in the schema language. The equivalent of adding square brackets to make a list is the GraphQLList type modifier. For example, to define a field that represents an array of strings, the type would be new GraphQLList(GraphQLString).

### 5.4.3 Custom object types

So far, we've created one object type to represent the root fields under the query type. To explore using custom object types, let's replace the sumNumbersInRange leaf field with a numbersInRange object field that supports the same begin and end arguments, and let's make it support two leaf fields for the sum and count of the whole numbers in the range.

Here's how the new numbersInRange field will be queried.

##### Listing 5.25 The numbersInRange field

```
{
  numbersInRange(begin: 2, end: 5) {
    sum
    count
  }
}
```

To implement this, we need to define a custom object type to represent the new "numbers in range" structure, which looks like an object that has sum and count properties. Let's name it NumbersInRange.

To organize the code for GraphQL object types, let's create a file for each, starting with this new type for the numbersInRange field.

Create a new directory api/src/schema/types, and create a numbers-in-range.js file there to implement the NumbersInRange type.

##### Listing 5.26 New file: api/src/schema/types/numbers-in-range.js

```
import {
  GraphQLObjectType,
  GraphQLInt,
  GraphQLNonNull,
} from 'graphql';

const NumbersInRange = new GraphQLObjectType({
  name: 'NumbersInRange',
  description: 'Aggregate info on a range of numbers',
  fields: {
    sum: {
      type: new GraphQLNonNull(GraphQLInt),
    },
    count: {
      type: new GraphQLNonNull(GraphQLInt),
    },
```

```
  },
});
```

```
export default NumbersInRange;
```

Besides the `name` property, we can give each type an optional `description` property to describe the type. Both of these will show up in GraphiQL's Docs explorer when the new `NumbersInRange` type is used in the main schema.

> **TIP** You can use rich-text formats like Markdown in these description properties and then have the client tool render them in a more readable way. GraphiQL supports rendering Markdown in descriptions out of the box!

Note that the `sum` and `count` fields in the `NumbersInRange` type do not have resolver functions. Although this design makes `sum` and `count` leaf fields, having resolver functions for them is optional. This is because these leaf fields can use the default trivial resolvers based on properties defined on their parent source object. For this to work, the object resolved as the parent object (which is of type `NumbersInRange`) has to respond to `sum` and `count` methods.

Let's create a function that takes `begin` and `end` as arguments, computes the sum/count, and returns an object with `sum` and `count` properties. Here's one way to implement that (you can put this code in the api/src/utils.js file).

##### Listing 5.27   Changes in api/src/utils.js

```
// ------

export const numbersInRangeObject = (begin, end) => {
  let sum = 0;
  let count = 0;
  for (let i = begin; i <= end; i++) {
    sum += i;
    count++;
  }
  return { sum, count };
};
```

> **TIP** There is a better way to compute the count and sum of consecutive numbers in a range without using a loop: you can use the arithmetic progression formulas. I used a loop for simplicity.

Now we need to change the `QueryType` object. It has a non-leaf field named `numbersInRange`, and that field needs to be resolved with the object returned by calling the `numbersInRangeObject` helper function.

##### Listing 5.28   Changes in api/src/schema/index.js

```
// ------
import NumbersInRange from './types/numbers-in-range';
import { numbersInRangeObject } from '../utils';
```

```
const QueryType = new GraphQLObjectType({
  name: 'Query',
  fields: {
    // ·—·—·

    // Remove the sumNumbersInRange field

    numbersInRange: {
      type: NumbersInRange,
      args: {
        begin: { type: new GraphQLNonNull(GraphQLInt) },
        end: { type: new GraphQLNonNull(GraphQLInt) },
      },
      resolve: function (source, { begin, end }) {
        return numbersInRangeObject(begin, end);
      },
    },
  },
});
// ·—·—·
```

That's it. If you test the API now, you should be able to execute a query like the following:

```
{
  numbersInRange(begin: 2, end: 5) {
    sum
    count
  }
}
```

And you will get this response:

```
{
  "data": {
    "numbersInRange": {
      "sum": 14,
      "count": 4
    }
  }
}
```

> **Challenge**
> Add an `avg` field to the `NumbersInRange` type, and make it return the `sum` divided by the `count`.

### 5.4.4  *Custom errors*

A GraphQL executor automatically handles any invalid queries or types used for arguments in the query. For example, if you omit one of the required arguments, you get the error shown in figure 5.3. If you use strings instead of integers for begin and end, you get the error shown in figure 5.4. And if you attempt to query for a nonexisting leaf field, you get the error shown in figure 5.5.

```
1 ▾ {                                              ▾ {
2     numbersInRange(begin: 2) {                   ▾   "errors": [
3         sum                                      ▾     {
4         count                                          "message": "Field \"numbersInRange\" argument
5     }                                            \"end\" of type \"Int!\" is required, but it was not
6 }                                                provided.",
7                                                   ▸       "locations": [ ↔ ]
                                                          }
                                                        ]
                                                   }|
```

**Figure 5.3   All required arguments must be present in the request.**

```
1 ▾ {                                              ▾ {
2     numbersInRange(begin: "A", end: "Z") {       ▾   "errors": [
3         sum                                      ▾     {
4         count                                            "message": "Int cannot represent non-integer
5     }                                            value: \"A\"",
6 }                                                 ▸       "locations": [ ↔ ]
7                                                         },
                                                   ▾     {
                                                           "message": "Int cannot represent non-integer
                                                   value: \"Z\"",
                                                   ▸       "locations": [ ↔ ]
                                                          }
                                                        ]
                                                    }
```

**Figure 5.4   Only the right data types are accepted.**

```
1 ▾ {                                              ▾ {
2 ▾   numbersInRange(begin: 2, end: 5) {           ▾   "errors": [
3         sum                                      ▾     {
4         count                                            "message": "Cannot query field \"avg\" on type
5         avg                                      \"NumbersInRange\".",
6     }                                            ▸       "locations": [ ↔ ]
7 }                                                       }
8 |                                                     ]
                                                    }
```

**Figure 5.5   Only fields published by the schema can be used.**

This is the power of a strongly typed schema. You get many great validations out of the box, but what about the custom cases? What should happen if a requester specifies an invalid range for the numbersInRange field (for example, using an end value that is less than the begin value)? The API currently ignores this case and just returns zeros, as shown in figure 5.6.

Let's fix this. Let's change the API to reject this input and, instead of returning zeros, return a custom error message to the requester. If the range is invalid, the

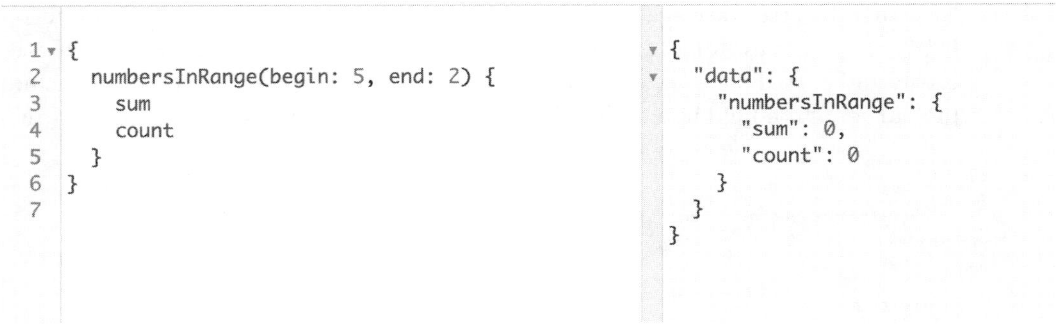

```
1 ▾ {
2     numbersInRange(begin: 5, end: 2) {
3       sum
4       count
5     }
6   }
7
```

```
▾ {
  ▾   "data": {
    ▾     "numbersInRange": {
            "sum": 0,
            "count": 0
          }
        }
      }
```

**Figure 5.6  To error or not to error?**

requester should be made aware of that fact, because otherwise, bugs might sneak into the code.

We do the check in the resolver function for the `numbersInRange` field and `throw` an error with our custom message.

**Listing 5.29  Changes in api/src/utils.js**

```
export const numbersInRangeObject = (begin, end) => {
  if (end < begin) {
    throw Error(`Invalid range because ${end} < ${begin}`);
  }
  // ------
};
```

Now, if you attempt to make an invalid range query, you get the message shown in figure 5.7.

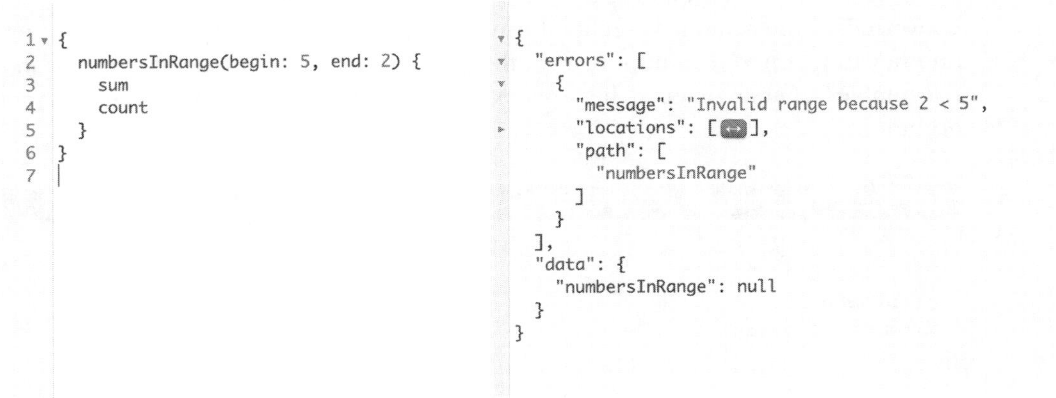

```
1 ▾ {
2     numbersInRange(begin: 5, end: 2) {
3       sum
4       count
5     }
6   }
7 |
```

```
▾ {
  ▾   "errors": [
    ▾     {
            "message": "Invalid range because 2 < 5",
            "locations": [ ⬌ ],
            "path": [
              "numbersInRange"
            ]
          }
        ],
        "data": {
          "numbersInRange": null
        }
      }
```

**Figure 5.7  A custom error message in the response**

Note that the errors are again delivered as part of the JSON response (and not through HTTP error codes, for example). In some cases, the JSON response may have both errors and partial data that is not affected by the errors. You can test that by including the `currentTime` field in a query with a bad range for `numbersInRange`; see figure 5.8.

```
1 ▾ {
2     numbersInRange(begin: 5, end: 2) {
3       sum
4       count
5     }
6     currentTime
7 }
8
```

```
▾ {
  ▾ "errors": [
    ▾ {
        "message": "Invalid range because 2 < 5",
        "locations": [ ⊟ ],
        "path": [
          "numbersInRange"
        ]
      }
    ],
    "data": {
      "numbersInRange": null,
      "currentTime": "21:51:08"
    }
  }
}
```

**Figure 5.8   The response has both errors and data.**

Did you notice how I made the `numbersInRange` field nullable in listing 5.28? For this particular case, a `numbersInRange` field may be absent from the response when the range it uses is invalid. This is another example of a case where nullability is okay because I am attaching a semantic meaning to it. Also, because `numbersInRange` is a root field, making it non-nullable will prevent having a partial response in other root fields (like `currentTime`) when there is an error in the range.

## 5.5    *Generating SDL text from object-based schemas*

The executable schema object that we created using the object-based method can be converted to the schema-language format using the `printSchema` function, which is another function we can import from the `graphql` package. We call it and pass in the executable schema object (the one exported by api/src/schema/index.js) as the argument.

**Listing 5.30   Changes in api/src/schema/index.js**

```
import {
  // .-.-.
  printSchema,
} from 'graphql';
// .-.-.

export const schema = new GraphQLSchema({
  query: QueryType,
});
console.log(printSchema(schema));
```

Here's what you'll see.

**Listing 5.31  Output of `printSchema`**

```
type Query {
  currentTime: String
  numbersInRange(begin: Int!, end: Int!): NumbersInRange
}
"""Aggregate info on a range of numbers"""
type NumbersInRange {
  sum: Int!
  count: Int!
}
```

This is the schema representation without the resolver functions, but it is a lot more concise and readable. My favorite part about this conversion is how the arguments to the `numbersInRange` field are defined in the schema language format:

```
(begin: Int!, end: Int!)
```

Compare that with:

```
args: {
  begin: { type: new GraphQLNonNull(GraphQLInt) },
  end: { type: new GraphQLNonNull(GraphQLInt) },
},
```

Note that the description of `NumbersInRange` is included right before it, surrounded by a set of three double quotes. Here's an example of a well-described version of the API we have so far.

**Listing 5.32  Example: using descriptions in SDL**

```
"""The root query entry point for the API"""
type Query {
  "The current time in ISO UTC"
  currentTime: String

  """
  An object representing a range of whole numbers
  from "begin" to "end" inclusive to the edges
  """
  numbersInRange(
    "The number to begin the range"
    begin: Int!,
    "The number to end the range"
    end: Int!
  ): NumbersInRange!
}
"""Aggregate info on a range of numbers"""
 type NumbersInRange {
```

```
"Sum of all whole numbers in the range"
sum: Int!
"Count of all whole numbers in the range"
count: Int!
}
```

**Current code**
Use `git checkout 5.4` to reset your local repo to the current progress in the code.

### 5.5.1    *The schema language versus the object-based method*

The schema language enables front-end developers to participate in designing the API and, more important, start using a mocked version of it right away. The frontend people on your team will absolutely love it. It enables them to participate in designing the API and, more important, start using a mocked version of it right away. The schema language text can serve as an early version of the API documentation.

However, completely relying on the full-schema text to create a GraphQL schema has a few drawbacks. You'll need to put in some effort to make the code modularized and clear, and you'll have to rely on coding patterns and tools to keep the schema-language text consistent with the tree of resolvers (aka *resolvers map*). These are solvable problems.

The biggest issue I see with the full-schema method is that you lose some flexibility in your code. All your types have to be written in that specific way that relies on the schema-language text. You can't use constructors to create *some* types when you need to. You're locked into this string-based approach. Although the schema-language text makes your types more readable, in many cases, you'll need flexibility over readability.

The object-based method is flexible and easier to extend and manage. It does not suffer from any of the problems I just mentioned. Your code will be modular with it because your schema will be a bunch of objects. You also don't need to merge modules, because these objects are designed and expected to work like a tree.

The only issue I see with the object-based method is that you have to deal with a lot more code around what's important to manage in your modules (types and resolvers). Many developers see that as noise, and I do not blame them.

If you're creating a small, well-defined GraphQL service, using the full-schema-string method is probably okay. However, in bigger and more agile projects, I think the more flexible and powerful object-based method is the way to go.

> **TIP**   You should still use the schema-language text even if you're using the object-based method. For example, at jsComplete.com, we use the object-based method, but every time the schema is built, we use the `printSchema` function to write the complete schema to a file. We commit and track that file in the project's Git repo, which has proven to be a very helpful practice!

## 5.6  *Working with asynchronous functions*

Both fields we have so far in this example are mapped to a normal synchronous resolver. However, if a field needs to do a lot of work to resolve its data, it should use an asynchronous resolver because, otherwise, the entire API service will be blocked and unable to serve other requests.

To demonstrate this problem, let's fake a delay in processing the `currentTime` field. JavaScript has no sleep function, but it's easy to accomplish something similar by comparing dates. Here's one way to make the `currentTime` resolver function synchronously take 5 seconds to complete.

---

**Listing 5.33  Delaying returning from `currentTime` by 5 seconds**

```
currentTime: {
  type: GraphQLString,
  resolve: () => {
    const sleepToDate = new Date(new Date().getTime() + 5000);
    while (sleepToDate > new Date()) {
      // sleep
    }
    const isoString = new Date().toISOString();
    return isoString.slice(11, 19);
  },
},
```

Now, each time you ask for the `currentTime` field, the server will spend 5 seconds doing nothing, and then it will return the answer. The problem is that during these 5 seconds, the whole node process for the server is completely blocked. A second requester cannot get any data from the API until the `while` loop in the first request is finished (see figure 5.9).

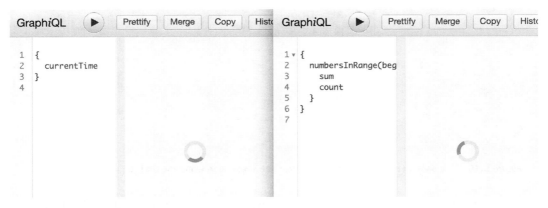

**Figure 5.9   The second request (right side) is waiting on the first request.**

You should never do that. Instead, all long-running processes should be done asynchronously either with native APIs offered by Node and its many packages or by forking the work over to a worker thread/process.

For example, to make the `currentTime` field fake-delay its response by 5 seconds but do so asynchronously, we can use the `setTimeout` method and wrap it in a promise object.

**Listing 5.34    Replacing existing code**

```
currentTime: {
  type: GraphQLString,
  resolve: () => {                              Resolver functions support
    return new Promise(resolve => {      ◁───   returning a promise object.
      setTimeout(() => {
        const isoString = new Date().toISOString();
        resolve(isoString.slice(11, 19));
      }, 5000);
    });
  },
};
```

**NOTE**  We don't need to `await` this promise. A resolver function can return a promise, and the executor will `await` that promise and use its data. This behavior is built into the GraphQL.js implementation.

With this change, each time you ask the API service for the `currentTime` field, it will still answer after 5 seconds, but the service process will not be blocked! Other requesters can ask for other parts of the API and get immediate responses while a requester is waiting for the `currentTime` (see figure 5.10).

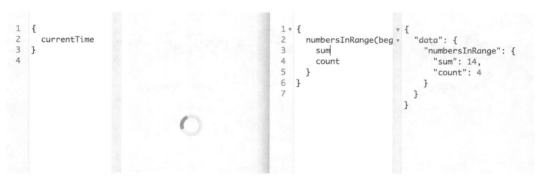

**Figure 5.10    The second requester (right side) can get a response while the first requester is waiting.**

This is going to be very handy when we work with objects coming from databases, because we should definitely use asynchronous APIs to make all communications with all the databases.

I think we're ready to do that!

**Current code**

For your reference, I put the code for the current-time sync-versus-async example in its own Git branch. You can use the command `git checkout 5.T1` to see that code.

I did not include this example in the current 5.4 branch (which you can go back to with the command `git checkout 5.4`).

## Summary

- A GraphQL service is centered around the concept of a schema that is made executable with resolver functions.
- A GraphQL implementation like GraphQL.js takes care of the generic tasks involved in working with an executable schema.
- You can interact with a GraphQL service using any communication interface. HTTP(S) is the popular choice for GraphQL services designed for web and mobile applications.
- You can convert from one schema representation to another using GraphQL.js helper functions like `buildSchema` and `printSchema`.
- You should not do long-running processes synchronously because doing so will block a GraphQL service process for all clients. Resolver functions in the GraphQL.js implementation can work with asynchronous promise-based operations out of the box.

# Working with database models and relations

Now that you've learned the core concepts of building a simple "static" schema and how to resolve its fields, it's time to get real and learn how to resolve fields from databases. It's time to implement the queries of the AZdev API. We'll go through them one by one as we designed them in chapter 4 and learn the concepts we need as we use them.

> ### Current code
> Use `git checkout 6.0` to reset your local repo to the current progress in the code. If you need to stash any local changes, use `git add . && git stash`. Remember to run `npm install` to install any missing dependencies.

## 6.1 Running and connecting to databases

The easiest way to get this project's databases up and running with sample data is to use Docker. Docker uses your OS virtualization to provide software in packaged containers. It's available on all three major operating systems.

I've prepared two Docker containers for this project: one for PostgreSQL and one for MongoDB. They both have the database structure created and the sample data imported. If you're new to Docker, no worries. It's really simple. All you need is to install Docker Desktop (az.dev/docker) on your OS and leave it running in the background.

> **NOTE** If you would like to use your own database services for the project, you can execute the dev-dbs/schema.* files to create the database entities and load the sample data.

Once Docker is running, you can run this command to start both databases.

---

**Listing 6.1  Command: start the database servers**

```
$ npm run start-dbs
```

This command will take a while the first time you run it as it will download the two containers on your machine. It will also start these containers and expose the database on their default ports. PostgreSQL will be running on port 5432 and MongoDB will be running on port 27017.

> **NOTE** I've also provided a Docker file to download and run clean blank databases if you would like to go through the steps to create a database schema and load it up with sample data.

Having sample data in all tables and collections is a great way to get started and enable us to test the GraphQL queries before dealing with the GraphQL mutations! Make sure you get some realistic data in all the database tables one way or another.

Take a look at the dev-dbs/schema.* files, and verify the structure of tables and collections that we designed in chapter 4. Note the `insert` statement I prepared there for the sample data.

**TIP**  The dev-dbs/schema.sql file uses the `pgcrypto` extension to manage the hashing of passwords and tokens in the `users` table. You can read the documentation for this extension at az.dev/pgcrypto.

If the database servers run successfully, you should have six Tasks with their Approaches and some extra dynamic data elements in MongoDB for each Approach. Use the following SQL queries to see the data in PostgreSQL.

**Listing 6.2    In `psql`: queries to read data**

```
SELECT * FROM azdev.users;

SELECT * FROM azdev.tasks;

SELECT * FROM azdev.approaches;
```

For the data in MongoDB, you can use this `find` command.

**Listing 6.3    In `mongo`: command to read the approaches data**

```
db.approachDetails.find({});
```

**TIP**  You can use database GUIs to inspect the databases and make sure they have the sample data loaded up. On my Mac, I use Postico for PostgreSQL (az.dev/postico) and Robo 3T for MongoDB (az.dev/robo).

Before a client can execute commands on a database and retrieve data from it, it needs to *connect* to it. There are many ways to connect to both PostgreSQL and MongoDB from the Node drivers. We can do a one-time connection per SQL statement in the `pg` driver, but a better way is to have the driver manage a pool of open connections and reuse them as needed (figure 6.1). Both drivers support this mode.

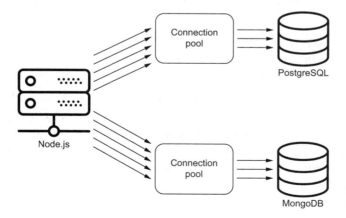

Figure 6.1  Keeping pools of open connections to databases

The code to connect to these databases is ready under api/src/db/. Take a look at pg-client.js and mongo-client.js and see if you need to do anything differently. If your local copy of the project fails to connect to databases, these two files are where you need to start troubleshooting.

Note that I tested the connections to both databases by counting the numbers of tables/collections. This step is optional, but it verifies that connections are successful when the server starts.

> **TIP** Note that I made both database client modules (under api/src/db) return an object with similar purposes. I find that kind of normalization helpful for entities in the project that are meant to do similar things.

## 6.2 *The taskMainList query*

To be able to work with Task records in the GraphQL schema, we need to define a new custom type for these records just like what we did for numbersInRange when we converted it from a leaf field into a non-leaf field. We need to create a custom type for each entity in the AZdev API: a Task type, an Approach type, and a User type.

Let's start by implementing the main Task type. Here is the SDL text we prepared for it.

**Listing 6.4 The `Task` type**

```
type Task implements SearchResultItem {
  id: ID!
  createdAt: String!
  content: String!
  tags: [String!]!
  approachCount: Int!

  # author: User!
  # approachList: [Approach!]!
}
```

The first query field that will use this Task type is the list of the latest Tasks that will be displayed on the main page of the AZdev app. We named that field taskMainList.

**Listing 6.5 Using the `Task` type in the `taskMainList` field on `Query`**

```
type Query {
  taskMainList: [Task!]
}
```

To learn the concepts in the right order, let's start with the five simple scalar leaf fields under this type: id, content, tags, approachCount, and createdAt.

Here's a GraphQL query that we can use to start testing this feature.

**Listing 6.6   The `taskMainList` query**

```
query {
  taskMainList {
    id
    content
    tags
    approachCount
    createdAt
  }
}
```

This query should return an array of Task records. Each item in that array is an object with five properties whose values will come from the PostgreSQL `azdev.tasks` table (which has columns matching the five field names). Let's implement this feature with the simplest code possible and improve it once we get it to work naively. As Kent Beck said, "Make it work. Make it right. Make it fast."

To implement this feature, we need to follow these three steps:

1  Define a new object type named `Task` that has the five scalar fields.
2  Write any non-default resolvers for the `Task` type. We have to do date-to-string conversion for the `created_at` database column. We also decided to expose the `tags` GraphQL field as an array of strings instead of the comma-separated string values in the database.
3  Modify the `Query` type to have a field named `taskMainList` that is a list of non-null `Task` items, and resolve it with an array of records from the `azdev.tasks` table.

Let's start by defining the `Task` type.

### 6.2.1   Defining object types

Here's a possible implementation of the new `Task` type (without any resolvers). Put this under api/src/schema/types/task.js.

**Listing 6.7   New file: api/src/schema/types/task.js**

```
import {
  GraphQLID,
  GraphQLObjectType,
  GraphQLString,
  GraphQLInt,
  GraphQLNonNull,
  GraphQLList,
} from 'graphql';

const Task = new GraphQLObjectType({
  name: 'Task',
  fields: {
    id: { type: new GraphQLNonNull(GraphQLID) },
```

```
      content: { type: new GraphQLNonNull(GraphQLString) },
      tags: {
        type: new GraphQLNonNull(
          new GraphQLList(new GraphQLNonNull(GraphQLString))
        ),
      },
      approachCount: { type: new GraphQLNonNull(GraphQLInt) },
      createdAt: { type: new GraphQLNonNull(GraphQLString) },
    },
  });
```

```
export default Task;
```

The `Task` object here is just a direct translation of the SDL text in listing 6.4. The six lines in the SDL version more than tripled with all the object-based method boiler-plate code. The worst part about this is probably the type for the `tags` field. The simple `[String!]!` had to be written with nested calls of three functions:

```
new GraphQLNonNull(
  new GraphQLList(
    new GraphQLNonNull(
      GraphQLString
    )
  )
)
```

There is no debate that the SDL text is a better way to present this type. This is why many tools were created to enable building GraphQL schemas based on SDL texts for types and other elements. The GraphQL.js `buildSchema` function itself was popular-ized by these tools. Some tools expanded the SDL syntax to enable modularizing an SDL-based schema into many parts. Other tools were introduced to merge multiple SDL-based schemas and resolve any conflicts between them. These tools are helpful and have practical uses, but I would like to keep this book focused purely on the GraphQL.js implementation and use the natively supported object-based method.

> **Using SDL with the object-based method**
>
> In the future, the GraphQL.js implementation might support an API that will allow you to use an SDL text with the object-based method (so it's not one way or the other).
>
> I wrote a package that enables a similar approach using the current GraphQL.js imple-mentation. I named it `graphql-makers`, and you can read about it at jscomplete .com/graphql-makers.

### 6.2.2 The context object

The next step is to modify the `Query` type to include the `taskMainList` field. This field is a list of non-null items where each item has the `Task` type introduced in listing 6.4.

This means the type for the `taskMainList` field should be `new GraphQLList(new GraphQLNonNull(Task))`. To resolve this field, we need to execute this SQL statement on the PostgreSQL database.

> **Listing 6.8   SQL statement for the `taskMainList` field**

```
SELECT *                          Don't include private Task objects.
FROM azdev.tasks
WHERE is_private = FALSE  ⟵┐      Sorts Tasks by creation date, newest first
ORDER BY created_at DESC  ⟵┘
LIMIT 100                 ⟵──────  Limits the results to 100 Task objects
```

Before we can execute this SQL query, we need to open the pool of connections to PostgreSQL. To do that, we need to import the api/src/db/pg-client.js module and invoke its default export (the `pgClient` function). But where exactly should we do this?

The pool of connections to a database should be started when the server is started and then made available to all the resolver functions that are going to use it. This is a lot more efficient than connecting to the database from within resolver functions.

The GraphQL.js implementation has a feature to help us make a pool of connections globally available to all resolvers. It's called the *context* object.

The special context object enables resolver functions to communicate and share information because it is passed to all of them (as their third argument). They can read it and write to it if needed. We only need a readable context for sharing the pool of database connections.

You can pass any object as the context object to the `graphql` executor function or the `graphqlHTTP` listener function. The object that we need to make part of the global context here is the `pgPool` object that is returned by the `pgClient` function.

Here are the changes we need in api/src/server.js to make the `pgPool` object available using the GraphQL context concept.

> **Listing 6.9   Changes in api/src/server.js**

```
// .-.-.
import pgClient from './db/pg-client';

async function main() {
  const { pgPool } = await pgClient();
  const server = express();
  // .-.-.

  server.use(
    '/',
    graphqlHTTP({
      schema,
      context: { pgPool },
      graphiql: true,
    }),
```

```
    );
    // ·—·—·
}
main();
```

Now all resolver functions will have access to the context object, and we can use the pgPool object to execute database queries in them!

The pgPool object has a query method we can use to execute a SQL statement. We can use it this way to execute the SELECT statement in listing 6.8.

**Listing 6.10  Example: executing a SQL statement with `pgPool`**

```
const pgResp = await pgPool.query(`
  SELECT *
  FROM azdev.tasks
  WHERE is_private = FALSE
  ORDER BY created_at DESC
  LIMIT 100
`);
```

The result of the query method is a promise that will resolve to an object, which I named pgResp. This pgResp object will have a rows property holding an array of objects representing the rows returned by the database.

**Listing 6.11  Example: shape of the `pgResp.rows` property**

```
[
  { id: 1, content: 'Task #1', approach_count: 1,  ·—·—·},
  { id: 2, content: 'Task #2', approach_count: 1,  ·—·—·},
  ·—·—·
]
```

Note that the pg package transforms every database row into a JavaScript object with the database field names as keys and the row values as the values for these keys. Also note that the key names use the snake-case format (for example, approach_count).

The context object is exposed to each resolver function as the third argument (after source and args).

**Listing 6.12  Example: the four arguments for each resolver function**

```
resolve: (source, args, context, info) => {}
```

> **NOTE** The fourth info argument will have information about the execution context, like what field/type this resolver is associated with. This argument is rarely used but is handy in a few advanced cases.

The taskMainList field should be resolved with an array of Task records (and the rows property on the pgPool.query response in listing 6.10 is that exact array). Remember from the previous chapter that you can return a promise from a resolver function, and GraphQL.js will do the right thing for it. We can just resolve taskMainList with the promise returned by the pgPool.query function.

---

**Listing 6.13   Changes in api/src/schema/index.js**

```
import {
  // .-.-.
  GraphQLList,
} from 'graphql';
// .-.-.
import Task from './types/task';

const QueryType = new GraphQLObjectType({
  name: 'Query',
  fields: {
    // .-.-.

    taskMainList: {
      type: new GraphQLList(new GraphQLNonNull(Task)),
      resolve: async (source, args, { pgPool }) => {
        const pgResp = await pgPool.query(`
          SELECT *
          FROM azdev.tasks
          WHERE is_private = FALSE
          ORDER BY created_at DESC
          LIMIT 100
        `);
        return pgResp.rows;
      },
    },
  },
});
// .-.-.
```

Go ahead and test things now. The API should be able to answer this query (see figure 6.2):

```
{
  taskMainList {
    id
    content
  }
}
```

**NOTE**   Task #5 does not show up in the response for the taskMainList query because it's a private Task in the sample data.

```
1 ▾ {
2     taskMainList {
3         id
4         content
5     }
6 }
```

QUERY VARIABLES

```
▾ {
  ▾   "data": {
    ▾     "taskMainList": [
          {
            "id": "1",
            "content": "Make an image in HTML change based on the theme
color mode (dark or light)"
          },
          {
            "id": "2",
            "content": "Get rid of only the unstaged changes since the
last git commit"
          },
          {
            "id": "3",
            "content": "The syntax for a switch statement (AKA case
statement) in JavaScript"
          },
          {
            "id": "4",
            "content": "Calculate the sum of numbers in a JavaScript
array"
          },
          {
            "id": "6",
            "content": "Create a secure one-way hash for a text value
```

**Figure 6.2  Server response for the `taskMainList` query**

If you try to ask for the `tags` or `createdAt` field, you'll get the following errors:

- For the `tags` field, you'll get this error message: "Expected Iterable, but did not find one for field Task.tags."
- For the `createdAt` field, you'll get this error message: "Cannot return null for non-null field Task.createdAt." The same error will occur for the `approach-Count` field.

Take a moment and try to figure out these error messages. I'll explain them in the next section.

---

**Using a subset of fields in SQL**

Since we did a `SELECT *` operation, all fields available in the `azdev.tasks` table will be available on the parent source object in the `Task` type. However, only the properties represented by the defined fields will be available in the API. You can optimize the SQL statement to only include the fields that the API is interested in.

For example:

```
SELECT id, content, tags, approach_count, created_at
FROM azdev.tasks
WHERE ·-·-·
```

---

### 6.2.3  *Transforming field names*

In some cases, we need the API to represent columns and rows in the database with a different structure. Maybe the database has a confusing column name; or maybe we want the API to consistently use camel-case for all field names, and the database uses snake-case for its columns. This latter situation is exactly what we have to deal with next. Columns on the `azdev.tasks` table are snake-case in the database (for example, `created_at`), and we planned to represent all fields as camel-case in the API (`createdAt`). This means we cannot rely on the default resolvers as we did for the `id` and `content` fields.

With camel-case fields, the default resolver tries to find the property `createdAt` on the row returned by the database. That property does not exist. That's why we got an error when we tried to ask for `createdAt`.

There are three main methods to deal with this issue.

### METHOD #1

We can simply perform a case map on all properties on each row when we get data back from the database. This way, the parent source object for the `Task` type will have the right property names, and all fields can be kept using the default resolvers. For example, if we have a function `caseMapper` that takes an object and makes all of its properties camel-case, we can modify the resolver of `taskMainList` as follows.

**Listing 6.14   Example: changing the structure of objects received from the database**

```
resolve: async (source, args, { pgPool }) => {
  const pgResp = await pgPool.query(
    // ------
  );
  return pgResp.rows.map(caseMapper);
},
```

> **TIP**   The `caseMapper` function implementation is omitted here, but you can use a function like `camelizeKeys` from the `humps` Node package. That function even supports converting an array of objects, and it will camel-case all properties on all objects in that array.

Can you spot a problem with this method? Actually, can you spot *two* problems with it? Not only are we looping over each row in the returned set (with the `map` method), but the `caseMapper` function loops over all the properties of a row object.

This is probably not a big deal if you're working with small sets of data. However, the GraphQL tree/resolver structure is already looping over fields and levels. We can use a field resolver to do the conversion manually when needed. That's method #2.

### METHOD #2

We can create custom resolvers for the fields that need to be converted. For example, we can change the `createdAt` field in listing 6.7 to include this `resolve` function.

**Listing 6.15   Example: using custom resolvers**

```
const Task = new GraphQLObjectType({
  name: 'Task',
  fields: {
```

```
// .-.-.
createdAt: {
  type: new GraphQLNonNull(GraphQLString),
  resolve: (source) => source.created_at,
},
},
});
```

This takes care of the case issue because we are resolving a `createdAt` field using the `created_at` property available on the parent source object (which is the row object coming from the database). You'll need to do this for each multiword field.

If you made this change, you can test the API by asking for a `createdAt` field on the `taskMainList` field, it will work (figure 6.3).

```
1 ▾ {
2 ▾   taskMainList {
3       id
4       content
5       createdAt|
6     }
7   }
```

```
▾ {
▾   "data": {
▾     "taskMainList": [
▾       {
          "id": "1",
          "content": "Make an image in HTML change based on the theme
color mode (dark or light)",
          "createdAt": "1596240182032"
        },
▾       {
          "id": "2",
          "content": "Get rid of only the unstaged changes since the
last git commit",
          "createdAt": "1596240182032"
```

**Figure 6.3  The `createdAt` field server response**

> **NOTE**  The `createdAt` reply is a 13-digit number. This is the number of milliseconds since midnight 01 January 1970 UTC. We'll change that value in the next section.

I like the readability of this method, and it's also helpful when you need to perform other custom logic on the value, not just map it as is. However, I am not a fan of mixing snake-case variable names with camel-case. It would be ideal if API server logic did not have to deal with snake-case variables. PostgreSQL has something up its sleeve to save us from needing to do the transformation in the first place! That's method #3.

> **NOTE**  Before you proceed, undo the `resolve` function changes in listing 6.15 (if you made them).

## METHOD #3

We can use the column alias feature in PostgreSQL to make it return the rows natively as camel-case. However, this solution requires listing all the leaf fields in the `SELECT` statement. For example, here's a version of the `taskMainList` resolver function to implement this method.

**Listing 6.16   Changes in api/src/schema/index.js**

```
resolve: async (source, args, { pgPool }) => {
  const pgResp = await pgPool.query(`
    SELECT id, content, tags,
           approach_count AS "approachCount", created_at AS "createdAt"
    FROM azdev.tasks
    WHERE // ·----
  `);
  return pgResp.rows;
},
```

Note that I use the `AS "approachCount"` and `AS "createdAt"` syntax to rename the returned columns. The quotes around the aliases are required because PostgreSQL is case insensitive. To force it to behave otherwise, you need to use quotes.

I think this is the better method because it makes the data come from PostgreSQL in the exact shape we need and because, in my opinion, having to list the column names that a statement needs is a good thing. Specificity is always the safer way.

**NOTE**  You will not need to write any SQL statements or aliases beyond this first example. All SQL statements with their aliased column names are available in api/src/db/sqls.js.

### 6.2.4   *Transforming field values*

GraphQL's default serialization for date objects in JavaScript is to call the `valueOf` method on them, and that method is equivalent to calling `getTime` (which returns the 13-digit milliseconds number). If we want to serialize fields (including date fields) differently, we can do that in custom resolver functions. For example, let's serialize all date-time fields for the AZdev API using UTC ISO format. We can use the JavaScript `toISOString` method for this. We'll need to implement the `createdAt` field's resolver function using the following.

**Listing 6.17   Changes in api/src/schema/types/task.js**

```
createdAt: {
  type: new GraphQLNonNull(GraphQLString),
  resolve: (source) => source.createdAt.toISOString(),
},
```

**NOTE**  Note that I used `source.createdAt` (and not `source.created_at`) since PostgreSQL returns data in camel-case object properties now.

Now the API displays values of `createdAt` using the ISO format (figure 6.4).

What about the `tags` field? Currently, the API is displaying this error for it: "Expected Iterable, but did not find one for field Task.tags."

This is because we defined the `tags` field as a `GraphQLList` type. The GraphQL executer expects its resolved value to be an *iterable*, like an array. The default resolver

```
1 ▾ {
2 ▾   taskMainList {
3       id
4       content
5       createdAt
6     }
7   }
```

```
▾ {
▾   "data": {
▾     "taskMainList": [
▾       {
            "id": "1",
            "content": "Make an image in HTML change based on the theme
color mode (dark or light)",
            "createdAt": "2020-08-01T00:03:02.032Z"
          },
▾         {
            "id": "2",
            "content": "Get rid of only the unstaged changes since the
last git commit",
            "createdAt": "2020-08-01T00:03:02.032Z"
          },
```

**Figure 6.4  The `createdAt` field as an ISO string**

for the `tags` field is currently resolving with what's in the `tags` database column: a string of comma-separated values (for example, `"node,git"`). We need to transform this value into an array of strings instead (so, `["node", "git"]`). We do that with a custom resolver function.

**Listing 6.18  Changes in api/src/schema/types/task.js**

```
tags: {
  type: new GraphQLNonNull(
    new GraphQLList(new GraphQLNonNull(GraphQLString))
  ),
  resolve: (source) => source.tags.split(','),
},
```

With that, the resolver will return an array when asked for the `tags` property (figure 6.5).

```
1 ▾ {
2 ▾   taskMainList {
3       id
4       content
5       tags
6     }
7   }
```

```
▾ {
▾   "data": {
▾     "taskMainList": [
▾       {
            "id": "1",
            "content": "Make an image in HTML change based on the theme
color mode (dark or light)",
            "tags": [
              "code",
              "html"
            ]
          },
▾         {
            "id": "2",
            "content": "Get rid of only the unstaged changes since the
last git commit",
            "tags": [
              "command",
              "git"
            ]
          },
```

**Figure 6.5  The `tags` comma-separated value exposed as an array in the API**

As you can see, it is fairly easy to control the shape of the GraphQL schema and use powerful transformation on the raw data returned by the database.

**Current code**

Use `git checkout 6.1` to reset your local repo to the current progress in the code.

### 6.2.5    *Separating interactions with PostgreSQL*

Before we continue implementing the author/approach relations on the `Task` type, let's do a small refactoring. Instead of using SQL statements directly in resolver functions, let's introduce a module responsible for communicating with PostgreSQL and just use that module's API in the resolver functions.

This separation of responsibilities will generally improve the readability of the API's code. The logic to fetch things from PostgreSQL will not be mixed with the logic to transform raw data into the public API. This new module will also improve the maintainability of the code! If the database driver changes its API or if a decision is made to use a different database driver, you can make these changes in one place instead of many. You'll also have one place where you can add logging or any other diagnostics around database calls. It will also be a lot easier to test this new module on its own, isolated from the other logic in the resolver functions, and to test the logic in the resolvers by mocking this new module.

I'll name this new module `pgApi`. We'll expose it in the context object instead of the driver's native `pgPool` object and make all read and write interactions with PostgreSQL through it.

Let's also move the line in api/src/server.js where we called the `pgClient` function to get a `pgPool` into this new `pgApi` module. This is an asynchronous operation, which means we need the `pgApi` module to be wrapped in an `async` function. I'll name this function `pgApiWrapper` and make it the default export in the new module.

Here's the implementation I came up with. Put this in api/src/db/pg-api.js.

**Listing 6.19    New file: api/src/db/pg-api.js**

```
import pgClient from './pg-client';
import sqls from './sqls';

const pgApiWrapper = async () => {
  const { pgPool } = await pgClient();
  const pgQuery = (text, params = {}) =>
    pgPool.query(text, Object.values(params));

  return {
    taskMainList: async () => {
      const pgResp = await pgQuery(sqls.tasksLatest);      ◁─┐  The tasksLatest SQL
      return pgResp.rows;                                     │  statement is already
    },                                                        │  in api/src/db/sqls.js.
  };
};

export default pgApiWrapper;
```

Note that I imported the `sqls` object from the provided ./sqls.js file and used `sqls`
`.tasksLatest`. That is the same SQL query as in listing 6.16. Having all the SQL statements in one place is a simple way to organize this module. Another way would be to create a file per database API function and have that file define the SQL statements it needs.
The latter is better for bigger projects, but I'll leave the simple two-file structure here. The
pg-api.js file will define the functions, and the sqls.js file will define the SQL statements.

   Also note that I introduced a new function, `pgQuery`, which is a wrapper for
`pgPool.query`. The `pgPool.query` function is the current driver's method, and it
expects query variables as an array. The `pgQuery` function is something we can control
any time when needed, and I made it receive query variables as an object (which will
make the code a bit more readable, in my opinion).

> **TIP** Wrapping third-party APIs is generally a good practice, but don't overdo
> it! For example, I have not wrapped the GraphQL.js API yet because the proj-
> ect's entire structure depends on it. The AZdev API code is not just using
> GraphQL.js; it's built around it. When GraphQL.js makes a non-backward-
> compatible change to its API, it will probably be time for a complete project
> overhaul. However, the other benefits to wrapping a third-party API still
> apply. For example, if we would like to change the syntax of creating type
> objects to reduce the boilerplate and use something similar to the SDL
> method, we can introduce a wrapper.

Now we need to change the context object in api/src/server.js to use the new `pgApi-`
`Wrapper` function instead of the driver-native `pgClient` function.

---

**Listing 6.20   Changes in api/src/server.js**

```
// .-.-.
import pgApiWrapper from './db/pg-api';        ◁——  This line replaces the
                                                     pg-client import line.
async function main() {
  const pgApi = await pgApiWrapper();          ◁——
                                                     This line replaces the
  // .-.-.                                           pgClient() call line.

  server.use(
    '/',
    graphqlHTTP({
      schema,
      context: { pgApi },
      graphiql: true,
    })
  );

  // .-.-.
}
```

Finally, we need to change the `resolve` function for `taskMainList` to use the new
`pgApi` instead of issuing a direct SQL statement.

**Listing 6.21 Changes in api/src/schema/index.js**

```
taskMainList: {
  type: new GraphQLList(new GraphQLNonNull(Task)),
  resolve: async (source, args, { pgApi }) => {
    return pgApi.taskMainList();
  },
},
```

That's it. You can test all these changes using the same query we've been using so far. Nothing changed on the public API service, but a lot has changed in the codebase. The code is off to a better start.

## 6.3 *Error reporting*

I would like to introduce one little modification here. By default, the GraphQL.js implementation does not report errors in logs, and that might cause frustration. It will still respond to API consumers with these errors, but as a backend developer, you don't see them.

Let's look at an example. Fake an error anywhere in the code that resolves data for the taskMainList field, something like the following.

**Listing 6.22 Temp changes in api/src/db/pg-api.js**

```
const QueryType = new GraphQLObjectType({
  name: 'Query',
  fields: {
    // ------
    taskMainList: {
      type: new GraphQLList(new GraphQLNonNull(Task)),
      resolve: async (source, args, { pgApi }) => {
        return pgApi.taksMainList();   <---| Typo!
      },
    },
  },
});
```

Now observe what happens when you ask for the taskMainList field in GraphiQL (figure 6.6).

```
1 ▾ {
2 ▾   taskMainList {
3       id
4       content
5       createdAt
6       tags
7     }
8   }
```

```
▾ {
    "errors": [
▾     {
        "message": "pgApi.taksMainList is not a function",
        "locations": [⊕],
        "path": [
          "taskMainList"
        ]
      }
    ],
    "data": {
      "taskMainList": null
    }
  }
```

**Figure 6.6 The backend error on the frontend app**

You see the error as a consumer (which is bad). You also don't see the error in the backend at all (which is also bad).

To solve that, the `express-graphql` package supports a `customFormatErrorFn` option, which is an optional function that can be used to format errors produced while the server is fulfilling GraphQL operations. We can use this function to report the error and return a generic error to the consumer (for example, in production).

##### Listing 6.23  Changes in api/src/server.js

```
async function main() {
  // ......

  server.use(
    '/',
    graphqlHTTP({
      schema,
      context: { pgApi },
      graphiql: true,
      customFormatErrorFn: (err) => {
        const errorReport = {
          message: err.message,
          locations: err.locations,
          stack: err.stack ? err.stack.split('\n') : [],      ◁—— Makes the error stack show up in development, which is very handy
          path: err.path,
        };
        console.error('GraphQL Error', errorReport);          ◁—— Logs the error in the server logs
        return config.isDev
          ? errorReport
          : { message: 'Oops! Something went wrong! :(' };      ◁—— Returns a generic error in production
      },
    }),
  );

  // ......
}
```

With that, if you execute the faulty `taskMainList` query now, the frontend consumer will see the generic error message while the backend developer will see the helpful error message in the API server logs.

> **TIP**  It's a common practice to not expose thrown errors to your API consumers in production. These often reveal implementation details and usually are not helpful to users. Only expose helpful error messages to your API consumers. We'll see examples when we work with mutations.

Don't forget to undo the intentional typo we made in listing 6.22.

#### Current code
Use `git checkout 6.2` to reset your local repo to the current progress in the code.

It's now time to talk about resolving relations. This will highlight one of the biggest challenges when creating GraphQL APIs: the infamous N+1 queries problem.

## 6.4    *Resolving relations*

The remaining fields on the `Task` type are `author` and `approachList`. We'll need to implement two new GraphQL types for them. I'll name them `Author` and `Approach`.

These fields will not be leaf fields in a query. They represent relations. A Task has one Author and many Approaches. To resolve these fields, the GraphQL server will have to execute SQL statements over many tables and return objects from these tables.

When we're done implementing the `author` and `approachList` fields, the API server should accept and reply to this query.

---

**Listing 6.24    The `taskMainList` complete query**

```
{
  taskMainList {
    id
    content
    tags
    approachCount
    createdAt

    author {
      id
      username
      name
    }

    approachList {
      id
      content
      voteCount
      createdAt

      author {
        id
        username
        name
      }
    }
  }
}
```

This is the complete query that should be supported by the API service. Note the nested fields `Task -> Author` and `Task -> Approach -> Author`.

> **NOTE**    An Approach also has an Author. To complete the `taskMainList` field, we will have to implement that relation as well.

With this query, we would like to get all the information about all the latest Tasks, who authored them, what approaches are defined on them, and who authored these approaches.

> **NOTE** The Latest Tasks UI view will not include Approaches. Approaches will be displayed only in the Single Task UI view. For simplicity, I used one Task type here, but type specificity can be used to match expected usage and enforce the acceptable ways to use the API. We'll see an example under the me root field.

### 6.4.1 *Resolving a one-to-one relation*

The author field has to be resolved from the azdev.users table. The foreign key that connects a Task object to a User object is the user_id field on the azdev.tasks table. When we resolved the taskMainList field with a list of Task objects, each of these objects had a value in its userId property. For each one, we have to execute another SQL statement to get information about the User who authored it. You can find that SQL statement under sqls.usersFromIds (in api/src/db/sqls.js).

**Listing 6.25   Second SQL statement in api/src/db/sqls.js**

```
// $1: userIds
usersFromIds: `
  SELECT id, username,
         first_name AS "firstName", last_name AS "lastName",
         created_at AS "createdAt"
  FROM azdev.users
  WHERE id = ANY ($1)
`,
```

Note that this SQL statement has a $1 in it. This is new. It's the syntax we can use with the pg driver to insert a variable into the SQL statement without resorting to string concatenation. The statement is expected to be executed with one variable, and that variable will be used to replace the $1 part.

> **NOTE** The ANY comparison construct can be used to fetch multiple records from the database using an array of IDs. This is going to help us reduce the number of SQL queries that the API server needs to execute. We'll see examples in chapter 7.

Next we need to design a function in the pgApi module to execute the sqls .usersFromIds statement. Let's design that function to accept a userId value as an argument.

**Listing 6.26   Changes in api/src/db/pg-api.sql**

```
const pgApiWrapper = async () => {
  // .....
  return {
```

```
    // ......
    userInfo: async (userId) => {
      const pgResp = await pgQuery(sqls.usersFromIds, { $1: [userId] });
      return pgResp.rows[0];
    },
  };
};
```

**Passes $I to the SQL statement as [userId]**

The `sqls.usersFromIds` statement is designed to work with multiple user IDs and return multiple user records. That's why the `$1` value was `[userId]`. However, since we're passing only a single `userId` value, the SQL statement will fetch one row or nothing (because the ID column is unique). The `pg` driver always returns the `rows` property on its response as an array, even when it's just one row. That's why the returned value was the first row from the statement's response (`pgResp.rows[0]`).

Note that I am designing the interactions with PostgreSQL first instead of starting with the GraphQL type and resolver functions and working my way down to the PostgreSQL interactions (which is what we did for the `taskMainList` field). What's important is that we can do each side of this task in complete isolation from the other!

To make the GraphQL server aware of the new `author` field, we need to define the `User` type. Everything in a GraphQL schema must have a type. In the SDL text, we had this structure for the `User` type.

---

**Listing 6.27   The `User` type**

```
type User {
  id: ID!
  username: String!
  name: String
  taskList: [Task!]!
}
```

**We'll implement the taskList field under the me root field.**

Remember the three steps we went through for the `Task` type? We need to do something similar for the `User` type:

1  Define a new object type named `User`, which has the three scalar fields.
2  Write any non-default resolvers for the `User` type. Let's combine the database `first_name` and `last_name` columns on table `azdev.users` into a single `name` field for the API.
3  Modify the `Task` type to have a field named `author` that is a non-null object of type `User` (the new type), and resolve this field with a record from the `azdev.users` table using the new `userInfo` function in listing 6.26.

Here's a possible implementation of the new `User` type along with its non-default resolver for the `name` field.

**Listing 6.28   New file: api/src/schema/types/user.js**

```
import {
  GraphQLID,
  GraphQLObjectType,
  GraphQLString,
  GraphQLNonNull,
} from 'graphql';

const User = new GraphQLObjectType({
  name: 'User',
  fields: {
    id: { type: new GraphQLNonNull(GraphQLID) },
    username: { type: GraphQLString },
    name: {
      type: GraphQLString,
      resolve: ({ firstName, lastName }) =>
        `${firstName} ${lastName}`,
    },
  },
});

export default User;
```

Note that for the `resolve` functions of the `name` field, I destructured the properties that are to be used in the resolver out of the first `source` argument.

> **NOTE** I did not include the `createdAt` field under this new type. I'll add it when we implement the `me` root field. The timestamp when the user was created should not appear under the `author` relation. It can be helpful under the `me` root field. For example, a UI can use it to show profile information for the currently logged-in user.

To use this new `User` type, we need to import it in the `Task` type and make the new `author` field use it. To resolve the `author` field, we just make a call to the `userInfo` function we added to `pgApi`.

**Listing 6.29   Changes in api/src/schema/types/task.js**

```
import User from './user';

const Task = new GraphQLObjectType({
  name: 'Task',
  fields: {
    // .-.-.

    author: {
      type: new GraphQLNonNull(User),
      resolve: (source, args, { pgApi }) =>
        pgApi.userInfo(source.userId),
    },
  },
});
```

That will do it. You can test the new relation with this query.

---

**Listing 6.30    Query to test the Task/Author relation**

```
{
  taskMainList {
    content
    author {
      id
      username
      name
    }
  }
}
```

The API displays the information about the Author for each Task, which is the same test account in the sample data we're using (figure 6.7).

```
1 ▾ {
2 ▾   taskMainList {
3       content
4 ▾     author {
5         id
6         username
7         name
8       }
9     }
10  }
```

```
▾ {
    "data": {
▾     "taskMainList": [
▾       {
          "content": "Make an image in HTML change based on the theme
  color mode (dark or light)",
▾         "author": {
            "id": "1",
            "username": "test",
            "name": "null null"
          }
        },
▾       {
          "content": "Get rid of only the unstaged changes since the
  last git commit",
▾         "author": {
            "id": "1",
            "username": "test",
            "name": "null null"
          }
        },
```

**Figure 6.7    Getting Author information for each Task object**

### DEALING WITH NULL VALUES

There is a small problem in the data response in figure 6.7: the Author name was returned as null null. Why is that?

The null concept is confusing. Different coders associate different meanings with it. You need to be careful to always consider the possibility of dealing with null. You should ask, "What if this is null?" about every variable you use in your code. This is one reason why languages like TypeScript and Flow are popular: they can help detect these problems.

When we used the template string ${firstName} ${lastName}, we should have asked ourselves that question! What if these properties are null? JavaScript will just insert "null" as a string. How do we solve this issue?

First, do we need to have first_name and last_name as nullable columns in the database? Will there ever be a semantic difference between null and an empty string in these columns? If not (which is the most likely answer), it would have been a better design decision to make these fields non-null in the database and maybe make them default to an empty string.

For the sake of example, let's assume that we don't have control over the structure of the database table and/or we cannot fix the data that's already there. This does not mean we should leak these problems out to the consumers of this API. We can make the API's name field non-null and make the server always return either the name or an empty string instead of nulls, or worse, nulls cast in a string.

There are many ways to implement that. Here's one.

##### Listing 6.31   Changes to the name field in api/src/schema/types/user.js

```
name: {
  type: new GraphQLNonNull(GraphQLString),
  resolve: ({ firstName, lastName }) =>
    [firstName, lastName].filter(Boolean).join(' '),
},
```

This way, the API will always return a string that will ignore null values in `firstName`, `lastName`, or both (figure 6.8).

```
1 ▾ {
2 ▾   taskMainList {
3         content
4 ▾       author {
5           id
6           username
7           name
8         }
9       }
10 }
```

```
{
  "data": {
    "taskMainList": [
      {
        "content": "Make an image in HTML change based on the theme
color mode (dark or light)",
        "author": {
          "id": "1",
          "username": "test",
          "name": ""
        }
      },
      {
        "content": "Get rid of only the unstaged changes since the
last git commit",
        "author": {
          "id": "1",
          "username": "test",
          "name": ""
        }
      },
```

**Figure 6.8   Making the name field always return a value (which could be an empty string)**

> **Current code**
> Use `git checkout 6.3` to reset your local repo to the current progress in the code.

#### THE N+1 QUERIES PROBLEM

Now that we have implemented a relation and made the GraphQL server execute multiple SQL statements for it, we can talk about the N+1 queries problem. It is the first big challenge when implementing GraphQL services. To see this problem in action, you'll need to enable logging for your PostgreSQL service and tail the logs while you execute GraphQL queries.

> **NOTE**   How to enable logging for PostgreSQL depends on your platform, OS, version, and many other factors, so you'll need to figure it out on your own. Make sure the server logs report a SQL query every time it is *executed* on the PostgreSQL service. The provided Docker image for PostgreSQL should do that out of the box.

Once you're tailing the logs, execute the query in listing 6.25 and find every instance in the log related to executing a SQL statement. Here are the SQL queries that were executed on my PostgreSQL server when I tested this.

---

**Listing 6.32   Excerpt from my PostgreSQL logs showing the N+1 problem**

```
LOG: statement:
SELECT ·-·-·
FROM azdev.tasks WHERE ·-·-·
LOG: execute <unnamed>:
SELECT ·-·-·
FROM azdev.users WHERE id = ANY ($1)
DETAIL:   parameters: $1 = '1'
LOG: execute <unnamed>:
SELECT ·-·-·
FROM azdev.users WHERE id = ANY ($1)
DETAIL:   parameters: $1 = '1'
LOG: execute <unnamed>:
SELECT ·-·-·
FROM azdev.users WHERE id = ANY ($1)
DETAIL:   parameters: $1 = '1'
LOG: execute <unnamed>:
SELECT ·-·-·
FROM azdev.users WHERE id = ANY ($1)
DETAIL:   parameters: $1 = '1'
LOG: execute <unnamed>:
SELECT ·-·-·
FROM azdev.users WHERE id = ANY ($1)
DETAIL:   parameters: $1 = '1'
```

**"1" is the ID value for the user I used in the sample data.**

---

If you're using Docker Desktop and the provided Docker images, you can see the PostgreSQL logs by opening the dashboard and navigating to the Logs view of the running `gia_pg` container (see figure 6.9). You can also see them in the output of the `npm run start-dbs` command.

> **TIP**   PostgreSQL will likely log a lot more lines around these executions. For example, you might see parse/bind lines as well. Look for entries that have a `statement` or `execute` label.

Why are we executing six SQL queries? Because we have one main query (for Tasks), and we have five public Task records in the sample data. For each Task record, we're asking the database about its associated User record. That's five queries for Users plus

**Figure 6.9    Docker container logs**

the main query. This 5 + 1 is the N+1 problem. If we had 41 public Task objects in the azdev.tasks table, we would be executing 42 SQL queries here.

Clearly this is a problem. We should not be doing that. There are many ways to fix this issue. I'll show you one of them here, and we will see a better one in the next chapter.

An easy way to fix this problem is through the direct use of database joins (or database views based on joins). Database joins are powerful. You can form a single SQL query that gets information from two or more tables at once. For example, if we're to find a Task record and get the information for its associated User in the same SQL response, we can do a join like this (you can put this in api/src/db/sqls.js).

**Listing 6.33    Changes in api/src/db/sqls.js**

```
const views = {
  tasksAndUsers: `
    SELECT t.*,
        u.id AS "author_id",
        u.username AS "author_username",
        u.first_name AS "author_firstName",
        u.last_name AS "author_lastName",
        u.created_at AS "author_createdAt"
    FROM azdev.tasks t
    JOIN azdev.users u ON (t.user_id = u.id)
  `,
};
// ......
```

The `tasksAndUsers` string can act like a view, and we can use it to create an actual database view object if we want to. However, let's just use it inline for this example.

You can test the `SELECT` statement in a PostgreSQL client (like `psql`). Docker Desktop provides a CLI button to give you command-line access to the running container (see figure 6.10).

```
[/ # psql azdev postgres
psql (12.2)
Type "help" for help.

azdev=#      SELECT t.*,
azdev-#          u.id AS "author_id",
azdev-#          u.username AS "author_username",
azdev-#          u.first_name AS "author_firstName",
azdev-#          u.last_name AS "author_lastName",
azdev-#          u.created_at AS "author_createdAt"
azdev-#      FROM azdev.tasks t
[azdev-#      JOIN azdev.users u ON (t.user_id = u.id);
 id |                             content
thor_id | author_username | author_firstName | author_lastName |
----+------------------------------------------------------------
--------+-----------------+------------------+-----------------+-
   1 | Make an image in HTML change based on the theme color mode
     1 | test            |                  |                 |
   2 | Get rid of only the unstaged changes since the last git con
     1 | test            |                  |                 |
   3 | The syntax for a switch statement (AKA case statement) in :
```

**Figure 6.10    The SQL view that has both Task and Author info**

Note that I used column aliases to prefix the `users` table columns with `"author_"`. If we don't do that, there might be a conflict in column names (for example, both tables have an `id` field). This prefixing will also make it easier for us to implement the GraphQL resolvers for this relation.

To use the `tasksAndUsers` view, instead of selecting from the `azdev.tasks` table for the `sqls.tasksLatest` SQL query, we can select from the new `tasksAndUsers` view.

**Listing 6.34    Changes in api/src/db/sqls.js**

```
taskMainList: `
  SELECT id, content, tags, · — · —·
    "author_id", "author_username", "author_firstName",
    "author_lastName", "author_createdAt"
  FROM (${views.tasksAndUsers})
  WHERE is_private = FALSE
  ORDER BY created_at DESC
  LIMIT 100
`,
```

With that, the parent source object used to resolve the `Task` type will also have `author_`-prefixed columns that hold the author information inline in the same object. No further SQL queries are necessary. However, we need to extract the prefixed columns into an object suitable to be the parent source object for the `User` type resolvers. Let's create a utility function to do that. I'll name it `extractPrefixedColumns`. Here's how we will use it in the `Task` type.

**Listing 6.35   Changes in api/src/schema/types/task.js**

```
// .-.-.
import { extractPrefixedColumns } from '../../utils';

const Task = new GraphQLObjectType({
  name: 'Task',
  fields: {
    // .-.-.

    author: {
      type: new GraphQLNonNull(User),
      resolve: prefixedObject =>
        extractPrefixedColumns({ prefixedObject, prefix: 'author' }),
    },
  },
});
```

The implementation of `extractPrefixedColumns` can be a simple `reduce` call to filter the columns and only include the prefixed columns, but without their prefixes.

**Listing 6.36   New function in api/src/utils.js**

```
export const extractPrefixedColumns = ({
  prefixedObject,
  prefix,
}) => {
  const prefixRexp = new RegExp(`^${prefix}_(.*)`);
  return Object.entries(prefixedObject).reduce(
    (acc, [key, value]) => {
      const match = key.match(prefixRexp);
      if (match) {
        acc[match[1]] = value;        ◁──┐  match[1] will be the prefixed column
      }                                  │  name without the prefix part.
      return acc;
    },
    {},
  );
};
```

That's it! You can test the query in listing 6.30, and it will work exactly the same—except instead of N+1 executed statements in the logs, there will be exactly one statement.

**Listing 6.37    Excerpt from my PostgreSQL logs showing that only one query was executed**

```
LOG: statement:
SELECT ·-·-·
   FROM (
   SELECT ·-·-·
   FROM azdev.tasks t
   JOIN azdev.users u ON (t.user_id = u.id)
) tau WHERE ·-·-·
```

This method is simple. It's efficient in terms of communicating with PostgreSQL. However, it does mean that for each returned row, we need to perform a loop over its objects to extract the prefixed keys. This issue can be improved by changing the `Author` type to resolve directly with the prefixed values. However, that means adding more complexity, which, I think, will make the code less readable. There is a better way, and we will discuss it in the next chapter.

I am going to undo all the view-based changes made to solve the N+1 problem to prepare for the other solution. However, before we talk about it, let's resolve the last remaining relation under `taskMainList`: the list of Approaches (and their Authors).

> **Current code**
>
> For your reference, I put the code for the view-based example in its own Git branch. You can use the command `git checkout 6.T1` to see that code.
>
> I did not include this example in the current 6.3 branch (which you can go back to with the command `git checkout 6.3`).

### 6.4.2    *Resolving a one-to-many relation*

We'll implement the `approachList` field starting from the types and resolvers. We need to modify the `Task` type to add the new `approachList` field. That field is a non-null list of non-null `Approach` objects (which is the new GraphQL type we need to introduce). To resolve the `approachList` field, we need a new function in `pgApi` that takes a `taskId` and returns an array of `Approach` objects associated with it. Let's name that function `approachList`.

**Listing 6.38    Changes in api/src/schema/types/task.js**

```
// ·-·-·
import Approach from './approach';

const Task = new GraphQLObjectType({
  name: 'Task',
  fields: {
    // ·-·-·
    approachList: {
      type: new GraphQLNonNull(
        new GraphQLList(new GraphQLNonNull(Approach))    ◁—— Approach is the new
```

Approach is the new GraphQL type we need to introduce.

```
    ),
    resolve: (source, args, { pgApi }) =>
      pgApi.approachList(source.id),      ◁──
  },
},
});
```

> pgApi.approachList receives the ID of a Task object (source.id) and should return a list of Approach objects.

**NOTE** This code uses two things that we do not have yet: the `Approach` type and the `pgApi.approachList` function.

Let's implement the `Approach` type next. This is the schema-language text we have for it.

**Listing 6.39   The `Approach` type in the schema-language text**

```
type Approach implement SearchResultItem {
  id: ID!
  createdAt: String!
  content: String!
  voteCount: Int!
  author: User!
  task: Task!
  detailList: [ApproachDetail!]!
}
```

> We'll implement the task and detailList fields in the next chapter.

The implementation of this type is mostly similar to the `Task` type. We can use the default resolvers for `id` and `content`, `voteCount`, the same ISO casting for `createdAt`, and the same code we used for the `author` field.

**Listing 6.40   New file: api/src/schema/types/approach.js**

```
import {
  GraphQLID,
  GraphQLObjectType,
  GraphQLString,
  GraphQLInt,
  GraphQLNonNull,
} from 'graphql';

import User from './user';

const Approach = new GraphQLObjectType({
  name: 'Approach',
  fields: {
    id: { type: new GraphQLNonNull(GraphQLID) },
    content: { type: new GraphQLNonNull(GraphQLString) },
    voteCount: { type: new GraphQLNonNull(GraphQLInt) },
    createdAt: {
      type: new GraphQLNonNull(GraphQLString),
      resolve: ({ createdAt }) => createdAt.toISOString(),
    },
    author: {
      type: new GraphQLNonNull(User),
```

```
      resolve: (source, args, { pgApi }) =>
        pgApi.userInfo(source.userId),
    },
  },
});
```

```
export default Approach;
```

The `approachList` field must be resolved from the `azdev.approaches` table. The foreign key that connects a Task object to a list of Approach objects is the `task_id` field in the `azdev.approaches` table. For each resolved Task object, we need to issue this SQL statement (which is already in the sqls.js file) to get the information about the list of Approach objects available under it.

**Listing 6.41    The `sqls.tasksApproachLists` statement**

```
tasksApproachLists: `                          The columns are aliased as camel-case.
  SELECT id, content, user_id AS "userId", task_id AS "taskId",
         vote_count AS "voteCount", created_at AS "createdAt"
  FROM azdev.approaches
  WHERE task_id = ANY ($1)                ◄──── This statement needs a Task
  ORDER BY vote_count DESC, created_at DESC       ID value to be passed as $1.
`,
```

**Sorts Approaches by their vote count (and then timestamp, if many records have the same vote count)**

**TIP**    Naming is hard, and I'm not always good at it. In the official open source repo for the AZdev API, you may see names other than the ones I use here in the book. In fact, if you can think of better names than those currently in the AZdev API GitHub repository, please open an issue or a pull request! You can find the GitHub repository for the AZdev project at az.dev/contribute.

The `sqls.approachesForTaskIds` statement will be used by the `pgApi.approachList` function that we will implement next.

**Listing 6.42    Changes in api/src/db/pg-api.js**

```
const pgApiWrapper = async () => {
  // .....

  return {
    // .....
    approachList: async (taskId) => {
      const pgResp = await pgQuery(sqls.approachesForTaskIds, {
        $1: [taskId],              ◄──── Passes $1 to the SQL
      });                                 statement as [taskId]
      return pgResp.rows;
    },
  };
};
```

I hope this is getting easier for you. We still have a lot more examples to go through, but the `taskMainList` example is finally complete (figure 6.11)! Go ahead and test the full query for it from listing 6.24.

```
1 ▾ {
2 ▾   taskMainList {
3         id
4         content
5         tags
6         approachCount
7         createdAt
8
9 ▾     author {
10        id
11        username
12        name
13      }
14
15 ▾    approachList {
16        id
17        content
18        voteCount
19        createdAt
20
21 ▾      author {
22          id
23          username
24          name
25        }
26    }
```

```
▾ {
▾   "data": {
▾     "taskMainList": [
▾       {
          "id": "1",
          "content": "Make an image in HTML change based on the theme
color mode (dark or light)",
          "tags": [
            "code",
            "html"
          ],
          "approachCount": 1,
          "createdAt": "2020-08-01T00:03:02.032Z",
►         "author": { ▣ },
▾         "approachList": [
▾           {
              "id": "1",
              "content": "<picture>\n  <source\n    srcset=\"settings-
dark.png\"\n    media=\"(prefers-color-scheme: dark)\"\n  />\n
<source\n    srcset=\"settings-light.png\"\n    media=\"(prefers-
color-scheme: light), (prefers-color-scheme: no-preference)\"\n  />\n
<img src=\"settings-light.png\" loading=\"lazy\" />\n</picture>",
              "voteCount": 0,
              "createdAt": "2020-08-01T00:03:02.035Z",
►             "author": { ▣ }
            }
          ]
        }
      ]
    }
```

**QUERY VARIABLES**

**Figure 6.11    The response for the complete `taskMainList` query**

Guess how many SQL statements we're sending to PostgreSQL to satisfy this GraphQL query?

- One for the main Task list.
- One for each Task's Author info (five total).
- One for each Task's list of Approaches (five total).
- One for each Approach on each Task to get that Approach's Author info. We have a total of six Approaches in the sample data.

That's a total of 17 SQL statements! We can still fix this with database views, but doing so will add a lot more complexity to the code. Let's explore the better option, which is to use the data-loader concept. We'll talk about that in the next chapter.

> **Current code**
> Use `git checkout 6.4` to reset your local repo to the current progress in the code.

## Summary

- Use realistic, production-like data in development to make your manual tests relevant and useful.
- Start with the simplest implementations you can think of. Make things work, and then improve on your implementations.

- You can use the GraphQL context object to make a pool of database connections available to all resolver functions.

- You can use fields' resolvers to transform the names and values of your data elements. The GraphQL API does not have to match the structure of the data in the database.

- Try to separate the logic for database interactions from other logic in your resolvers.

- It's a good practice to wrap third-party APIs with your own calls. This gives you some control over their behavior and makes the code a bit more maintainable going forward.

- Resolving database relations involves issuing SQL statements over many tables. This causes an N+1 queries problem by default because of the graph-resolving nature of GraphQL. We can solve this problem using database views, but that complicates the code in the GraphQL service. In the next chapter, we will learn about the DataLoader library, which offers a better way to deal with the N+1 problem and make your GraphQL service more efficient in general.

# Optimizing data fetching

**This chapter covers**

- Caching and batching data-fetch operations
- Using the DataLoader library with primary keys and custom IDs
- Using GraphQL's union type and field arguments
- Reading data from MongoDB

Now that we have a GraphQL service with a multimodel schema, we can look at one of GraphQL's most famous problems, the N+1 queries problem. We ended the previous chapter with a GraphQL query that fetches data from three database tables.

**Listing 7.1   The N+1 query example**

```
{
  taskMainList {
    // ......
    author {
      // ......
    }
    approachList {
```

```
      // ......
      author {
        // ......
      }
    }
  }
}
```

Because the GraphQL runtime traverses the tree field by field and resolves each field on its own as it does, this simple GraphQL query resulted in a lot more SQL statements than necessary.

---

**Current code**

Use `git checkout 7.0` to reset your local repo to the current progress in the code. If you need to stash any local changes, use `git add . && git stash`. Remember to run `npm install` to install any missing dependencies.

---

## 7.1   Caching and batching

To analyze a solution to this problem, let's go back to the simpler query from listing 6.30.

---

**Listing 7.2   The `taskMainList` query**

```
{
  taskMainList {
    content
    author {
      id
      username
      name
    }
  }
}
```

If you remember, this query was issuing six SQL `SELECT` statements to the database, which is an example of the N+1 problem (N being five Task records). We've seen how to use database join views to make it execute only one SQL statement, but that solution is not ideal. It's not easy to maintain or scale.

Another solution is to use the concepts of caching and batching for all the necessary SQL statements in a single GraphQL operation:

- *Caching*—The least we can do is cache the response of any SQL statements issued and then use the cache the next time we need the exact same SQL statement. If we ask the database about user x, do not ask it again about user x; just use the previous response. Doing this in a single API request (from one consumer) is a no-brainer, but you can also use longer-term, multisession caching if you need to optimize things further. However, caching by itself is not enough. We also need to group queries asking for data from the same tables.

- *Batching*—We can delay asking the database about a certain resource until we figure out the IDs of all the records that need to be resolved. Once these IDs are identified, we can use a single query that takes in a list of IDs and returns the list of records for them. This enables us to issue a SQL statement per table, and doing so will reduce the number of SQL statements required for the simple query in listing 7.2 to just two: one for the `azdev.tasks` table and one for the `azdev.users` table.

Manually managing these caching and batching operations would still be a lot of work. However, this is the type of work that can be abstracted to a separate library. After releasing the GraphQL.js reference implementation, the Facebook team also released a reference implementation for such a library. They named it DataLoader (az.dev/data-loader).

> **TIP** While the DataLoader JavaScript project originated at Facebook as another reference implementation mirroring Facebook's own internal data-loading library, it has since moved to the GraphQL foundation and it is now maintained by the GraphQL community. It's a stable, battle-tested project; and despite being young, it's already part of thousands of open source projects and is downloaded millions of times each month.

DataLoader is a generic JavaScript utility library that can be injected into your application's data-fetching layer to manage caching and batching operations on your behalf.

To use DataLoader in the AZdev API project, we need to install it first.

---

**Listing 7.3  Command: installing the `dataloader` package**

```
$ npm install dataloader
```

This npm package has a default export that we usually import as `DataLoader`. This default export is a JavaScript class that we can use to instantiate a `DataLoader` instance. The `DataLoader` class constructor expects a function as its argument, and that function is expected to do the data fetching. This function is known as the *batch-loading function* because it expects an array of key IDs and should fetch all records associated with those IDs in one batch action and then return the records as an array that has the same order as the array of input IDs.

For example, here's one way to create a loader responsible for loading user records.

---

**Listing 7.4   Example: the `DataLoader` syntax**

```
import DataLoader from 'dataloader';

const userLoader = new DataLoader(
  userIds => getUsersByIds(userIds)
);
```

> The userIds argument is an array, and getUsersByIds is the batch-loading function that takes an array of IDs and returns an array of user records representing these IDs (in order).

Once you have the logic of fetching a list of user records based on a list of ID values, you can start using the `userLoader` object to fetch multiple users. For example, imagine that a request in your API application needs to load information about users in the following order.

---

**Listing 7.5   Example: using a `DataLoader` object**

```
const promiseA = userLoader.load(1);
const promiseB = userLoader.load(2);

// await on something async

const promiseC = userLoader.load(1);
```

`DataLoader` takes care of batching the first two statements into a single SQL statement because they happen in the same frame of execution, which is known in Node.js as a single *tick* of the event loop (az.dev/event-loop).

For the third statement, Dataloader uses its memoization cache of `.load()` calls. User 1 has already been fetched from the database (in the previous frame of execution, but still in the same request). Fetching it again would be redundant.

This minimization of SQL statements and elimination of redundant loads relieves pressure on your data-storage services. It also creates fewer objects overall, which may relieve memory pressure on your API application as well.

---

### Why DataLoader?

While you can do the batching and caching manually, `DataLoader` enables you to decouple the data-loading logic in your application without sacrificing the performance of the caching and batching optimizations. `DataLoader` instances present a consistent API over your various data sources (PostgreSQL, MongoDB, and any others). This allows you to focus on your application's logic and safely distribute its data-fetching requirements without worrying about maintaining minimal requests to your databases and other sources of data.

Note that `DataLoader` uses simple single-resource batching and short-term caching. There are other GraphQL-to-database execution layers that use multiresource batching (without caching and its many problems) to achieve similar (and often better) performance improvements. However, I think the `DataLoader` approach is simpler, more flexible, and easier to maintain.

## 7.1.1 *The batch-loading function*

A batch-loading function like getUsersByIds in listing 7.4 accepts an array of IDs (or generic keys) and should return a promise object that resolves to an array of records. To be compatible with DataLoader, the resulting array must be the exact same length as the input array of IDs, and each index in the resulting array of records must correspond to the same index in the input array of IDs.

For example, if the getUsersByIds batch function is given the input array of IDs [ 2, 5, 3, 1 ], the function needs to issue one SQL statement to fetch all user records for those IDs. Here's one way to do that in PostgreSQL.

---
**Listing 7.6  Example: using the SQL IN operator**

```
SELECT *
FROM azdev.users
WHERE id IN (2, 5, 3, 1);
```

> **TIP** If an ORDER BY clause is not specified in a SELECT statement, the database will pick the most efficient way to satisfy the statement. The order of the returned rows will not be guaranteed.

For the sake of this example, let's assume that for this SQL statement, the database returned three user records (instead of four) in the following order:

```
{ id: 5, name: 'Luke' }       ◁── The results order is different from
{ id: 1, name: 'Jane' }            the order of IDs in the input array.
{ id: 2, name: 'Mary' }       ◁── The database did not have a user
                                   corresponding to the input id 3.
```

The getUsersByIds batch-loading function *cannot* use the result of that SQL statement as is. It needs to reorder the records and ensure that each item aligns with the original order of IDs: [ 2, 5, 3, 1 ]. If an ID has no corresponding record in the result, it should be represented with a null value:

```
[
  { id: 2, name: 'Mary' },
  { id: 5, name: 'Luke' },
  null,
  { id: 1, name: 'Jane' }
]
```

In chapter 6, we wrote the pgApi.userInfo function in api/src/db/pg-api.js. Let's convert that into a batch-loading function and see what we need to do to make it Data-Loader-compatible.

First, we should rename it to usersInfo now that it will be used to return an array of user records. We should also rename its argument to userIds to indicate that it expects a list of user IDs.

The `sqls.usersFromIds` statement is already designed to work with an array of user IDs (using the `ANY` construct).

> ## The ANY comparison construct
>
> There are many ways to fetch multiple records from the database using an array of IDs. The easiest is to use the `ANY` PostgreSQL comparison construct because we can feed it an array directly (so no array manipulation is needed).
>
> The SQL statement in listing 7.6 can be written with `ANY` as follows:
>
> ```
> SELECT *
> FROM azdev.users
> WHERE id = ANY ('{2, 5, 3, 1}');
> ```
>
> Note that the array syntax in PostgreSQL uses curly brackets instead of square brackets. This might look a bit weird, but we don't have to deal with this issue ourselves as the driver we're using will take care of that conversion for us.

We need to change the $1 value we pass to be the new `userIds` argument, which itself should be an array.

Finally, we need to reorder the list of user records coming from the database to match the order in the input array of `userIds`. We can use a simple `.map`/`.find` combination to do that.

Here are all the changes we need to make the `pgApi.usersInfo` a `DataLoader`-compatible batch-loading function.

### Listing 7.7   Changes in api/src/db/pg-api.js

```
const pgApiWrapper = async () => {
  // -.-.-.
  return {                                      Passes $1 as userIds, which
    // -.-.-.                                    is now an array of user IDs
    usersInfo: async (userIds) => {
      const pgResp = await pgQuery(sqls.usersFromIds, { $1: userIds });
Plural   return userIds.map((userId) =>
names      pgResp.rows.find((row) => userId === row.id)
      );
    },                              Uses a .map call on the input array to
    // -.-.-.                       ensure that the output array has the exact
  };                               same length and order. DataLoader will not
};                                 work properly if you don't do that.
```

**TIP**  The `.map`/`.find` method is *not* the most efficient way to accomplish the task in listing 7.7, but it is simple. You should consider converting the `pgReps.rows` array into an object and do a constant time lookup within the `.map` loop. I'll leave that as an exercise for you. Look at the final codebase for the project (az.dev/contribute) to see the optimization we are doing for this part.

This batch-loading function is ready. Let's use it.

## 7.1.2 *Defining and using a DataLoader instance*

`DataLoader` caching is not meant to be part of your application-level caching that's shared among requests. It's meant to be a simple memoization to avoid repeatedly loading the same data in the context of a single request in your application. To do that, you should initialize a loader object for each request in your application and use it only for that request.

Since we're using the Express.js framework to manage requests to the AZdev API, to make the "Users loader" scoped to a single request, we can define it inside the listener function of the `server.use` call in api/src/server.js.

However, the code currently delegates the entire listener function argument to the `graphqlHTTP` higher-order function. We'll need to change that. Here's one way of doing so.

##### Listing 7.8 Changes in the `server.use` call in api/src/server.js

```
// .-.-.
import DataLoader from 'dataloader';

async function main() {
  // .-.-.

  server.use('/', (req, res) => {
    const loaders = {
      users: new DataLoader((userIds) => pgApi.usersInfo(userIds)),
    };
    graphqlHTTP({
      schema,
      context: { pgApi, loaders },
      // .-.-.
    })(req, res);
  }
);
```

This change introduces a new function as the listener function for `server.use`, defines the `users` loader within this new request-scoped context, and then delegates the rest of the work back to the `graphqlHTTP` function. With that, we're now able to make the new `loaders` object part of the GraphQL context object.

Note that I made `loaders` into an object that has the `usersDataLoader` instance as a property because we will be introducing more loaders for more database models.

Also note that `graphqlHTTP` is a higher-order function that returns another function. Its returned function expects the `req` and `res` arguments (coming from the Express listener function). We are basically doing the same thing as before; but now that we've introduced a wrapper listener function, we need to pass these `req` and `res` objects manually.

**TIP**   I defined the `loaders` object for both `POST` and `GET` requests. Ideally, in a production environment, it should be defined only for `POST` requests. I'll leave that part for you to optimize.

That's it for initializing the loaders. Each time there is a request, we create a Data-Loader instance for the Users model that uses the `pgApi.usersInfo` batch-loading function that we have prepared. Let's now replace the manual direct fetching of users in the codebase with this new `DataLoader` instance. We need to modify the two GraphQL types that previously used `pgApi.userInfo`. Look that up: we used it in the `Task` and `Approach` types.

Here's how to change both of these places to use the new `usersDataLoader` instance. First, here is the `Task` type.

**Listing 7.9   Changes in the `Task` type in api/src/schema/types/task.js**

```
const Task = new GraphQLObjectType({
  name: 'Task',
  fields: {
    // ·—·—·

    author: {
      type: new GraphQLNonNull(User),
      resolve: (source, args, { loaders }) =>
        loaders.users.load(source.userId),
    },

    // ·—·—·
  },
});
```

And here is the `Approach` type.

**Listing 7.10   Changes in the `Approach` type in api/src/schema/types/approach.js**

```
const Approach = new GraphQLObjectType({
  name: 'Approach',
  fields: {
    // ·—·—·

    author: {
      type: new GraphQLNonNull(User),
      resolve: (source, args, { loaders }) =>
        loaders.users.load(source.userId),
    },

    // ·—·—·
  },
});
```

The changes to these types are identical. We use the new `loaders` object in the resolver's context object (instead of the previous `pgApi` object) and then use a `.load` call on the `usersDataLoader` instance.

`DataLoader` takes care of the rest! When multiple `.load` calls are made in the same execution context while the GraphQL query is being resolved, `DataLoader` batches the calls. It prepares an array from all the loaded IDs and executes the batch-loading function just once. It then uses the response for that single call to satisfy all user data requirements that were made in the query.

If we try the same GraphQL query in listing 7.2 now while tailing the logs of Postgre-SQL, we will see something like the following excerpt from my PostgreSQL logs:

```
LOG:   statement: SELECT ... FROM azdev.tasks WHERE ...
LOG:   execute <unnamed>: SELECT ... FROM azdev.users WHERE id = ANY ($1)
DETAIL:   parameters: $1 = '{1}'     ◄——
                                          "1" is the ID value for the
                                          test user in the sample data.
```

Note that the parameter value is {1}, which represents an array in PostgreSQL. More important, note that only *one* SQL statement was issued for the `users` table (instead of five, as previously).

We added a lot of value with just a few lines of code. But to appreciate it more, let's exclusively load the other ID-based data fetching through `DataLoader` instances. Remember the GraphQL query that made 17 SQL statements at the end of chapter 6? Let's see how many SQL statements it will make after converting all data-fetching logic to go through `DataLoader` instances.

> **Current code**
>
> Use `git checkout 7.1` to reset your local repo to the current progress in the code.

### 7.1.3  *The loader for the approachList field*

The other ID-based fetching we have done so far is in the `pgApi.approachList` function in api/src/db/pg-api.js. This function is a bit different than the `pgApi.usersInfo` function as it takes a `taskId` and returns an array of `Approach` records. This means when we switch it to work with an array of keys instead of a single value, it will take an array of `taskIds`, and it should return an *array of arrays* (each array representing the list of Approaches for one Task).

`DataLoader`, in this case, will be concerned about the order of the top-level array. The order of the items in the inner-level arrays is an application-level concern.

`sqls.approachesForTaskIds` accepts an array of Task IDs, but it will return a single list of all the Approach records under all the input Task IDs. We'll need to split this list and group Approach records by Task IDs while keeping the order of the top-level array matching the order of the input array.

We can use a `.map`/`.filter` combination to do that. Here are all the changes I made to this function.

##### Listing 7.11   Changes in api/src/db/pg-api.js

```
const pgApiWrapper = async () => {
  // ·-·-·
  return {
    // ·-·-·
    approachLists: async (taskIds) => {
      const pgResp = await pgQuery(sqls.approachesForTaskIds, {
        $1: taskIds,
      });
      return taskIds.map((taskId) =>
        pgResp.rows.filter((row) => taskId === row.taskId),
      );
    },
  };
};
```

*Plural names* → `approachLists`, `taskIds`

← **Passes $I as the taskIds array** `$1: taskIds`

◁ **Splits the rows and groups them under their corresponding taskId value. The filter call will group the items in the response by the taskId value. The returned result is an array of approach arrays.**

The `pgApi.approachLists` batch-loading function is now compatible with `Data-Loader`. To use it, we instantiate a new loader instance in api/src/server.js.

##### Listing 7.12   Changes in api/src/server.js

```
const loaders = {
  users: new DataLoader((userIds) => pgApi.usersInfo(userIds)),
  approachLists: new DataLoader((taskIds) =>
    pgApi.approachLists(taskIds),
  ),
};
```

Then we use this new instance in the GraphQL types that previously used a direct database fetch to list Approaches. The only type that did that is the `Task` type.

##### Listing 7.13   Changes in api/src/schema/types/task.js

```
const Task = new GraphQLObjectType({
  name: 'Task',
  fields: {
    // ·-·-·
    approachList: {
      type: new GraphQLNonNull(
        new GraphQLList(new GraphQLNonNull(Approach))
      ),
      resolve: (source, args, { loaders }) =>
        loaders.approachLists.load(source.id),
    },
  },
});
```

That should do it. Go ahead and test the same query we tested at the end of chapter 6 (listing 6.24) while tailing the PostgreSQL logs. You should see something like this excerpt from my PostgreSQL logs:

```
LOG:  statement: SELECT ... FROM azdev.tasks WHERE ...;
LOG:  execute <unnamed>: SELECT ... FROM azdev.users WHERE id = ANY ($1)
DETAIL:  parameters: $1 = '{1}'
LOG:  execute <unnamed>: SELECT ... FROM azdev.approaches WHERE task_id = ANY
➥ ($1) ...
DETAIL:  parameters: $1 = '{1,2,3,4,6}'
```

The key thing to notice here is that we're using a single SQL query to fetch Approaches for all Tasks. This same query will be used whether we have 100 or 1,000 Tasks.

With the new `DataLoader` instances in place, the query that used 17 SQL statements before is now using only 3 statements (one statement per database table). We did not need to do any join statements or field renaming. This is a win!

This win also contributes to making the server more resilient to denial-of-service attacks using intentionally complicated queries: for example, if we used GraphQL's alias concept to ask for Approach data multiple times, as follows.

**Listing 7.14  An intentionally complicated query example**

```
{
  taskMainList {
    id
    author {
      id
    }
    a1: approachList {
      id
      author {
        id
      }
    }
    a2: approachList {
      id
      author {
        id
      }
    }
    a3: approachList {
      id
      author {
        id
      }
    }
  }
}
```

The `DataLoader` instances would take care of not going to the database multiple times per alias. This intentionally complicated query would still only execute three statements over the wire. We should certainly put more protection layers between public queries and the backend schema, but it's good to know that if something slipped through the cracks, we have a level of optimization to fall back on.

---

**Current code**

Use `git checkout 7.2` to reset your local repo to the current progress in the code.

---

Note that we did not need to optimize the `sqls.tasksLatest` statement because it does not depend on IDs (so no batching is needed). However, we can still use Data-Loader to take advantage of the caching of any query asking for the `taskMainList` field. We'll do that soon, but first let's implement the `task` field under an Approach object and learn about circular dependencies with GraphQL types.

## 7.2    *Single resource fields*

In our schema plan, the `taskInfo` root query root field is supposed to fetch the information for a single Task record identified by an ID that the API consumer can send as a field argument.

---

**Listing 7.15   The `taskInfo` root field and its `id` argument**

```
type Query {
  taskInfo(id: ID!): Task
  // ------
}
```

Here's a query that we can use to work through this field.

---

**Listing 7.16   Example query for the `taskInfo` field**

```
query taskInfoTest {
  taskInfo(id: 3) {
    id
    content
    author {
      id
    }
    approachList {
      content
    }
  }
}
```

Note that this field has to support the nested `author` and `approachList` information. But guess what? We don't need to do anything new. We have already implemented these relationships under `taskMainList`. The `taskInfo` field uses the same output type (Task).

You might be tempted to think that since this `taskInfo` field works with a single record, there is no need to use `DataLoader` for it. However, using `DataLoader` is preferable for many reasons. For one thing, having all database fetch requests go through `DataLoader` is simply a good code abstraction practice, but there is still performance value for composite queries. For example, take a look at this query.

```
query manyTaskInfoTest {
  task1: taskInfo(id: 1) {
    id
    content
    author {
      id
    }
  }
  task2: taskInfo(id: 2) {
    id
    content
    author {
      id
    }
  }
}
```

If we don't use a `DataLoader` instance for the `taskInfo` field, this query will ask the database about two Task records using two SQL statements. With a `DataLoader` instance, these two statements are batched into one.

Before we implement the `taskInfo` field, let's do a little refactoring. The api/src/schema/index.js file is currently doing two things that are logically separate: it defines the main `Query` type and uses it to create a schema. Let's split these two tasks into two files instead of one.

```
import { GraphQLSchema, printSchema } from 'graphql';

import QueryType from './queries';

export const schema = new GraphQLSchema({
  query: QueryType,
});

console.log(printSchema(schema));
```

Move everything else that was in the file to api/src/schema/queries.js, and export the main `QueryType` from that file.

**Listing 7.19   New file: api/src/schema/queries.js**

```javascript
import {
  GraphQLObjectType,
  GraphQLString,
  GraphQLInt,
  GraphQLNonNull,
  GraphQLList,
} from 'graphql';

import NumbersInRange from './types/numbers-in-range';
import { numbersInRangeObject } from '../utils';

import Task from './types/task';

const QueryType = new GraphQLObjectType({
  name: 'Query',
  fields: {
    currentTime: {
      type: GraphQLString,
      resolve: () => {
        const isoString = new Date().toISOString();
        return isoString.slice(11, 19);
      },
    },
    numbersInRange: {
      type: NumbersInRange,
      args: {
        begin: { type: new GraphQLNonNull(GraphQLInt) },
        end: { type: new GraphQLNonNull(GraphQLInt) },
      },
      resolve: function (source, { begin, end }) {
        return numbersInRangeObject(begin, end);
      },
    },
    taskMainList: {
      type: new GraphQLList(new GraphQLNonNull(Task)),
      resolve: async (source, args, { pgApi }) => {
        return pgApi.taskMainList();
      },
    },
  },
});

export default QueryType
```

**Current code**

Use `git checkout 7.3` to reset your local repo to the current progress in the code.

**TIP**   Note that I made the refactoring changes in a separate Git commit. This is a good practice to keep the history of changes in a Git repo clean and easy to understand.

Let's make this change with a top-down approach this time (so far, we've been using a bottom-up approach). We'll first define the `taskInfo` root query (in the new api/src/schema/queries.js file). Note that—for the first time so far—we're going to use a field argument (the `id` argument for `taskInfo`). In the definition of the `taskInfo` field, we have to include the type of that `id` argument. We can use the `GraphQLID` type for it.

**Listing 7.20  Changes in api/src/schema/queries.js**

```
import {
  GraphQLID,
  GraphQLObjectType,
  GraphQLString,
  GraphQLInt,
  GraphQLNonNull,
  GraphQLList,
} from 'graphql';
// ·—·—·

const QueryType = new GraphQLObjectType({
  name: 'Query',
  fields: {
    // ·—·—·
    taskInfo: {
      type: Task,
      args: {
        id: { type: new GraphQLNonNull(GraphQLID) },
      },
      resolve: async (source, args, { loaders }) => {
        return loaders.tasks.load(args.id);
      },
    },
  },
});
```

When a consumer passes values for a field's arguments, the values are captured as one object passed as the second argument for each resolve method (commonly named args).

Defines the name/type of a field argument

Reads the value a consumer used for the id argument out of the resolve method's args object

The `loaders.tasks` function does not exist yet. I often start planning for a change in the codebase just like this. I find it helpful to think about the new objects and functions I need and *use* them before I write them. This approach helps me come up with better, more practical designs. The new loader function goes in api/src/server.js.

**Listing 7.21  Changes in api/src/server.js**

```
const loaders = {
  // ·—·—·
  tasks: new DataLoader((taskIds) => pgApi.tasksInfo(taskIds)),
};
```

Following the top-down analysis, we now need to define the `pgApi.tasksInfo` function. I have prepared a `sqls.tasksFromIds` statement for it in api/src/db/sqls.js.

**Listing 7.22    The `sqls.tasksFromIds` statement**

```
// $1: taskIds
// $2: userId (can be null)
tasksFromIds: `
  SELECT ...
  FROM azdev.tasks
  WHERE id = ANY ($1)
  AND (is_private = FALSE OR user_id = $2)
`,
```

Something new and important is introduced in this statement. It takes two variables: one is the IDs of tasks to be loaded, and the other is a `userId` argument. The query will then make sure the looked-up Task is either public or owned by the user identified by the `userId` value. Without that condition, private Tasks can be looked up using the `taskInfo` field (which will use this SQL statement).

This SQL statement can be used without a `userId` value (which is what we need to do first); for that case, it will only fetch information about public Task records.

Here's the `pgApi` DataLoader-compatible function to execute the SQL statement.

**Listing 7.23    Changes in api/src/db/pg-api.js**

```
const pgApiWrapper = async () => {
  // .-.-.

  return {
    // .-.-.
    tasksInfo: async (taskIds) => {
      const pgResp = await pgQuery(sqls.tasksFromIds, {
        $1: taskIds,
        $2: null, // TODO: pass logged-in userId here.
      });
      return taskIds.map((taskId) =>              Note the loose equality
        pgResp.rows.find((row) => taskId == row.id),  ◁——  operator (==) here.
      );
    },
  };
};

export default pgApiWrapper;
```

**Challenge**

Can you think of the reason why I used the abstract (or loose) equality operator in listing 7.23?

Answer: The `id` argument in the `taskInfo` root field is defined with the `GraphQLID` type. GraphQL casts any value you pass to a `GraphQLID` field to a string. The actual `id` values coming from PostgreSQL are integers (because all primary key fields were defined using the `serial` type). Comparing integers to strings is one of the rare cases where the loose equality operator is useful.

> Alternatively, you can do the number-to-string casting yourself before making the comparison.

That's it! Go ahead and test the `taskInfoTest` query in listing 7.16.

> **TIP** The `$1`/`$2` variables have to be defined in order. The `pgQuery` wrapper is designed to pass their values in order as positional items in an array.

> **Current code**
> Use `git checkout 7.4` to reset your local repo to the current progress in the code.

## 7.3 Circular dependencies in GraphQL types

We designed the `Approach` type to have a `task` field so that we can display the parent Task information when a search result item is an Approach record. To implement this relation, we can reuse the loaders and `pgApi` function we wrote for the `taskInfo` root field.

However, this relation is the inverse of the `Task` –> `Approach` relation we implemented for the `approachList` field. This means it will introduce a circular dependency in the graph: `Task` –> `Approach` –> `Task` –> `Approach` –> …

To see this problem in action, let's try to implement the new relation. The only change we need to make is the `Approach` type.

Since the `Approach` type now needs to use the `Task` type, and since that `Task` type already uses the `Approach` type, the `Approach` type will hit the circular dependency problem. Check it out: here are the necessary changes.

> **Listing 7.24 Changes in api/src/schema/types/approach.js**

```
// .-.-.
import Task from './task';

const Approach = new GraphQLObjectType({
  name: 'Approach',
  fields: {
    // .-.-.
    task: {
      type: new GraphQLNonNull(Task),          <-┐   This line is the problem.
      resolve: (source, args, { loaders }) =>        Task uses Approach,
        loaders.tasks.load(source.taskId)            which now uses Task.
    },
  },
});

export default Approach;
```

The server logs will report this problem:

```
ReferenceError: Task is not defined
```

Luckily, there is a simple solution. Instead of using types directly under the `fields` property, that property can be a function whose return value is the object representing the fields. GraphQL.js supports this out of the box, and it's handy for situations like these.

> **Listing 7.25    Changes in api/src/schema/types/approach.js**

```
const Approach = new GraphQLObjectType({
  name: 'Approach',
  fields: () => ({              ◁——— Note the new function syntax here!
    // ·-·-·
    task: {
      type: new GraphQLNonNull(Task),
      resolve: (source, args, { pgApi }) =>
        pgApi.tasks.load(source.taskId),
    },
  }),
});
```

Changing the `fields` configuration property to be a function delays this dependency and uses it dynamically instead of statically. That function is basically executed after Node.js loads all modules. This function is often referred to as a *thunk*, which is a fancy name for a function that is used to delay a calculation until results are needed (among a few other applications).

The `ReferenceError` should be gone now. Verify that, and test the `task` field under the `approachList` field.

It is a good practice to *always* use the function signature for the `fields` configuration property instead of the object form. Go ahead and make that change, and retest the queries we already finished.

> **Current code**
>
> Use `git checkout 7.5` to reset your local repo to the current progress in the code.

### 7.3.1   *Deeply nested field attacks*

When you implement two-way relations, you should think of a way to prevent the deeply nested field attacks discussed in chapter 1. For example, the new `Approach ->` `Task` relation will open the door for a query like this (figure 7.1).

You can protect your API server against this type of attack in many ways. The simplest solution is just to count the nesting levels and block the query after a certain threshold. The fourth argument of each resolver has a `path` property that can be used

```
 1 ▼ {
 2 ▼   taskMainList {
 3 ▼     approachList {
 4 ▼       task {
 5 ▼         approachList {
 6 ▼           task {
 7 ▼             approachList {
 8 ▼               task {
 9 ▼                 approachList {
10 ▼                   task {
11 ▼                     approachList {
12 ▼                       task {
13 ▼                         approachList {
14 ▼                           task {
15 ▼                             approachList {
16 ▼                               task {
17 ▼                                 approachList {
18 ▼                                   task {
19 ▼                                     approachList {
20 ▼                                       task {
21 ▼                                         approachList {
22 ▼                                           task {
23 ▼                                             approachList {
24 ▼                                               task {
25 ▼                                                 approachList {
26 ▼                                                   task {
27 ▼                                                     approachList {
28 ▼                                                       task {
29 ▼                                                         approachList {
30 ▼                                                           task {
31                                                              approachList {
32                                                                id
33                                                              }
34                                                            }
35                                                          }
36                                                        }
37                                                      }
38                                                    }
39                                                  }
40                                                }
41                                              }
42                                            }
43                                          }
44                                        }
45                                      }
46                                    }
47                                  }
48                                }
49                              }
50                            }
51                          }
52                        }
53                      }
54                    }
55                  }
56                }
57              }
58            }
59          }
60        }
61      }
62    }
63 }
64
```

**Figure 7.1   Example:
deeply nested fields in a query**

for that purpose if you want to selectively do this check in certain fields (like `task` on the `Approach` type). However, a better way here would be to do this validation per operation rather than per resolver.

You can also design your schema such that nested attacks are not even possible. For example, we can come up with a different type for a "search-result-approach-object" and define the `task` field only on that type rather than the main `Approach` type. Similarly, the `approachList` field can be made available only under the `taskInfo` root field and not under the `taskMainList` field (where it is actually not needed in the UI). Check out the AZdev GitHub repo (az.dev/contribute) to see examples of using more specific types to prevent deeply nested field attacks. We'll also see an example of this concept in the next chapter under the root `me` field.

> **TIP**  The deeply nested field attack is just one example of many ways an API server can be attacked with intentionally complicated operations. To protect your server from all of them, you can analyze each operation to be executed, estimate how much time and data it will use, and block operations beyond certain thresholds. There are libraries out there to help you do that. You can also just let all queries run but implement a timeout to cancel operations that take a long time. Or, you can implement a timeout based on custom cost factors you define on specific operations and block an operation if its total cost goes beyond a certain threshold.

## 7.4    Using DataLoader with custom IDs for caching

Although a `DataLoader` batch-loading function is often associated with a list of input IDs, you don't need actual IDs coming from primary fields in the database. You can come up with your own ID-to-result association and use `DataLoader` with the custom map you designed. This is usually helpful when you are using the caching aspect of `DataLoader`. For example, you can come up with SQL statements and give each statement a unique label. That label becomes one of the IDs you can use with a `Data-Loader` instance.

Many examples in the GraphQL schema we designed could benefit from that approach. One of them is the `taskMainList` field.

### 7.4.1    The taskMainList field

Let's test how many SQL statements the following GraphQL query will currently issue. Can you guess?

> **Listing 7.26    An example of a query using multiple aliases**

```
{
  a1: taskMainList {
    id
  }
  a2: taskMainList {
    id
```

```
  }
  a3: taskMainList {
    id
  }
  a4: taskMainList {
    id
  }
}
```

Since we have not used `DataLoader` for `taskMainList`, this GraphQL query will issue the same `SELECT` statement four times.

Here's the related excerpt from my PostgreSQL logs:

```
LOG: statement: SELECT ... FROM azdev.tasks WHERE ....;
LOG: statement: SELECT ... FROM azdev.tasks WHERE ....;
LOG: statement: SELECT ... FROM azdev.tasks WHERE ....;
LOG: statement: SELECT ... FROM azdev.tasks WHERE ....;
```

We can use `DataLoader` to cache the data response it gets the first time it loads this list and then not go back to the database for the same request. However, `DataLoader` is wired to fetch a value for a key. You can think of the "value" here as the list of the latest Task records, but there are no keys in this case. To make this database statement work with `DataLoader`, we need to come up with a custom key for this `SELECT` statement. A key here is just any unique label for it. I'll use the label `latest` for this one.

Let's do this change with a top-down approach. The type that needs to be resolved with the latest Tasks is the root `Query` type. Instead of issuing `pgApi.taskMainList()`, let's assume we have a `tasksByTypes` loader that can fetch any list of Task records by a particular type, and let's fetch the `latest` type.

**Listing 7.27  Changes in api/src/schema/queries.js**

```
const QueryType = new GraphQLObjectType({
  name: 'Query',
  fields: () => ({
    // ......
    taskMainList: {
      type: new GraphQLList(new GraphQLNonNull(Task)),
      resolve: async (source, args, { loaders }) => {
        return loaders.tasksByTypes.load('latest');
      },
    },
  }),
});
```

Note that I am using a top-down approach here as well. Let's now write the `tasksBy-Types` loader. We'll need to add it to the listener function (in api/src/server.js).

**Listing 7.28   Changes in api/src/server.js**

```
const loaders = {
  // .-.--.
  tasksByTypes: new DataLoader((types) =>
    pgApi.tasksByTypes(types),
  ),
};
graphqlHTTP({
  schema,
  context: { loaders },          ◁──  Note that the pgApi object was removed from the
  graphiql: true,                     context object. We don't need to query the database
  // .-.--.                           directly anymore. All database communication
})(req, res);                         should happen through a loader object.
```

Again, I've used a `tasksByTypes` property that does not exist on `pgApi` yet. This is my plan for the new batch-loading function. We'll write that next.

The new `pgApi.tasksByTypes` batch-loading function is special in this case. It currently only supports loading the `latest` type, but we still have to write it in a way that makes it accept an array of types and return an array of results associated with these types.

**Listing 7.29   Changes in api/src/db/pg-api.js**

```
const pgApiWrapper = async () => {
  // .-.--.

  return {
    tasksByTypes: async (types) => {          ◁──  Replaces the
      const results = types.map(async (type) => {     taskMainList function
        if (type === 'latest') {
          const pgResp = await pgQuery(sqls.tasksLatest);
          return pgResp.rows;
        }
        throw Error('Unsupported type');
      });
      return Promise.all(results);
    },
    // .-.--.
  };
};
```

Note that the SQL query is invoked within the `.map` call, making the map callback function return a pending promise, which makes the `results` object an array of pending promises. That's why I wrap the returned result with a `Promise.all` call. Depending on what other types we end up adding (or not adding), this particular way of fetching within a map call can be optimized. It's okay as is for now because we're really just faking the batching nature of this list.

That's it. No matter how many aliases you add to fetch the `taskMainList` root field, `DataLoader` will only ask the database about that list once. Verify that.

With `DataLoader` in the stack, we can now continue implementing other fields and either use existing loaders or define new ones as needed.

> **Current code**
> Use `git checkout 7.6` to reset your local repo to the current progress in the code.

### 7.4.2 *The search field*

The `search` field takes an argument—the search term—and returns a list of matching records from both the Task and Approach models through the interface type they implement: `SearchResultItem`.

**Listing 7.30 The search field**

```
type Query {
  # ...
  search(term: String!): [SearchResultItem!]
}
```

The search term, in this case, is the unique key that can be used with a `DataLoader` batch-loading function.

The search feature has a new concept that we're going to implement for the first time: the GraphQL interface type. Here are the parts of the schema related to it.

```
interface SearchResultItem {
  id: ID!
  content: String!
}

type Task implements SearchResultItem {
  # ...
}

type Approach implements SearchResultItem {
  # ...
}
```

For each record in the search results, the new interface type needs a way to determine what type it is. It needs to tell the API consumer that a search result is a Task object or an Approach object. We can do that using the `resolveType` configuration property, which is a function whose argument is the object that implements the `SearchResultItem` type; it needs to return which GraphQL type represents that object. Let's design the search results objects to have a `type` property that holds a `task` or `approach` string value. We can use that to implement the `resolveType` function logic.

Here's one implementation of the `SearchResultItem` type that's based on this plan. Put this in api/src/schema/types/search-result-item.js.

**Listing 7.31   New file: api/src/schema/types/search-result-item.js**

```
import {
  GraphQLID,
  GraphQLInterfaceType,
  GraphQLNonNull,
  GraphQLString,
} from 'graphql';

import Task from './task';
import Approach from './approach';

const SearchResultItem = new GraphQLInterfaceType({
  name: 'SearchResultItem',
  fields: () => ({
    id: { type: new GraphQLNonNull(GraphQLID) },
    content: { type: new GraphQLNonNull(GraphQLString) },
  }),
  resolveType(obj) {
    if (obj.type === 'task') {
      return Task;
    }
    if (obj.type === 'approach') {
      return Approach;
    }
  },
});

export default SearchResultItem;
```

We can now use this new type to define the root search field. We also need to define the arguments this field expects. We designed it to expect a `term` value, which is a string. To resolve the search field, let's assume that we have a loader named `searchResults` whose key is the search term.

Here's one possible implementation of the field.

**Listing 7.32   Changes in api/src/schema/queries.js**

```
// .....

import SearchResultItem from './types/search-result-item';

const QueryType = new GraphQLObjectType({
  name: 'Query',
  fields: () => ({
    // .....

    search: {
      type: new GraphQLNonNull(
        new GraphQLList(new GraphQLNonNull(SearchResultItem)),
      ),
      args: {
        term: { type: new GraphQLNonNull(GraphQLString) },
      },
      resolve: async (source, args, { loaders }) => {
```

Defines the name/type of a field argument ⤳

```
        return loaders.searchResults.load(args.term);
      },
    },
  }),
});
```

**Reads the value a consumer used for the term field argument out of the resolve method's args object**

Now, to make the `Task` and `Approach` types implement this new interface type, we used the `interfaces` property of the `GraphQLObjectType` configuration object. The value of this property is an array of all the interface types an object type implements.

---

**Listing 7.33  Changes in api/src/schema/types/task.js**

```
// .-.-.
import SearchResultItem from './search-result-item';

const Task = new GraphQLObjectType({
  name: 'Task',
  interfaces: () => [SearchResultItem],
  fields: () => ({
    // .-.-.
  }),
});
```

---

**Listing 7.34  Changes in api/src/schema/types/approach.js**

```
// .-.-.
import SearchResultItem from './search-result-item';

const Approach = new GraphQLObjectType({
  name: 'Approach',
  interfaces: () => [SearchResultItem],
  fields: () => ({
    // .-.-.
  }),
});
```

---

Note that I wrapped the interfaces array as a thunk just as we are now doing for the `fields` property.

Following the top-down analysis, we now need to define a `DataLoader` instance named `searchResults`. Let me pause here and ask this question: do we really need a caching/batching loader for a search query?

Probably not. It's unlikely an API consumer will do multiple searches in one query. And unless they are intentionally trying to overload the API service, it's unlikely they will search for the same term many times!

However, as we've seen in `taskMainList`, using a loader provides some protection against bad queries (whether they were malicious or not). Imagine a UI application with a bug that causes a search query to repeat 100 times in a GraphQL request. You don't want your API server to issue 100 full-text-search SQL statements to the database in that case.

Another reason to use a loader for this case is for consistency. `DataLoader` is now an abstraction layer in our stack, and all database communication should happen through it. Mixing some direct database communication here would be a code smell.

The `searchResults` batch-loading function takes a list of search query terms, and it should do a full-text-search operation for each.

Let's assume that the `pgApi` module has a `searchResults` method to do the SQL communication. Here's what I came up with for the loader definition.

#### Listing 7.35  Changes in api/src/server.js

```
async function main() {
  // ·—·—·

  server.use('/', (req, res) => {
    const loaders = {
      // ·—·—·
      searchResults: new DataLoader((searchTerms) =>
        pgApi.searchResults(searchTerms),
      ),
    };
    // ·—·—·
  });

  // ·—·—·
};
```

The final piece of this puzzle is the `pgApi.searchResults` method and the full-text-search logic it executes. Luckily, PostgreSQL has built-in support for full-text search. I prepared a single SQL statement that retrieves search results from both the `azdev.tasks` and `azdev.approaches` tables; check it out at `sqls.searchResults`.

#### Listing 7.36  The `sqls.searchResults` full-text-search statement

```
// $1: searchTerm
// $2: userId (can be null)
searchResults: `
  WITH viewable_tasks AS (
    SELECT *
    FROM azdev.tasks n
    WHERE (is_private = FALSE OR user_id = $2)
  )
  SELECT id, "taskId", content, tags, "approachCount", "voteCount",
         "userId", "createdAt", type,
         ts_rank(to_tsvector(content), websearch_to_tsquery($1)) AS rank
  FROM (
    SELECT id, id AS "taskId", content, tags,
           approach_count AS "approachCount", null AS "voteCount",
           user_id AS "userId", created_at AS "createdAt",
           'task' AS type
    FROM viewable_tasks
```

```
      UNION ALL
      SELECT a.id, t.id AS "taskId", a.content, null AS tags,
             null AS "approachCount", a.vote_count AS "voteCount",
             a.user_id AS "userId", a.created_at AS "createdAt",
             'approach' AS type
        FROM azdev.approaches a JOIN viewable_tasks t ON (t.id = a.task_id)
    ) search_view
    WHERE to_tsvector(content) @@ websearch_to_tsquery($1)
    ORDER BY rank DESC, type DESC
  `,
```

This SQL statement uses a few cool PostgreSQL tricks. For example, it uses an inline view (`viewable_tasks`) to make sure the operation only works on viewable Task records, which are either public or owned by a `userId` value. The `userId` value can be null, in which case the statement will only work for public Task records.

The statement uses a `UNION ALL` operator to combine result sets from multiple database tables into a single set. It then uses this combined set as the source for the full-text search, which it performs using the `to_tsvector`, `websearch_to_tsquery`, and `ts_rank` PostgreSQL functions. This is just one set of many functions and operators that can be used to perform and optimize this search, but those are beyond the scope of this book. You can read more about PostgreSQL full-text-search capabilities at az.dev/pg-fts.

Here's how we can use this SQL statement in the `pgApi` module.

---

**Listing 7.37   Changes in api/src/db/pg-api.js**

```
const pgApiWrapper = async () => {
  // ·—·—·

  return {
    // ·—·—·
    searchResults: async (searchTerms) => {
      const results = searchTerms.map(async (searchTerm) => {
        const pgResp = await pgQuery(sqls.searchResults, {
          $1: searchTerm,
          $2: null, // TODO: pass logged-in userId here.
        });
        return pgResp.rows;
      });
      return Promise.all(results);
    },
  };
};
```

---

Note that this function uses the same "promise-map" method we used for `tasksBy-Types` to be `DataLoader` compatible. Also note that I passed the $2 value as null for now. Once we enable API consumers to log in, we need to figure out how to make the current `userId` value available for this function. We'll do that in the next chapter.

We can test now! Here's an example of how to query the new `search` field in GraphQL.

---

**Listing 7.38  An example query to test the search field**

```
{
  search(term: "git OR sum") {
    content
    ... on Task {
      approachCount
    }
    ... on Approach {
      task {
        id
        content
      }
    }
  }
}
```

This search should return three records from the sample data: two Task records and one Approach record (figure 7.2).

```
 1 ▾ {
 2 ▾   search(term: "git OR sum") {
 3       content
 4       ... on Task {
 5         approachCount
 6       }
 7 ▾     ... on Approach {
 8         task {
 9           id
10           content
11         }
12       }
13     }
14   }
```

```
▾ {
▾   "data": {
▾     "search": [
▾       {
            "content": "git diff | git apply --reverse",
            "task": {
              "id": "2",
              "content": "Get rid of only the unstaged changes
            }
          },
          {
            "content": "Get rid of only the unstaged changes si
            "approachCount": 1
          },
          {
            "content": "Calculate the sum of numbers in a JavaS
            "approachCount": 1
          }
        ]
      }
    }
```

**Figure 7.2   Executing the `search` query in GraphiQL**

Note the power of the PostgreSQL text-search capabilities. The example uses OR, and the search results are ranked based on relevance. Try a few other search terms, and explore the many other features we enabled.

**TIP** If an interface type is implemented by many types, the `resolveType` property can become difficult to maintain. It's not ideal that you need to edit it every time you add another type that implements your interface. GraphQL.js supports another method to determine the type of the implementing object. You can define an `isTypeOf` function on every object type that implements an interface, and GraphQL.js will pick the first object type whose `isTypeOf` returns true. If you define `isTypeOf` on all objects that implement an interface, you won't need the `resolveType` property.

---

**Current code**

Use `git checkout 7.7` to reset your local repo to the current progress in the code.

---

Let's now implement the `detailList` field under an Approach record. I've delayed implementing this one because of its complexity and because we really should do it through `DataLoader`. I think we're ready for it.

## 7.5 *Using DataLoader with MongoDB*

Since we've decided to store the dynamic Details of an Approach record in MongoDB, we need to make a `DataLoader` instance that fetches data from there. This is the first time we will be reading data from MongoDB, so we need to create an API module for MongoDB, instantiate it on the main server, and use it to define a `DataLoader` instance.

Let's do this one with a top-down approach as well. Similar to how we named objects for PostgreSQL and where we stored its modules, let's come up with a `mongoApi` module and assume that it has a batch-loading function named `detailLists` to load a list of Detail objects given a list of Approach IDs.

Here are the changes I came up with for api/src/server.js (mirroring what's there for PostgreSQL).

**Listing 7.39   Changes in api/src/server.js**

```
// .-.-.
import mongoApiWrapper from './db/mongo-api';

async function main() {
  const pgApi = await pgApiWrapper();
  const mongoApi = await mongoApiWrapper();

  // .-.-.

  server.use('/', (req, res) => {
    const loaders = {
      // .-.-.
```

```
      detailLists: new DataLoader((approachIds) =>
        mongoApi.detailLists(approachIds)
      ),
    };
    // .-.-.
  });

  // .-.-.
};
```

The new `mongoApi` module will host all the interactions with MongoDB. Here's the implementation I came up with for it (also mirroring what we have so far for api/src/db/pg-api.js). Put this in api/src/db/mongo-api.

Listing 7.40   New file: `api/src/db/mongo-api`

```
import mongoClient from './mongo-client';

const mongoApiWrapper = async () => {
  const { mdb } = await mongoClient();

  const mdbFindDocumentsByField = ({
    collectionName,
    fieldName,
    fieldValues,
  }) =>
    mdb
      .collection(collectionName)
      .find({ [fieldName]: { $in: fieldValues } })
      .toArray();

  return {
    detailLists: async (approachIds) => {
      // TODO: Use mdbFindDocumentsByField to
      // implement the batch-loading logic here
    },
  };
};

export default mongoApiWrapper;
```

Note that I placed the current `mongo-client` driver's logic to find a list of documents in a MongoDB collection into its own function named `mdbFindDocumentsByField` (just as I did for `pgQuery`). Eventually, there will be more functions of this nature, and they can be abstracted, maintained, and tested separately from the application-level logic that's going to use them. In fact, I'm already thinking these functions should be moved to the client files, but I'll keep them next to their usage for simplicity.

**TIP** The abstraction I did for `mdbFindDocumentsByField` is a bit more detailed than what I did for `pgQuery` because the `mongo` driver API uses Java-Script objects (versus SQL text statements in the `pg` driver). The level of abstraction is a matter of preference, but what I tried to achieve here is to keep everything related to the `mongo` driver separate from the application-level logic (to make the code `DataLoader` compatible, for example). An argument can be made that this is a premature abstraction, but I have been down this road many times, and I've found these abstractions very helpful as the project grows.

Because the `mongoApi.detailLists` function is used as the batch-loading function for a `DataLoader` instance, it needs to maintain the size and order of the input array of `approachIds`. Let's figure out what we need here, one piece at a time.

First, remember that the `approachIds` value is coming from PostgreSQL, which means we will need to filter the response we get out of MongoDB for the `approach-Details` collection using the `pgId` field on a document to find each document associated with each Approach. If there is no match in MongoDB, that means the Approach record has no Detail records.

Using the same `.map`/`.find` trick we did in `pgApi.usersInfo`, here's the skeleton of what we need in `mongoApi.detailLists`.

**Listing 7.41   Changes in api/src/db/mongo-api**

```
const mongoApiWrapper = async () => {
  // ......

  return {
    detailLists: async (approachIds) => {
      const mongoDocuments = await mdbFindDocumentsByField({
        collectionName: 'approachDetails',
        fieldName: 'pgId',
        fieldValues: approachIds,
      });

      return approachIds.map((approachId) => {
        const approachDoc = mongoDocuments.find(
          (doc) => approachId === doc.pgId
        );

        if (!approachDoc) {
          return [];
        }

        const { explanations, notes, warnings } = approachDoc;
                                                   ◁

        // ......
      });
    },
  };
};
```

These destructured variables will each hold an array of values. They can also be undefined.

◁— We need to restructure the raw MongoDB data here to match our GraphQL schema design.

Once the ID-to-document map is finished, each `approachDetails` document in MongoDB is an object whose properties represent the three content categories that we designed for the `ApproachDetail` ENUM type.

**Listing 7.42   The `ApproachDetail` ENUM type**

```
enum ApproachDetailCategory {
  NOTE
  EXPLANATION
  WARNING
}
```

Each of these properties holds an array of text values. However, remember that we designed the `ApproachDetail` type to have a `category` field and a `content` field.

**Listing 7.43   The `ApproachDetail` type in the SDL text**

```
type ApproachDetail {
  category: ApproachDetailCategory!
  content: String!
}
```

This means we need a bit of logic to take an object:

```
{
  explanations: [explanationsValue1, ·····],
  notes: [notesValue1, ·····],
  warnings: [warningsValue1, ·····],
}
```

And we convert the object to the following:

```
[
  {
    content: explanationsValue1,
    category: "EXPLANATION"
  },
  {
    content: notesValue1,
    category: "NOTE"
  },
  {
    content: warningsValue1,
    category: "WARNING"
  },
  ·····
]
```

Furthermore, the content categories are optional in an `approachDetail` document. One category might have 10 values while another category might not exist (and be undefined in listing 7.41).

Considering all these points, here's one way to do the necessary conversion for the schema.

**Listing 7.44 Changes in api/src/db/mongo-api.js**

```javascript
const mongoApiWrapper = async () => {
  // .-.-.

  return {
    detailLists: async (approachIds) => {
      // .-.-.

      return approachIds.map((approachId) => {
        // .-.-.

        const approachDetails = [];
        if (explanations) {
          approachDetails.push(
            ...explanations.map((explanationText) => ({
              content: explanationText,
              category: 'EXPLANATION',
            }))
          );
        }
        if (notes) {
          approachDetails.push(
            ...notes.map((noteText) => ({
              content: noteText,
              category: 'NOTE',
            }))
          );
        }
        if (warnings) {
          approachDetails.push(
            ...warnings.map((warningText) => ({
              content: warningText,
              category: 'WARNING',
            }))
          );
        }
        return approachDetails;
      });
    },
  };
};
```

We start with an empty array of objects (`approachDetails`). Then, for each array values property on an `approachDetail` document, if that array value exists, we push into the `approachDetails` array all the items in that array value after mapping them to the `{ content: '·-·-·', category: '·-·-·' }` structure.

**TIP**  There is certainly a chance to do the three `if` statements in listing 7.44 dynamically with one loop and allow for future values in an Approach Detail category. I'll leave that for you as an exercise.

Next, we need to define two new types in this GraphQL schema: `ApproachDetail` and `ApproachDetailCategory`. Let's start with the latter. It's an `ENUM` with three fixed values. To define an `ENUM` type, the GraphQL.js API provides a `GraphQLEnumType` constructor that takes a configuration object representing the `ENUM` values. Here's what I did to define the `ApproachDetailCategory` type. Put this in a new file at api/src/schema/types/approach-detail-category.js.

---

**Listing 7.45    New file: api/src/schema/types/approach-detail-category.js**

```
import { GraphQLEnumType } from 'graphql';

const ApproachDetailCategory = new GraphQLEnumType({
  name: 'ApproachDetailCategory',
  values: {
    NOTE: {},
    EXPLANATION: {},
    WARNING: {},
  },
});

export default ApproachDetailCategory;
```

> These objects can be used to specify a description per value or deprecate a value. Also, if the values in the database are stored differently, such as with numbers, you can do the string-to-number map in each value's configuration object.

---

Now we can define the `ApproachDetail` type, which uses the `ApproachDetailCategory` type. The `ApproachDetail` type is a simple instance of `GraphQLObjectType`. Create a new file for it at api/src/schema/types/approach-detail.js.

---

**Listing 7.46    New file: api/src/schema/types/approach-detail.js**

```
import {
  GraphQLObjectType,
  GraphQLString,
  GraphQLNonNull,
} from 'graphql';

import ApproachDetailCategory from './approach-detail-category';

const ApproachDetail = new GraphQLObjectType({
  name: 'ApproachDetail',
  fields: () => ({
    content: {
      type: new GraphQLNonNull(GraphQLString),
    },
    category: {
      type: new GraphQLNonNull(ApproachDetailCategory),
```

```
    },
  }),
});
```

```
export default ApproachDetail;
```

Finally, we need to define the `detailList` field itself on the `Approach` type. This is where we use the new DataLoader instance, and it's exactly the same as we did for the previous types. Hopefully this is getting easier now!

**Listing 7.47  Changes in api/src/schema/types/approach.js**

```
import {
  // ......
  GraphQLList,
} from 'graphql';
// ......
import ApproachDetail from './approach-detail';
const Approach = new GraphQLObjectType({
  name: 'Approach',
  fields: () => ({
    // ......

    detailList: {
      type: new GraphQLNonNull(
        new GraphQLList(new GraphQLNonNull(ApproachDetail))
      ),
      resolve: (source, args, { loaders }) =>
        loaders.detailLists.load(source.id),
    },
  },
});
```

You can test this new feature using the following query (see figure 7.3).

**Listing 7.48  An example query to test the `detailList` field**

```
{
  taskMainList {
    content
    approachList {
      content
      detailList {
        content
        category
      }
    }
  }
}
```

**Figure 7.3   Output of the `taskMainList` query**

For each of the five public Tasks in our sample data, this query fetches all Approaches from PostgreSQL and then fetches all Details on every Approach from MongoDB. Guess how many times it reaches out to MongoDB?

*One* time.

Thanks to the `DataLoader` instance, all of the MongoDB operations are batched into a single one.

> **Current code**
>
> Use `git checkout 7.7` to reset your local repo to the current progress in the code.

The only root query field remaining is the `me` field, but to properly test it we need a valid authentication token. Let's first implement the mutations we designed for the schema. Then, once we can issue the mutation to get a valid `authToken` value, we will implement the `me` field and do the TODOs we left in the code that require passing the ID for the current user (as identified by an `authToken`).

## Summary

- To optimize data-fetching operations in a generic, scalable way, you can use the concepts of caching and batching. You can cache SQL responses based on unique values like IDs or any other custom unique values you design in your API service. You can also delay asking the database about a specific resource until you figure out all the unique IDs of all the records needed from that resource and then send a single request to the database to include all the records based on all the IDs.

- `DataLoader` is a generic JavaScript library that can be used as part of your application's data-fetching layer to provide a simplified, consistent API over various data sources and abstract the use of batching and caching. This enables you to focus on your application's logic and safely distribute its data-fetching requirements without worrying about maintaining minimal requests to your databases and other sources of data.

- `DataLoader` instances are meant to be scoped for a single request. They can be used for both ID-based SQL statements and more complex statements like fetching lists or even full-text-search requests.

- If you use `DataLoader` in your stack, it's a good practice to do all database communications through it. Your GraphQL resolvers will then delegate the task of resolving the data to the `DataLoader` instances. This makes the code cleaner and more maintainable.

# Implementing mutations 8

**This chapter covers**

- Implementing GraphQL's mutation fields
- Authenticating users for mutation and query operations
- Creating custom, user-friendly error messages
- Using powerful database features to optimize mutations

We implemented most of the query tree for the AZdev GraphQL API in chapter 7. It's now time to implement the mutation operations we planned, starting with the userCreate mutation to enable AZdev users to create an account and use other mutations (and queries) that require authenticated requests.

Since this is the very first mutation we're creating, we need to do some groundwork to wire things up for all mutations. We basically need to make the schema ready to host mutations.

> **Current code**
> Use `git checkout 8.0` to reset your local repo to the current progress in the code.
> If you need to stash any local changes, use `git add . && git stash`. Remember
> to run `npm install` to install any missing dependencies.

## 8.1 *The mutators context object*

We've abstracted all database READ operations to go through DataLoader instances
using the loaders object we passed to each resolver as part of the global GraphQL
context. It's time to think about the WRITE operations. Every mutation operation will
perform an INSERT, UPDATE, or DELETE SQL statement or a MongoDB operation (or a
combination of them). These WRITE operations do not need to go through Data-
Loader. Although we could make the mutations' READ parts go through DataLoader, I
think that would be a case of overengineering.

> **TIP** A mutation can contain multiple fields, resulting in the server executing
> multiple database WRITE/READ operations. However, unlike query fields,
> which are executed in parallel, mutation fields run in a series, one after the
> other. If an API consumer sends two mutation fields, the first is guaranteed to
> finish before the second begins. This is to ensure that a race condition does
> not happen, but it also complicates the task of something like DataLoader.

Let's add to the global context another object responsible for mutations. I'll name it
mutators. This object will host all the database mutation operations (for both
PostgreSQL and MongoDB). In fact, let's plan to group all database operations under
a mutators property in the database API objects. Add a mutators property to both
pgApi and mongoApi.

**Listing 8.1 Changes in api/src/db/pg-api.js**

```
const pgApiWrapper = async () => {
  // .-.-.

  return {
    // .-.-.

    mutators: {

    },
  };
};
```

**Listing 8.2    Changes in `api/src/db/mongo-api.js`**

```
const mongoApiWrapper = async () => {
  // .-.-.

  return {
    // .-.-.

    mutators: {

    },
  };
};
```

Each future mutation operation will be a sub-property of these new `mutators` properties.

> **TIP** You can also group all the `pgApi` functions used by `DataLoader` under a `loaders` property, but I'll skip that here to keep things simple. Ideally, every loader or mutator function should have its own file and host its own database statements. I'll leave this refactoring for you as an exercise.

Now, in api/src/server.js, let's create a new object to host all database mutation operations (from both databases) and make that object part of the global context.

**Listing 8.3    Changes in api/src/server.js**

```
async function main() {
  // .-.-.

  server.use('/', (req, res) => {
    // .-.-.

    const mutators = {
      ...pgApi.mutators,
      ...mongoApi.mutators,
    };

    graphqlHTTP({
      schema,
      context: { loaders, mutators },
      graphiql: true,
    })(req, res);
  });

  // .-.-.
};
```

Now all mutation resolvers will have access to all database mutation operations.

> **TIP** Resolvers for query fields will also have access to this new `mutators` object. However, they should never use it. Query fields should be pure and never cause side effects.

## 8.2 The Mutation type

Just as we defined a `QueryType` that held all the root query fields that API consumers could start with, we need to define a `MutationType` to hold all the mutation fields that API consumers can invoke. We do that in api/src/schema/index.js, mirroring what we already have there for `QueryType`.

**Listing 8.4 Changes in api/src/schema/index.js**

```
import QueryType from './queries';
import MutationType from './mutations';

export const schema = new GraphQLSchema({
  query: QueryType,
  mutation: MutationType,
});
```

The new mutations.js file will be under api/src/schema, and it will use a regular `GraphQLObjectType` object.

**Listing 8.5 New file: api/src/schema/mutations.js**

```
import { GraphQLObjectType } from 'graphql';
const MutationType = new GraphQLObjectType({
  name: 'Mutation',
  fields: () => ({
    // .-.-.
  }),
});

export default MutationType;
```

## 8.3 User mutations

Now that we have the skeleton to support mutation operations, let's tackle the first two mutations that will allow a consumer of this API to create an account (userCreate) and then obtain an authentication token to use other mutations (userLogin).

Remember that for each mutation, in addition to the main mutation field, we need to define two types: an input type and a payload type. For the first mutation, we also need to define the `UserError` type, which we planned to use to represent user-friendly error messages when users send the mutation bad input (for example, a short password).

### 8.3.1 The userCreate mutation

Here's the part of the SDL that we need to focus on for the `userCreate` mutation.

**Listing 8.6 SDL for `userCreate` and its dependencies**

```
input UserInput {
  username: String!
  password: String!
```

```
    firstName: String
    lastName: String
}

type UserError {
  message: String!
}

type UserPayload {
  errors: [UserError!]!
  user: User
  authToken: String!
}

type Mutation {
  userCreate(input: UserInput!): UserPayload!

  # More mutations
}
```

The generic `UserError` type is a simple instance of `GraphQLObjectType`. Put it under api/src/schema/types/user-error.js.

**Listing 8.7    New file: api/src/schema/types/user-error.js**

```
import {
  GraphQLObjectType,
  GraphQLString,
  GraphQLNonNull,
} from 'graphql';

const UserError = new GraphQLObjectType({
  name: 'UserError',
  fields: () => ({
    message: {
      type: new GraphQLNonNull(GraphQLString),
    },
  }),
});

export default UserError;
```

We can now define the `UserPayload` type, which uses the `UserError` type. The User-Payload type is used in two mutations (`userCreate` and `userLogin`), so let's put it in its own file under api/src/schema/types/payload-user.js.

**Listing 8.8    New file: api/src/schema/types/payload-user.js**

```
import {
  GraphQLObjectType,
  GraphQLString,
  GraphQLNonNull,
  GraphQLList,
```

```
} from 'graphql';

import User from './user';
import UserError from './user-error';

const UserPayload = new GraphQLObjectType({
  name: 'UserPayload',
  fields: () => ({
    errors: {
      type: new GraphQLNonNull(
        new GraphQLList(new GraphQLNonNull(UserError)),
      ),
    },
    user: { type: User },
    authToken: { type: GraphQLString },
  }),
});

export default UserPayload;
```

Now we can implement the mutation field and its `UserInput` type. To use this mutation, the consumer has to supply a username address and a password; they can optionally supply first and last names. Usually, you want the consumer's input to include at least all the non-null fields in the database: in this case, `username` and `password`. We cannot create a `User` record without these.

> **TIP** Note that I named the file payload-user.js instead of user-payload.js. I did that to have the payload types grouped together in the types directory. In a bigger project, you can organize different GraphQL types under different directories for categories or API features.

For the `UserInput` type, we need to use a `GraphQLInputObjectType` object. This is another GraphQL.js constructor object that is similar to `GraphQLObjectType`.

---

**Listing 8.9  New file: api/src/schema/types/input-user.js**

```
import {
  GraphQLInputObjectType,
  GraphQLString,
  GraphQLNonNull,
} from 'graphql';

const UserInput = new GraphQLInputObjectType({
  name: 'UserInput',
  fields: () => ({
    username: { type: new GraphQLNonNull(GraphQLString) },
    password: { type: new GraphQLNonNull(GraphQLString) },
    firstName: { type: GraphQLString },
    lastName: { type: GraphQLString },
  }),
});

export default UserInput;
```

Now we can import both the `UserPayload` and `UserInput` types into api/src/schema/mutations.js and define the `userCreate` field object—which, just like query fields, has `type`, `args`, and `resolve` properties.

> **Listing 8.10    Changes in api/src/schema/mutations.js**

```
import { GraphQLObjectType, GraphQLNonNull } from 'graphql';
import UserPayload from './types/payload-user';
import UserInput from './types/input-user';

const MutationType = new GraphQLObjectType({
  name: 'Mutation',
  fields: () => ({
    userCreate: {
      type: new GraphQLNonNull(UserPayload),
      args: {
        input: { type: new GraphQLNonNull(UserInput) },
      },
      resolve: async (source, { input }, { mutators }) => {
        return mutators.userCreate({ input });        ◁─┐  The mutators.userCreate
      },                                                 │  method does not exist yet.
    },
  }),
});

export default MutationType;
```

Finally, we need to implement `mutators.userCreate`, which we used in the `resolve` function. It expects an object with an `input` property (which itself is an object of type `UserInput`).

> **TIP**  Note that I matched the `mutators` function name to the field that's using it. This is just a style preference on my part to keep methods grouped by their subject, which I think is a useful practice to follow everywhere. However, in a bigger codebase, you should consider adding a suffix to methods to make them easy to find and replace. For example, you can do something like `userCreateLoader` and `userCreateMutator`.

Remember that a GraphQL mutation is always a `WRITE` operation followed by a `READ` operation. The `type` of a mutation is what can be read after it's finished. In this case, it's a `UserPayload` record, which includes the newly created user record from the database. The newly created user record has to be read from the database because it needs to include the values that are autofilled by the database (like the serial ID and creation timestamp information). This means we need an `INSERT` statement followed by a `SELECT` statement.

That's when PostgreSQL will surprise you. We can actually tell PostgreSQL to return a newly created record using the same `INSERT` statement. Here's an example.

> **Listing 8.11 Example: PostgreSQL's RETURNING clause**

```
INSERT INTO azdev.users (username, password)
  VALUES ('janedoe', 'ChangeMe')
RETURNING id, username, created_at
```

Did you notice that RETURNING part? Not only will this INSERT statement insert a row in the table, but it will also SELECT columns from that new row and return them in the same database operation. That's one of my favorite features in PostgreSQL.

With this magic, all we need to do is read the input values and pass them to a version of that INSERT statement, but with a few more details to hash the password and alias the columns. I'll also include an example for you to use the UserError structure in the payload by blocking the mutation operation if the consumer sends a password value with fewer than six characters.

Here's what I came up with for the mutators.userCreate function.

> **Listing 8.12 New mutator method in api/src/db/pg-api.js**

```
// .-.-.

import { randomString } from '../utils';

const pgApiWrapper = async () => {
  // .-.-.

  return {
    // .-.-.

    mutators: {
      // .-.-.

      userCreate: async ({ input }) => {
        const payload = { errors: [] };
        if (input.password.length < 6) {
          payload.errors.push({
            message: 'Use a stronger password',
          });
        }
        if (payload.errors.length === 0) {
          const authToken = randomString();
          const pgResp = await pgQuery(sqls.userInsert, {
            $1: input.username.toLowerCase(),
            $2: input.password,
            $3: input.firstName,
            $4: input.lastName,
            $5: authToken,
          });
          if (pgResp.rows[0]) {
            payload.user = pgResp.rows[0];
            payload.authToken = authToken;
          }
```

**The randomString function returns a random string. It's already implemented in api/src/utils.js.**

**The userInsert SQL statement inserts a row into the azdev.users table. It's already implemented in api/src/db/sqls.js.**

```
      }
      return payload;
    },
  },
};
};
```

Remember that an `auth_token` acts like a temporary password. That's why its value is hashed as well, but the user is expected to use the plain-text version (which is generated at random).

Note that just like the `resolve` functions for query fields, a mutation's `resolve` function can also return a promise, and GraphQL.js will do the "awaiting" for us. Also note that the "short password" error completely blocks the `INSERT` statements (otherwise, what's the point?), but sometimes user errors may be captured during the `INSERT` statement. For example, to make sure the supplied username value is not one that's already used, instead of issuing an extra `SELECT` statement before the `INSERT` statement, we can simply let the `INSERT` statement fail because the database already has a validation on that column. Let me leave that here as an exercise for you. Also, make a validation around the `firstName` and `lastName` input values. For example, don't allow numbers. If the consumer sends the name as `{ firstName: "James", lastName: "007" }`, fail that operation with a user error.

To test the `userCreate` mutation, here's a request you can use in GraphiQL.

---

**Listing 8.13   Example mutation request to test `userCreate`**

```
mutation userCreate {
  userCreate(input: {
    username: "janedoe"
    password: "123"          ◁──┐  Try it first with a short password to
    firstName: "Jane"           │  see the UserError response, and then
    lastName: "Doe"             │  try it with a valid password.
  }) {
    errors {
      message
    }
    user {
      id
      name
    }
    authToken
  }
}
```

Figure 8.1 shows the response you should get when you try a short password.

> **TIP**  The stored `auth_token` value should expire after a certain time. One way to do that is to add another column to `azdev.users` to manage the time validity of each token.

```
 1 ▾ mutation userCreate {                  ▾ {
 2 ▾   userCreate(input: {                  ▾   "data": {
 3       username: "janedoe"                ▾     "userCreate": {
 4       password: "123"                    ▾       "errors": [
 5       firstName: "Jane"                            {
 6       lastName: "Doe"                                "message": "Use a stronger password"
 7 ▾   }) {                                           }
 8       errors {                                   ],
 9         message                                  "user": null,
10       }                                          "authToken": null
11       user {                                   }
12         id|                                  }
13         name                             }
14       }
15       authToken
16     }
17 }
```

**Figure 8.1   A user-error data response**

**Current code**

Use `git checkout 8.1` to reset your local repo to the current progress in the code.

### 8.3.2   *The userLogin mutation*

To offer returning users a way to obtain a new `auth_token` value, we need to implement the `userLogin` mutation. Here's the part of the SDL text to implement for it.

**Listing 8.14   SDL for `userLogin` and its dependencies**

```
input AuthInput {
  username: String!
  password: String!
}

type Mutation {
  userLogin(input: AuthInput!): UserPayload!

  # ⋯⋯⋯
}
```

We've already implemented the `UserPayload` type, so we can reuse it here, but we need to create the `AuthInput` type. This is simple, and it's similar to the `UserInput` type. Put the following in api/src/schema/types/input-auth.js.

**Listing 8.15   New file: api/src/schema/types/input-auth.js**

```
import {
  GraphQLInputObjectType,
  GraphQLString,
```

```
    GraphQLNonNull,
} from 'graphql';

const AuthInput = new GraphQLInputObjectType({
  name: 'AuthInput',
  fields: () => ({
    username: { type: new GraphQLNonNull(GraphQLString) },
    password: { type: new GraphQLNonNull(GraphQLString) },
  }),
});

export default AuthInput;
```

The userLogin mutation field needs to be defined under MutationType (in api/src/
schema/mutations.js). This is also similar to the userCreate field, except that it will
use a different mutators function.

---

**Listing 8.16   Changes in api/src/schema/mutations.js**

```
// .-.-.

import AuthInput from './types/input-auth';

const MutationType = new GraphQLObjectType({
  name: 'Mutation',
  fields: () => ({
    // .-.-.
    userLogin: {
      type: new GraphQLNonNull(UserPayload),
      args: {
        input: { type: new GraphQLNonNull(AuthInput) },
      },
      resolve: async (source, { input }, { mutators }) => {
        return mutators.userLogin({ input });
      },
    },
  }),
});

export default MutationType;
```

While it's possible to do this mutation operation with a single database UPDATE statement, I'll do it with two statements: one to validate the input username/password values (sqls.userFromCredentials) and one to update the auth_token user field in the
database (sqls.userUpdateAuthToken). Take a look at these two prepared statements
in api/src/db/sqls.js.

> **TIP** Both SQL statements use PostgreSQL's crypt function from the
> pgcrypto extension (az.dev/pgcrypto).

For input validation on this mutators function, let's make sure the username/password
values are not empty. Here's the implementation I came up with for this function.

**Listing 8.17  Changes in api/src/db/pg-api.js**

```
const pgApiWrapper = async () => {
  // ·—·—·

  return {
    // ·—·—·

    mutators: {
      // ·—·—·
      userLogin: async ({ input }) => {
        const payload = { errors: [] };
        if (!input.username || !input.password) {
          payload.errors.push({
            message: 'Invalid username or password',
          });
        }
        if (payload.errors.length === 0) {
          const pgResp = await pgQuery(sqls.userFromCredentials, {
            $1: input.username.toLowerCase(),
            $2: input.password,
          });
          const user = pgResp.rows[0];
          if (user) {
            const authToken = randomString();
            await pgQuery(sqls.userUpdateAuthToken, {
              $1: user.id,
              $2: authToken,
            });
            payload.user = user;
            payload.authToken = authToken;
          } else {
            payload.errors.push({
              message: 'Invalid username or password'
            });
          }
        }
        return payload;
      },
    },
  };
};
```

We start by checking the values in input.username and input.password and pushing a user error to the payload if they are empty. Although these input fields were defined in the input object as not-null, empty values will still pass the GraphQL validation. Then, if the username and password are valid, we can update the users table to store a hashed value for a new, randomly generated authToken value and return the plaintext version of it as part of the payload.

> **TIP**  We don't need to distinguish the invalidity of passwords from the invalidity of usernames. Grouping the two validations in one is more secure.

To test the userLogin mutation, here's a request you can use in GraphiQL.

**Listing 8.18   Request to test `userLogin`**

```
mutation userLogin {
  userLogin(input: {
    username: "test",
    password: "123456"
  }) {
    errors {
      message
    }
    user {
      id
      name
    }
    authToken
  }
}
```

←── The "test/123456" credentials are valid (from the sample development data).

Try this mutation with a valid and an invalid password (figures 8.2 and 8.3), and make sure both cases work okay.

```
1 ▾ mutation userLogin {                    ▾ {
2     userLogin(input: {                    ▾   "data": {
3       username: "test",                   ▾     "userLogin": {
4       password: "42"                      ▾       "errors": [
5 ▾   }) {                                            {
6       errors {                                        "message": "Invalid username or password"
7         message                                     }
8       }                                           ],
9       user {                                      "user": null,
10        id                                        "authToken": null
11        name                                    }
12      }                                       }
13      authToken                           }
14    }
15  }
```

**Figure 8.2   Testing the `userLogin` mutation with invalid credentials**

```
1 ▾ mutation userLogin {                    ▾ {
2     userLogin(input: {                    ▾   "data": {
3       username: "test",                   ▾     "userLogin": {
4       password: "123456"                          "errors": [],
5 ▾   }) {                                          "user": {
6       errors {                                      "id": "1",
7         message                                     "name": ""
8       }                                           },
9       user {                                      "authToken": "078a4a415c12a88af7bd35f6ec8be
10        id                                      }
11        name                                  }
12      }                                     }
13    |   authToken
14    }
15  }
```

**Figure 8.3   Testing the `userLogin` mutation with valid credentials**

**TIP** Save the returned valid `authToken` value, as we need it in the next section.

> **Current code**
>
> Use `git checkout 8.2` to reset your local repo to the current progress in the code.

## 8.4 Authenticating API consumers

Now that we can use the API to get a valid `authToken` value, we need to figure out how to include that token in the headers of future requests so that we can use it with GraphQL operations that require a valid user session.

The GraphiQL editor that comes bundled with the `express-graphql` package supports a headers editor (similar to the variables editor). To enable it, make the following change in api/src/server.js.

**Listing 8.19 Changes in api/src/server.js**

```
async function main() {
  // .-.-.

  server.use('/', (req, res) => {
    // .-.-.
    graphqlHTTP({
      schema,
      context: { loaders, mutators },
      graphiql: { headerEditorEnabled: true },
      // .-.-.
    })(req, res);
  });

  // .-.-.
}
```

The GraphiQL editor should now show the REQUEST HEADERS editor (figure 8.4).

**Figure 8.4 The REQUEST HEADERS section in GraphiQL**

We can use the `Authorization` request header to include the `authToken` value with every request made by GraphiQL. The syntax for that request header is shown next.

---
**Listing 8.20    Example: syntax for the `Authorization` header**

```
Authorization: <type> <credentials>
```
⟵  The main types of authentication are Basic, Bearer, Digest, HOBA, Mutual, Client, and Form Based. The credentials depend on the type.

Since we're using a single string value `authToken`, we can use the `Bearer` type (which is a token-based system).

> **TIP**    The `Bearer` type is the basis for OAuth open standard and JWT. My plan here is to implement the most basic form of token-based authentication and let you build on that. If you're interested in learning more about API security, check out the book *API Security in Action* by Neil Madden (Manning, 2019) at www.manning.com/books/api-security-in-action.

Remember the TODOs we left in `pgApi` functions that passed null as the current `userId` value? One was for the `taskInfo` root query field, and the other was for the `search` root query field. Let's fix these first.

Use the `userLogin` mutation to obtain a valid `authToken` value using the "test/123456" credentials. That user owns a private Task record that should show up if they send the following GraphQL query.

---
**Listing 8.21    Searching for a private Task record**

```
{
  search(term: "babel") {
    content
  }
}
```

To include the `authToken` value, put this in the request headers editor:

```
{
  "Authorization": "Bearer AUTH_TOKEN_VALUE_HERE"
}
```
⟵  Replace this with the valid authToken value you get from the userLogin mutation.

This query currently returns no data, and we need to make it work because the consumer is now sending the server a valid `authToken` value.

I've prepared a SQL statement (`sqls.userFromAuthToken`) to find a user record using an `authToken` value. Let's create a `pgApi.userFromAuthToken` function to use that statement, in api/src/db/pg-api.js.

---

**Listing 8.22  Changes in api/src/db/pg-api.js**

```
const pgApiWrapper = async () => {
  // .-.-.

  return {
    userFromAuthToken: async (authToken) => {
      if (!authToken) {
        return null;
      }
      const pgResp = await pgQuery(sqls.userFromAuthToken, {
        $1: authToken,
      });
      return pgResp.rows[0];
    },

    // .-.-.
  };
};
```

The `pgApi.userFromAuthToken` function is special. It is not going to be used by a Data-Loader instance. It's not even part of GraphQL resolving logic. We'll need it before communicating with GraphQL.

Don't do the authentication within GraphQL resolving logic. It's better to have a different layer handling it either before or after the GraphQL service layer. We'll do the authentication work in the Express request-handling layer (where we also prepared the `loaders` object). Then we can pass a `currentUser` value to the search logic to include it in the `sqls.searchResults` statement (which is designed to accept a user ID value).

In api/src/server.js, add the following before the `loaders` object.

---

**Listing 8.23  Changes in api/src/server.js**

```
async function main() {
  // .-.-.

  server.use('/', async (req, res) => {  ◁──┐
    const authToken =
      req && req.headers && req.headers.authorization
        ? req.headers.authorization.slice(7) // "Bearer "
        : null;
    const currentUser = await pgApi.userFromAuthToken(authToken);
    if (authToken && !currentUser) {
      return res.status(401).send({
        errors: [{ message: 'Invalid access token' }],
      });
    }

    // .-.-.
  });

  // .-.-.
}
```

Note the new async keyword, which is needed since the new code uses the await keyword on the userFromAuthToken async function.

When there is an authorization header (as parsed by Express), we will validate the authToken value through the pgApi.userFromAuthToken function.

Note that I made the server return a 401 error when there is an invalid authToken (no user record found). This is preferable to just silently failing and not considering the user as logged in. The user should be notified that they are using an invalid authToken value (for example, it could be expired, and they need to log out and log in again). Also note that I formatted the returned error to match GraphQL's own root errors (an array of error objects with a message property). This logic is still executed as part of a GraphQL request, and it should conform to the way GraphQL formats errors.

Now we'll take care of the pgApi methods where we left a TODO to include a userId value that can use the new currentUser variable. Both pgApi.tasksInfo and pgApi.searchResults need it. Let's change their argument into an object so that we can include the currentUser value.

---
**Listing 8.24    Changes in api/src/server.js**

```
async function main() {
  // .-.-.

  server.use('/', async (req, res) => {
    // .-.-.

    const loaders = {
      users: new DataLoader((userIds) => pgApi.usersInfo(userIds)),
      approachLists: new DataLoader((taskIds) =>
        pgApi.approachLists(taskIds),
      ),
      tasks: new DataLoader((taskIds) =>
        pgApi.tasksInfo({ taskIds, currentUser }),
      ),
      tasksByTypes: new DataLoader((types) =>
        pgApi.tasksByTypes(types),
      ),
      searchResults: new DataLoader((searchTerms) =>
        pgApi.searchResults({ searchTerms, currentUser }),
      ),
      detailLists: new DataLoader((approachIds) =>
        mongoApi.detailLists(approachIds),
      ),
    };

    // .-.-.
  });

  // .-.-.
}
```

Then, change the pgApi function to account for the new argument design and current-User value.

**Listing 8.25  Changes in api/src/db/pg-api.js**

```
const pgApiWrapper = async () => {
  // .-.-.

  return {
    // .-.-.
    tasksInfo: async ({ taskIds, currentUser }) => {
      const pgResp = await pgQuery(sqls.tasksFromIds, {
        $1: taskIds,
        $2: currentUser ? currentUser.id : null,
      });
      return taskIds.map((taskId) =>
        pgResp.rows.find((row) => taskId == row.id),
      );
    },
    searchResults: async ({ searchTerms, currentUser }) => {
      const results = searchTerms.map(async (searchTerm) => {
        const pgResp = await pgQuery(sqls.searchResults, {
          $1: searchTerm,
          $2: currentUser ? currentUser.id : null,
        });
        return pgResp.rows;
      });
      return Promise.all(results);
    },

    // .-.-.
  };
};
```

That's it. You can test the "babel" search query now, and it should work. Test it with an invalid `authToken` value as well (figures 8.5 and 8.6).

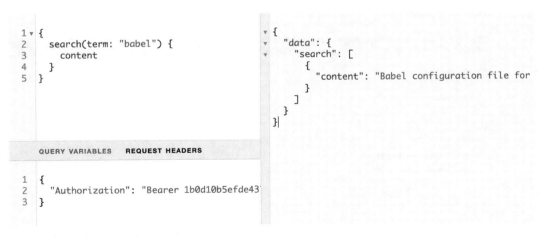

**Figure 8.5  Sending a request header with a GraphQL query**

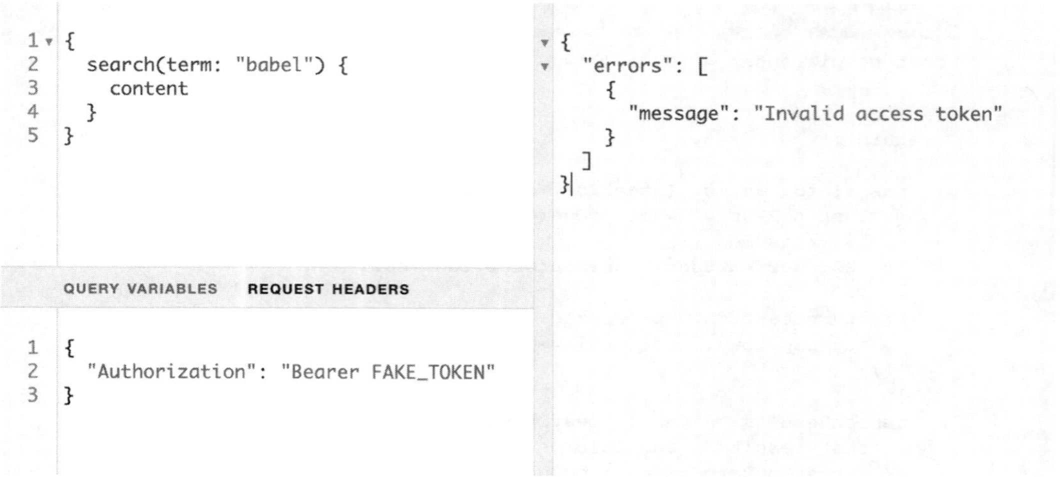

```
1 ▾ {
2       search(term: "babel") {
3         content
4       }
5   }
```

```
  ▾ {
  ▾   "errors": [
          {
            "message": "Invalid access token"
          }
        ]
     }
```

**QUERY VARIABLES    REQUEST HEADERS**

```
1   {
2       "Authorization": "Bearer FAKE_TOKEN"
3   }
```

**Figure 8.6   Testing an invalid `Authorization` request header**

The `taskInfo` root query field should also work for Task 5 when you're using a valid `authToken` value for the test user.

> **Current code**
> Use `git checkout 8.3` to reset your local repo to the current progress in the code.

### 8.4.1   *The me root query field*

Let's implement the `me` root query field next. The following is the part of the SDL related to that field.

**Listing 8.26   SDL text for the `me` field**

```
type Query {
  // ......
  me: User
}

type User {
  id: ID!
  createdAt: String!
  username: String!
  name: String
  taskList: [Task!]!
}
```

We implemented the `User` type but without the `taskList` field. Now that we are implementing the `me` field, it's time to also support the `taskList` field on the `User` type but restrict it to only be available within the `me` field scope.

Let's start with the me field itself. Here's a query we can use to test it when it's finished.

##### Listing 8.27 Example query to test the me root field

```
{
  me {
    id
    username
  }
}
```

To support this new root field, we will need to add its definition under QueryType (in api/src/schema/queries.js). Since we are already getting the currentUser record (for a valid authToken value) in the Express listener function (in api/src/server.js), we can make currentUser part of the GraphQL's context object and just return it directly from the resolve function of the new me field.

##### Listing 8.28 Changes in api/src/server.js

```
async function main() {
  // .-.-.

  server.use('/', async (req, res) => {
    // .-.-.
    graphqlHTTP({
      schema,
      context: { loaders, mutators, currentUser },
      graphiql: { headerEditorEnabled: true },
      // .-.-.
    })(req, res);
  });

  // .-.-.
}
```

##### Listing 8.29 Changes in api/src/schema/queries.js

```
// .-.-.
import User from './types/user';

const QueryType = new GraphQLObjectType({
  name: 'Query',
  fields: () => ({
    // .-.-.
    me: {
      type: User,
      resolve: async (source, args, { currentUser }) => {
        return currentUser;
      },
    },
  }),
});
```

This is a special field since the database statement is not executed within the GraphQL resolver. That's why we don't even need to use a `DataLoader` for it.

Go ahead and test the query in listing 8.27 (with a valid `authToken` in the request headers). See figure 8.7.

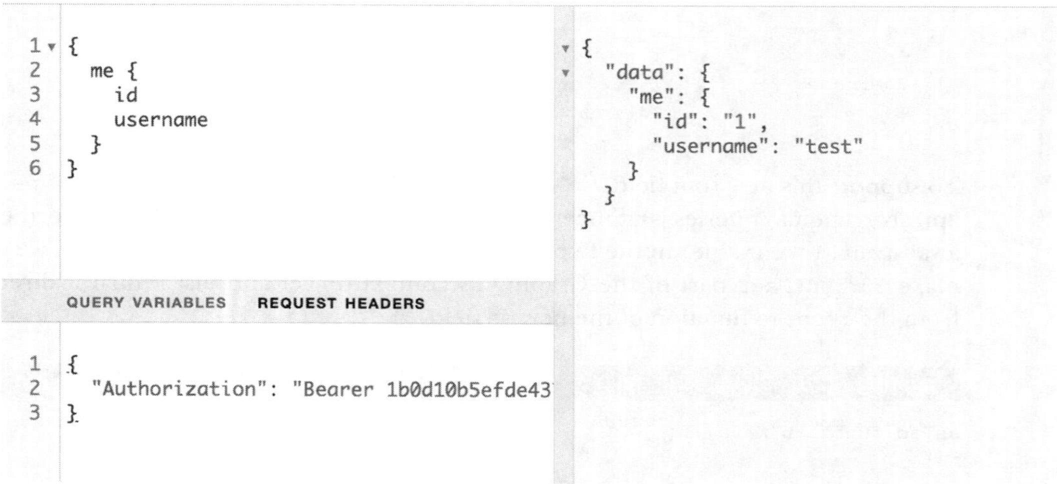

```
1 ▾ {
2     me {
3       id
4       username
5     }
6   }
```

```
  ▾ {
  ▾   "data": {
        "me": {
          "id": "1",
          "username": "test"
        }
      }
    }
```

QUERY VARIABLES    REQUEST HEADERS

```
1   {
2     "Authorization": "Bearer 1b0d10b5efde43
3   }
```

Figure 8.7   Testing the me field

However, we designed the root me field to give authorized users a way to see all their Task records. We need to implement the `taskList` field under the `User` type next.

To do that, we need to distinguish between a `taskList` field used on any user record (in any scope) and a `taskList` field used within the me root field scope.

There are ways to do that dynamically. One of them is to utilize the fourth `info` argument to figure out the path for a `taskList` field. This might work okay, but I am going to use a simpler method.

Let's just create two `User` types! We will keep the one we have and introduce a new one for the me field. The new type gets the `taskList` field. To implement that without duplicating the `User` type fields, we can make its `fields` configuration property a function that returns the `fields` object with or without a `taskList` field.

Here's what I came up with.

Listing 8.30   New code in api/src/schema/types/user.js

```
import {
  // .....
  GraphQLList,
} from 'graphql';

import Task from './task';
```

```
const fieldsWrapper = ({ meScope }) => {
  const userFields = {
    id: { type: new GraphQLNonNull(GraphQLID) },
    username: { type: GraphQLString },
    name: {
      type: GraphQLString,
      resolve: ({ firstName, lastName }) =>
        [firstName, lastName].filter(Boolean).join(' '),
    },
  };

  if (meScope) {
    userFields.taskList = {
      type: new GraphQLNonNull(
        new GraphQLList(new GraphQLNonNull(Task)),
      ),
      resolve: (source, args, { loaders, currentUser }) => {
        return loaders.tasksForUsers.load(currentUser.id);
      },
    };
  }

  return userFields;
};
const User = new GraphQLObjectType({
  name: 'User',
  fields: () => fieldsWrapper({ meScope: false }),
});

export const Me = new GraphQLObjectType({
  name: 'Me',
  fields: () => fieldsWrapper({ meScope: true }),
});

export default User;
```

The loaders.tasksForUsers function does not exist yet.

This way, the module has two exports. The default is the generic User type that can be used anywhere, and the other is a named export (Me) to be used under the me field scope.

Here's how to use the new me type.

**Listing 8.31  Changes in api/src/schema/queries.js**

```
// ·--·-·
import { Me } from './types/user';

const QueryType = new GraphQLObjectType({
  name: 'Query',
  fields: () => ({
    // ·--·-·
    me: {
      type: Me,
      resolve: async (source, args, { currentUser }) => {
```

Replaces the default User import line

```
          return currentUser;
        },
      },
    }),
});
```

Let's define the `loaders.tasksForUsers` function and its batch-loading `pgApi` function.

**Listing 8.32   Changes in api/src/server.js**

```
const loaders = {
  // .-.-.

  tasksForUsers: new DataLoader((userIds) =>
    pgApi.tasksForUsers(userIds),
  ),
};
```

The implementation of `pgApi.tasksForUsers` is similar to the other batch-loading function we wrote earlier. It will use the `sqls.tasksForUsers` statement and map the input array of IDs into an array of lists. We're only going to use this function with the current user ID value, but keeping all database fetching logic within resolvers the same is a good practice.

**Listing 8.33   Changes in api/src/db/pg-api.js**

```
const pgApiWrapper = async () => {
  // .-.-.

  return {
    // .-.-.

    tasksForUsers: async (userIds) => {
      const pgResp = await pgQuery(sqls.tasksForUsers, {
        $1: userIds,
      });
      return userIds.map((userId) =>
        pgResp.rows.filter((row) => userId === row.userId),
      );
    },

    // .-.-.
  };
};
```

You can now test that the `taskList` field is available under the `me` field (don't forget to include a valid `authToken` in the request headers). See figure 8.8.

---

**Listing 8.34  Query to test `taskList` under `me`**

```
{
  me {
    id
    username
    taskList {
      content
    }
  }
}
```

```
1 ▾ {
2 ▾   me {
3       id
4       username
5       taskList {
6         content
7       }
8     }
9   }

    QUERY VARIABLES    REQUEST HEADERS

1   {
2     "Authorization": "Bearer 1b0d10b5efde43
3   }
```

```
▾ {
▾   "data": {
▾     "me": {
        "id": "1",
        "username": "test",
▾       "taskList": [
          {
            "content": "Make an image in HTML change based on the theme color
mode (dark or light)"
          },
          {
            "content": "Get rid of only the unstaged changes since the last git
commit"
          },
          {
            "content": "The syntax for a switch statement (AKA case statement)
in JavaScript"
          },
          {
            "content": "Calculate the sum of numbers in a JavaScript array"
          },
          {
```

**Figure 8.8  The `taskList` field under the me field**

You can also make sure that the `taskList` field is not available under the `author` field using this query. See figure 8.9.

---

**Listing 8.35  Query to test `taskList` under `author`**

```
{
  taskMainList {
    content
    author {
      username
      taskList {        ◁——  The taskList field should not be available
        content               under the author field scope.
      }
    }
  }
}
```

---

**Current code**

Use `git checkout 8.4` to reset your local repo to the current progress in the code.

```
 1 ▾ {                                   ▾ {
 2 ▾   taskMainList {                    ▾   "errors": [
 3       content                         ▾     {
 4 ▾     author {                              "message": "Cannot query field \"taskList\" on type \"User\".",
 5         username                      ▾       "locations": [
 6         taskList {                              {
 7           content                               "line": 6,
 8         }                                       "column": 7
 9       }                                       }
10     }                                       ],
11   }                                         "stack": [
                                                "GraphQLError: Cannot query field \"taskList\" on type \"User\".",
```

**Figure 8.9**  The `taskList` field is not available under the `author` field scope.

## 8.5    *Mutations for the Task model*

Let's implement the `taskCreate` mutation field next. Here's the part of the SDL text for it.

---
**Listing 8.36    SDL text for Task mutations and their dependencies**

```
input TaskInput {
  content: String!
  tags: [String!]!
  isPrivate: Boolean!
}

type TaskPayload {
  errors: [UserError!]!
  task: Task
}

type Mutation {
  taskCreate(input: TaskInput!): TaskPayload!

  # ......
}
```

Let's create a new type under api/src/schema/types to host the `TaskInput` type. Here's the implementation I came up with.

---
**Listing 8.37    New file: api/src/schema/types/input-task.js**

```
import {
  GraphQLInputObjectType,
  GraphQLString,
  GraphQLNonNull,
  GraphQLBoolean,
  GraphQLList,
} from 'graphql';

const TaskInput = new GraphQLInputObjectType({
  name: 'TaskInput',
```

```
    fields: () => ({
      content: { type: new GraphQLNonNull(GraphQLString) },
      tags: {
        type: new GraphQLNonNull(
          new GraphQLList(new GraphQLNonNull(GraphQLString)),
        ),
      },
      isPrivate: { type: new GraphQLNonNull(GraphQLBoolean) },
    }),
});

export default TaskInput;
```

The TaskPayload type is a standard GraphQLObjectType that uses the Task type and the UserError type (which are both defined already).

---

**Listing 8.38  New file: api/src/schema/types/payload-task.js**

```
import {
  GraphQLObjectType,
  GraphQLNonNull,
  GraphQLList,
} from 'graphql';

import Task from './task';
import UserError from './user-error';

const TaskPayload = new GraphQLObjectType({
  name: 'TaskPayload',
  fields: () => ({
    errors: {
      type: new GraphQLNonNull(
        new GraphQLList(new GraphQLNonNull(UserError)),
      ),
    },
    task: { type: Task },
  }),
});

export default TaskPayload;
```

We can now import these two new types to create the taskCreate mutation field.

---

**Listing 8.39  Changes in api/src/schema/mutations.js**

```
// ...
import TaskPayload from './types/payload-task';
import TaskInput from './types/input-task';

const MutationType = new GraphQLObjectType({
  name: 'Mutation',
  fields: () => ({
    // ...
```

```
      taskCreate: {
        type: TaskPayload,
        args: {
          input: { type: new GraphQLNonNull(TaskInput) },
        },
        resolve: async (                              The mutators.taskCreate
          source,                                     method does not exist yet.
          { input },
          { mutators, currentUser },
        ) => {
          return mutators.taskCreate({ input, currentUser });
        },
      },
    },
  }),
});
```

For the `mutators.taskCreate` method, we have to first validate the input values. For example, let's make sure the `content` field has at least 15 characters. This would be similar to what we did for the `password` field in `mutators.userCreate`.

If input validation is successful, we can insert the new Task record and return it as part of the mutation payload. The SQL statement I prepared for this mutation is `sqls.taskInsert`.

**Listing 8.40   Changes in api/src/db/pg-api.js**

```
const pgApiWrapper = async () => {
  // .-.-.

  return {
    // .-.-.
    mutators: {
      // .-.-.
      taskCreate: async ({ input, currentUser }) => {
        const payload = { errors: [] };
        if (input.content.length < 15) {
          payload.errors.push({
            message: 'Text is too short',
          });
        }
        if (payload.errors.length === 0) {
          const pgResp = await pgQuery(sqls.taskInsert, {
            $1: currentUser.id,
            $2: input.content,
            $3: input.tags.join(','),       ◁── Remember that tags are stored as
            $4: input.isPrivate,                comma-separated values in the database,
          });                                    but the API consumer sends them as an
                                                 array of strings. That's why we needed a
          if (pgResp.rows[0]) {                  join call here.
            payload.task = pgResp.rows[0];
          }
        }
```

```
        return payload;
      },
    },
  };
};
```

Here's a request you can use in GraphiQL to test the `taskCreate` mutation.

**Listing 8.41  Request to test `taskCreate`**

```
mutation taskCreate {
  taskCreate (
    input: {
      content: "Use INSERT/SELECT together in PostgreSQL",
      tags: ["sql", "postgresql"]
      isPrivate: false,
    }
  ) {
    errors {
      message
    }
    task {
      id
      content
      tags
      author {
        id
      }
      createdAt
    }
  }
}
```

Test it with and without a valid `authToken` value in the request headers.

**Current code**
Use `git checkout 8.5` to reset your local repo to the current progress in the code.

**Challenge**
Give API consumers a way to update a Task record if they own it.

## 8.6  *Mutations for the Approach model*

Let's now implement the two mutations to add an Approach to a Task (`approachCreate`) and vote on existing Approaches (`approachVote`).

### 8.6.1   *The approachCreate mutation*

Here's the part of the SDL that we need to focus on to implement the `approachCreate` mutation.

#### Listing 8.42   SDL for `approachCreate` and its dependencies

```
input ApproachDetailInput {
  content: String!
  category: ApproachDetailCategory!
}

input ApproachInput {
  content: String!
  detailList: [ApproachDetailInput!]!
}

type ApproachPayload {
  errors: [UserError!]!
  approach: Approach
}

type Mutation {
  approachCreate(
    taskId: ID!
    input: ApproachInput!
  ): ApproachPayload!

  # .-.-.-
}
```

Let's start with the mutation field this time, which goes in api/src/schema/mutations.js. Let's plan on having a `mutators.approachCreate` function to invoke database statements.

Because an Approach record may have extra Detail elements, this mutation has to insert a record in PostgreSQL and then insert a document in MongoDB. The MongoDB operation depends on the PostgreSQL operation. The simplest way to implement that is to use a dependency injection and make the main `mutators.approachCreate` function do the work in both databases in order. One way to do that is to pass the context-level `mutators` object to the main mutator function as an argument.

#### Listing 8.43   Changes in api/src/schema/mutations.js

```
import {
  // .-.-.-
  GraphQLID,
} from 'graphql';
// .-.-.-
import ApproachPayload from './types/payload-approach';    ┤ We did not implement
import ApproachInput from './types/input-approach';        ┤ these types yet.
```

```
const MutationType = new GraphQLObjectType({
  name: 'Mutation',
  fields: () => ({
    // .-.-.

    approachCreate: {
      type: ApproachPayload,
      args: {
        taskId: { type: new GraphQLNonNull(GraphQLID) },
        input: { type: new GraphQLNonNull(ApproachInput) },
      },
      resolve: async (
        source,
        { taskId, input },
        { mutators, currentUser },
      ) => {
        return mutators.approachCreate({        ⟵──  The main mutator (not
          taskId,                                     implemented yet)
          input,
          currentUser,
          mutators,       ⟵──┐  Note that the mutators
        });                   │  object is passed here.
      },
    },
  }),
});
```

This way, the `mutators.approachCreate` function can start with the PostgreSQL insert
and then invoke a different mutator function to do the insert in MongoDB. Alterna-
tively, we could invoke the two database operations with two different functions within
the `resolve` function, but I think having one mutator function responsible for the
complete Approach insert operation is cleaner.

> **TIP** Instead of passing `mutators` as an argument, we could rely on the fact
> that `mutators` is the caller of `approachCreate`, make `approachCreate` a regu-
> lar (not arrow) function, and then access `mutators` in it using the `this` key-
> word. I think the argument approach is more readable.

Let's create the payload and input types this mutation uses. We have `ApproachPayload`,
which is a simple instance of `GraphQLObjectType`.

**Listing 8.44  New file: api/src/schema/types/payload-approach.js**

```
import {
  GraphQLList,
  GraphQLNonNull,
  GraphQLObjectType,
} from 'graphql';

import Approach from './approach';
import UserError from './user-error';
```

```
const ApproachPayload = new GraphQLObjectType({
  name: 'ApproachPayload',
  fields: () => ({
    errors: {
      type: new GraphQLNonNull(
        new GraphQLList(new GraphQLNonNull(UserError)),
      ),
    },
    approach: { type: Approach },
  }),
});

export default ApproachPayload;
```

The ApproachDetailInput and ApproachInput types are both instances of the Graph-QLInputObjectType.

**Listing 8.45   New file: api/src/schema/types/input-approach-detail.js**

```
import {
  GraphQLInputObjectType,
  GraphQLString,
  GraphQLNonNull,
} from 'graphql';

import ApproachDetailCategory from './approach-detail-category';

const ApproachDetailInput = new GraphQLInputObjectType({
  name: 'ApproachDetailInput',
  fields: () => ({
    content: { type: new GraphQLNonNull(GraphQLString) },
    category: {
      type: new GraphQLNonNull(ApproachDetailCategory),
    },
  }),
});

export default ApproachDetailInput;
```

**Listing 8.46   New file: api/src/schema/types/input-approach.js**

```
import {
  GraphQLInputObjectType,
  GraphQLString,
  GraphQLNonNull,
  GraphQLList,
} from 'graphql';

import ApproachDetailInput from './input-approach-detail';

const ApproachInput = new GraphQLInputObjectType({
  name: 'ApproachInput',
  fields: () => ({
```

```
    content: { type: new GraphQLNonNull(GraphQLString) },
    detailList: {
      type: new GraphQLNonNull(
        new GraphQLList(new GraphQLNonNull(ApproachDetailInput)),
      ),
    },
  }),
});

export default ApproachInput;
```

To implement `mutators.approachCreate`, we can use the `sqls.approachInsert` statement to insert the main Approach record into PostgreSQL. If that is successful, we pass the ID of the newly created Approach record to a MongoDB `mutators` method. Furthermore, we need to increment the `approach_count` column in the `azdev.tasks` table. I prepared the statement `sqls.approachCountIncrement` to do that.

---

**Listing 8.47  Changes in api/src/db/pg-api.js**

```
const pgApiWrapper = async () => {
  // .-.-.

  return {
    // .-.-.

    mutators: {
      // .-.-.

      approachCreate: async ({
        taskId,
        input,
        currentUser,                                          Invokes the PostgreSQL
        mutators,                                             operation to create the
      }) => {                                                 Approach record
        const payload = { errors: [] };
          if (payload.errors.length === 0) {
            const pgResp = await pgQuery(sqls.approachInsert, {   ◁
              $1: currentUser.id,
              $2: input.content,
              $3: taskId,
            });
          if (pgResp.rows[0]) {                               The Approach record is
            payload.approach = pgResp.rows[0];                created. Increment the
            await pgQuery(sqls.approachCountIncrement, {  ◁── Task's approachCount.
              $1: taskId,
            });
            await mutators.approachDetailCreate(    ◁──  Continue to add its
              payload.approach.id,                         details in MongoDB.
              input.detailList,
            );
          }
        }
```

```
        return payload;
      },
    },
  };
};
```

Remember how, when we implemented the `detailList` field under the `approaches` field, we had to convert the list from an object (as stored in MongoDB) to an array (as defined for the `detailList`)? We'll need to do the exact inverse conversion for the `approachDetailCreate` method. We need to convert this format (as we designed it for the `ApproachDetailInput` type):

```
[
  {
    content: explanationsValue1,
    category: "EXPLANATION"
  },
  {
    content: notesValue1,
    category: "NOTE"
  },
  {
    content: warningsValue1,
    category: "WARNING"
  },
  ·—·—·
]
```

Here is the format we will convert it into, which is expected by the `approachDetails` MongoDB collection:

```
{
  explanations: [explanationsValue1, ·—·—·],
  notes: [notesValue1, ·—·—·],
  warnings: [warningsValue1, ·—·—·],
}
```

A simple loop can do the trick. Here's what I came up with for this conversion and for inserting the MongoDB record.

**Listing 8.48    Changes in api/src/db/mongo-api.js**

```
const mongoApiWrapper = async () => {
  // ·—·—·

  return {
    // ·—·—·

    mutators: {
      approachDetailCreate: async (approachId, detailsInput) => {
```

```
      const details = {};
      detailsInput.forEach(({ content, category }) => {
        details[category] = details[category] || [];
        details[category].push(content);
      });
      return mdb.collection('approachDetails').insertOne({
        pgId: approachId,
        ...details,
      });
    },
  },
};
};
```

However, while this is the right direction for what we have to do, it will not work. There is a problem with this code. Can you spot it?

The forEach loop in listing 8.48 is optimized to use the category VALUES as keys for the new object. However, the values stored in the database are lowercase plurals (that is, notes), while the values exposed to the consumers (and used in inputs) are uppercase singulars (that is, NOTE). Instead of doing that conversion in the code, GraphQL's ENUM type offers a way to change the values of items to match what's stored in the database and still expose a different value to API consumers. Here's how to do that.

**Listing 8.49  Changes in api/src/schema/types/approach-detail-category.js**

```
const ApproachDetailCategory = new GraphQLEnumType({
  name: 'ApproachDetailCategory',
  values: {
    NOTE: { value: 'notes' },
    EXPLANATION: { value: 'explanations' },
    WARNING: { value: 'warnings' },
  },
});
```

This way, the consumer sees the uppercase version but GraphQL will convert that to the lowercase version when it communicates with the database. However, we now need to change the first conversion we made to work with this ENUM type change.

**Listing 8.50  Changes in api/src/db/mongo-api.js**

```
const mongoApiWrapper = async () => {
  // .-.-.

  return {
    detailLists: async (approachIds) => {
      // .-.-.
      return approachIds.map((approachId) => {
        // .-.-.
```

```
      if (explanations) {
        approachDetails.push(
          ...explanations.map((explanationText) => ({
            content: explanationText,
            category: 'explanations',
          }))
        );
      }
      if (notes) {
        approachDetails.push(
          ...notes.map((noteText) => ({
            content: noteText,
            category: 'notes',
          }))
        );
      }
      if (warnings) {
        approachDetails.push(
          ...warnings.map((warningText) => ({
            content: warningText,
            category: 'warnings',
          }))
        );
      }
      return approachDetails;
    });
  },

  // ·-·-·

};
};
```

That's it! You can test the `approachCreate` mutation with the following request.

**Listing 8.51    Request to test `approachCreate`**

```
mutation approachCreate {
  approachCreate(
    taskId: 42 # Get this value from a taskCreate mutation call
    input: {
      content: "INSERT INTO tableName ·-·-·] ) ] SELECT-STATEMENT",
      detailList: [
        {
          content: "You can still use a RETURNING clause after that",
          category: NOTE,
        },
        {
          content: "The INSERT statement only works if the SELECT statement
          ➡ does",
          category: EXPLANATION,
        },
      ],
    }
  ) {
```

```
    errors {
      message
    }
    approach {
      id
      content
      voteCount
      author {
        username
      }
      detailList {
        content
        category
      }
    }
  }
}
```

**TIP** Error handling becomes more challenging when using different data sources for entities that are related. For example, think of what needs to be done if an error occurs in MongoDB while creating an Approach. What should happen to the Approach record in PostgreSQL?

One way to handle cross-database-related operations is to use database transactions, which allow us to group multiple operations and treat them as one unit of work that can either happen in full or not happen at all. In PostgreSQL, a transaction is set up by surrounding the SQL commands of the transaction with BEGIN and COMMIT commands; and a transaction can be cancelled using the ROLLBACK command. Combining that with a try/catch statement in JavaScript offers a way to ensure that cross-database-related work is either complete or should be reported back to the consumer as an error.

**Current code**
Use git checkout 8.6 to reset your local repo to the current progress in the code.

**Challenge**
Give API consumers a way to add more details to existing Approach records.

**TIP** Instead of using a separate SQL statement to increment the approach_count column after an Approach object is inserted, we can use the power of PostgreSQL triggers to do that in the database.

### 8.6.2    *The approachVote mutation*

We planned to give AZdev API consumers a way to vote on Approach records. They can vote either up or down on any Approach.

Here's the part of the SDL text that we need to focus on for the approachVote mutation.

**Listing 8.52    SDL for approachVote and its dependencies**

```
input ApproachVoteInput {
  """true for up-vote and false for down-vote"""
  up: Boolean!
}

type Mutation {
  approachVote(
    approachId: ID!
    input: ApproachVoteInput!
  ): ApproachPayload!

  # .-.--
}
```

At this point, I would be seriously disappointed if you don't try to implement this mutation on your own. To leave you no excuse for not trying, I've prepared the sqls.approachVote statement that you can use.

**Listing 8.53    approachVote SQL statement in api/src/db/sqls.js**

```
// $1: approachId
// $2: voteIncrement
approachVote: `
  UPDATE azdev.approaches
  SET vote_count = vote_count + $2
  WHERE id = $1
  RETURNING id, content, ·-··;
`,
```

The sqls.approachVote statement expects input in this order:

1    The ID of the Approach on which the user is voting
2    The voteIncrement value, which should be either 1 or -1, depending on the type of vote (1 for up, -1 for down)

Here's a request you can use in GraphiQL to test your implementation.

**Listing 8.54    Request to test approachVote**

```
mutation approachVote {
  approachVote(
    approachId: 42 # Get this value from approachCreate
```

```
    input: { up: false }
  ) {
    errors {
      message
    }
    approach {
      content
      voteCount
    }
  }
}
```

Here are the changes I made to implement the `approachVote` mutation.

---

**Listing 8.55   New file: api/src/schema/types/input-approach-vote.js**

```
import {
  GraphQLInputObjectType,
  GraphQLBoolean,
  GraphQLNonNull,
} from 'graphql';

const ApproachVoteInputType = new GraphQLInputObjectType({
  name: 'ApproachVoteInput',
  description: "true for up-vote and false for down-vote",
  fields: () => ({
    up: { type: new GraphQLNonNull(GraphQLBoolean) },
  }),
});

export default ApproachVoteInputType;
```

---

**Listing 8.56   Changes in api/src/schema/mutations.js**

```
// .-.-.-.
import ApproachVoteInput from './types/input-approach-vote';

const MutationType = new GraphQLObjectType({
  name: 'Mutation',
  fields: () => ({
    // .-.-.-.
    approachVote: {
      type: ApproachPayload,
      args: {
        approachId: { type: new GraphQLNonNull(GraphQLID) },
        input: { type: new GraphQLNonNull(ApproachVoteInput) },
      },
      resolve: async (
        source,
        { approachId, input },
        { mutators },
      ) => {
        return mutators.approachVote({ approachId, input });
```

```
        },
      },
    }),
  });
```

**Listing 8.57    Changes in api/src/db/pg-api.js; new `mutators` function**

```
const pgApiWrapper = async () => {
  // .-.-.

  return {
    // .-.-.
    mutators: {
      // .-.-.
      approachVote: async ({ approachId, input }) => {
        const payload = { errors: [] };
        const pgResp = await pgQuery(sqls.approachVote, {
          $1: approachId,
          $2: input.up ? 1 : -1,
        });

        if (pgResp.rows[0]) {
          payload.approach = pgResp.rows[0];
        }

        return payload;
      },
    },
  };
};
```

Go ahead and test the mutation request in listing 8.54 (which should down-vote an Approach object).

> **NOTE**    I did not check for the existence of a valid user session for this muta-
> tion. That means guest users can vote as well. I left out that part so we have an
> example mutation that we can test without request headers.

**Current code**
Use `git checkout 8.7` to reset your local repo to the current progress in the code.

## 8.7    *The userDelete mutation*

The last remaining mutation we planned for the AZdev API is to give users a way to
delete their accounts. Here's the SDL part we prepared.

---
**Listing 8.58   SDL text for deleting a user**

```
type UserDeletePayload {
  errors: [UserError!]!
  deletedUserId: ID
}

type Mutation {
  userDelete: UserDeletePayload!

  #  . - . - .
}
```

Try implementing this on your own first. I've prepared the sqls.userDelete statement. UserDeletePayload is a simple instance of GraphQLObjectType.

---
**Listing 8.59   New file: api/src/schema/types/payload-user-delete.js**

```
import {
  GraphQLList,
  GraphQLNonNull,
  GraphQLObjectType,
  GraphQLID,
} from 'graphql';

import UserError from './user-error';

const UserDeletePayload = new GraphQLObjectType({
  name: 'UserDeletePayload',
  fields: () => ({
    errors: {
      type: new GraphQLNonNull(
        new GraphQLList(new GraphQLNonNull(UserError)),
      ),
    },
    deletedUserId: { type: GraphQLID },
  }),
});

export default UserDeletePayload;
```

Let's implement the mutator function next. It will receive the currentUser object in
its argument, invoke the sqls.userDelete statement, and then return the deleted-
UserId value as part of its payload.

---
**Listing 8.60   Changes in api/src/db/pg-api.js**

```
const pgApiWrapper = async () => {
  // . - . - .

  return {
    // . - . - .

    mutators: {
```

```
      // .-.-.

      userDelete: async ({ currentUser }) => {
        const payload = { errors: [] };
        try {
          await pgQuery(sqls.userDelete, {
            $1: currentUser.id,
          });
          payload.deletedUserId = currentUser.id;
        } catch (err) {
          payload.errors.push({
            message: 'We were not able to delete this account',
          });
        }

        return payload;
      },
    },
  };
};
```

Finally, we use this mutator function in the resolve function of the new mutation field.

---
**Listing 8.61    Changes in api/src/schema/mutations.js**

```
// .-.-.
import UserDeletePayload from './types/payload-user-delete';

const MutationType = new GraphQLObjectType({
  name: 'Mutation',
  fields: () => ({
    // .-.-.

    userDelete: {
      type: UserDeletePayload,
      resolve: async (source, args, { mutators, currentUser }) => {
        return mutators.userDelete({ currentUser });
      },
    },
  }),
});
```

That's it. To test this mutation, create a new user account using the userCreate mutation example in listing 8.13, use that account's authToken value in the request headers editor, and send the following mutation request.

---
**Listing 8.62    Example mutation request to test userDelete**

```
mutation userDelete {
  userDelete {
    errors {
```

```
      message
    }
    deletedUserId
  }
}
```

Note that this mutation will work only if the user does not own any Task or Approach records. Otherwise, the foreign key constraints in these relations will block the delete operation. As an example for your reference, I used a `try/catch` statement on this operation to catch any database errors and expose the problem with a generic user error message. Test that as well.

> **TIP**  If you want to enable deleting a User record even if the user owns other records in the database, PostgreSQL supports an `ON DELETE` option on foreign key constraints that automatically deletes (or updates) all records referenced by a record to be deleted. This is a much better approach than executing many `DELETE` SQL statements.

### Current code
Use `git checkout 8.8` to reset your local repo to the current progress in the code.

### Challenge
Give API consumers a way to delete their own Task records.

With that, this GraphQL schema is in good executable shape to offer an API that can be used to build a working UI product, and that's exactly what we will be doing in part 3 of this book.

> **NOTE**  To keep things simple, short, and easy to follow in all the implementations so far, I have skipped over many changes that I wanted to make. For example, all these mutations require a lot more input validation. Furthermore, the code could use many optimizations and abstractions and, in some cases, much-needed guards. For example, the `approachVote` mutation allows anyone to vote as many times as they want and even vote on private needs. That should not happen. Check out the code repository at az.dev/contribute to see the history of the changes beyond what is presented in this book. Feel free to ask any questions about the final code at the jsComplete help channel at jscomplete.com/help.

**The subscription operations**

GraphQL.js has some support for creating subscriptions, but it is still evolving. Also, to use subscriptions, a transport server that supports web sockets must be used. The simple express.js server setup that we have used so far does not support that. GraphiQL also does not support testing subscriptions yet (to be more accurate, you can do some testing with GraphiQL, but that setup is a bit complicated).

The good news is that tools are available to create, test, and use subscriptions without complicated setups. Apollo server/client is the most popular. There is also the `graphql-yoga` package, which contains some great abstractions to help implement subscriptions.

While going the complicated route would be a good educational example, the practical solution here is to use one of the tools that has well-tested support for subscriptions. Since the last chapter of this book is focused on the Apollo ecosystem, we will implement and use the subscription operations there.

## *Summary*

- To host mutations, a GraphQL schema must define a root mutation type.
- To organize database operations for mutations, you can group them on a single object that you expose as part of the global context for resolvers.
- User-friendly error messages can and should be included as part of any mutation response.
- The PostgreSQL RETURNING clause can be used to do a WRITE operation followed by a READ operation in a single SQL statement. The INSERT/SELECT combination enables us to make a WRITE operation depend on a READ operation in a single SQL statement.
- A hashed token value can be used as a temporary password for mutation operations and query operations that should behave differently for authenticated users.
- Some mutation operations depend on each other. Dependency injection can be used in these cases.

# Part 3

# Using GraphQL APIs

In part 2 of the book, we built a data API and implemented various GraphQL types to support many query and mutation operations. In part 3, we'll explore how to use these operations in a frontend application. We'll do that with and without a dedicated GraphQL client library.

In chapter 9, we'll explore how to use a GraphQL API with direct Ajax requests. You'll learn about UI components and their data requirements, you'll see examples of using tokens in GraphQL requests to implement authentication and authorization, and you'll learn about the value of GraphQL fragments when coupled with UI components.

Chapter 10 is a long but fun ride to explore the power of the most popular GraphQL client library: Apollo Client. You'll learn how to use it both in plain JavaScript and in React. You'll learn about its core concepts, like links, cache, hook functions, and local app state, as well as how to implement and use GraphQL subscriptions.

# Using GraphQL APIs
## without a client library

*9*

**This chapter covers**

- Analyzing UI components to determine their GraphQL data requirements
- Performing Ajax POST requests for GraphQL operations
- Using tokens in request headers to identify the API consumer
- Using fragments to make every UI component responsible for its own data requirements
- Using GraphQL features to simplify and generalize the UI code

In the last chapter, we finished the implementation of the AZdev GraphQL API service. It's now time to explore how to use that API practically in a frontend web application.

When it comes to using GraphQL in web applications, you can use it either directly with a simple Ajax library (like `axios` or `fetch`) or with a fully featured

GraphQL client (like Relay or Apollo) to manage all GraphQL communications. We'll explore using a GraphQL API with client libraries in the next chapter. In this chapter, we will start by exploring how to use the AZdev GraphQL API without a client library. However, to make this example as close as possible to a real-life project, we're going to use a UI library to manage what happens in the browser.

> **TIP**  Remember to check out az.dev/gia-updates to see any API updates you might need for this chapter.

## 9.1    *Using a web UI library*

I contemplated demonstrating how to use GraphQL without using a UI library (like React or Angular). While that would be a good exercise to learn the DOM API, it's really not practical. For many reasons (beyond the scope of this book), no one builds frontend applications today without a UI library. It's simply messy. UI libraries decrease the complexities of dealing with the DOM API and offer a declarative alternative to it. That is especially important if the web UI gets frequent UI updates.

The most popular UI libraries today are Vue and React. I'll use React in this book because it's closer to GraphQL's ecosystem and design principles. Besides the fact that both React and GraphQL originated at Facebook, React offers a language to declaratively describe user interfaces (web or otherwise), and GraphQL offers a language to declaratively describe data requirements. React offers composability with its components, and GraphQL offers composability with its fragments. These similarities allow for a great match between React and GraphQL.

In addition, the most popular clients for GraphQL are designed for React first. You can certainly use some clients with other UI libraries, but their built-in support for React is first class. You can also use GraphQL in iOS and Android mobile applications with React Native.

If you don't know React at all, it will not be a problem in this chapter. I'll provide all the React-related code for the project. I also intentionally kept everything as simple as possible without making the example too trivial. I want you to focus on how GraphQL fits in a frontend application. Using a GraphQL API without a client in other UI libraries is very similar. You just need to find the points to hook GraphQL-related actions.

If you want to brush up on React before proceeding with this chapter, I put all the basics in one article that does not assume you know anything about React. It's available at jscomplete.com/learn-react.

> **NOTE**  I am also picking React simply because I like it a lot more than the other options (and I have tried most of them). If you're interested in my reasons for preferring React, you can read my "Why React" article at jscomplete.com/why-react.

## 9.2 Running the web server

If you've been following the code we wrote in part 2 of the book, you should have a Node web server running on port 4321 (by default) and serving a GraphQL API service on its root endpoint.

So far, we've been modifying files under the api directory in the book's Git repository (available at az.dev/gia-repo). We'll now start modifying the files under the web directory structure (figure 9.1).

> **NOTE** You need to have PostgreSQL and MongoDB both started and ready with the AZdev schema and have the API server running as well. See the instructions in the repo's README file if you skipped over part 2 of the book.

**Figure 9.1   The api and web top-level directories**

### Current code

Use `git checkout 9.0` to reset your local repo to the current progress in the code. If you need to stash any local changes, use `git add . && git stash`. Remember to run `npm install` to install any missing dependencies.

With the database and API servers running, use the following command to run the web server.

**Listing 9.1   Command: starting the web-server process**

```
$ npm run web-server
```

This command will run a process that bundles all code and serves it on http://localhost:1234. If everything works okay, you should be able to access the development web server main page. It should look as shown in figure 9.2.

Take a look around the web directory and get familiar with its structure (figure 9.3). This is a pure React project that mounts a simple single-page app. There are no helper libraries like Redux or React Router. All React components are in web/src/components. The top-level component is `Root`, which is defined in web/src/components/Root.js. The components that can show up on their own in this example are exported in

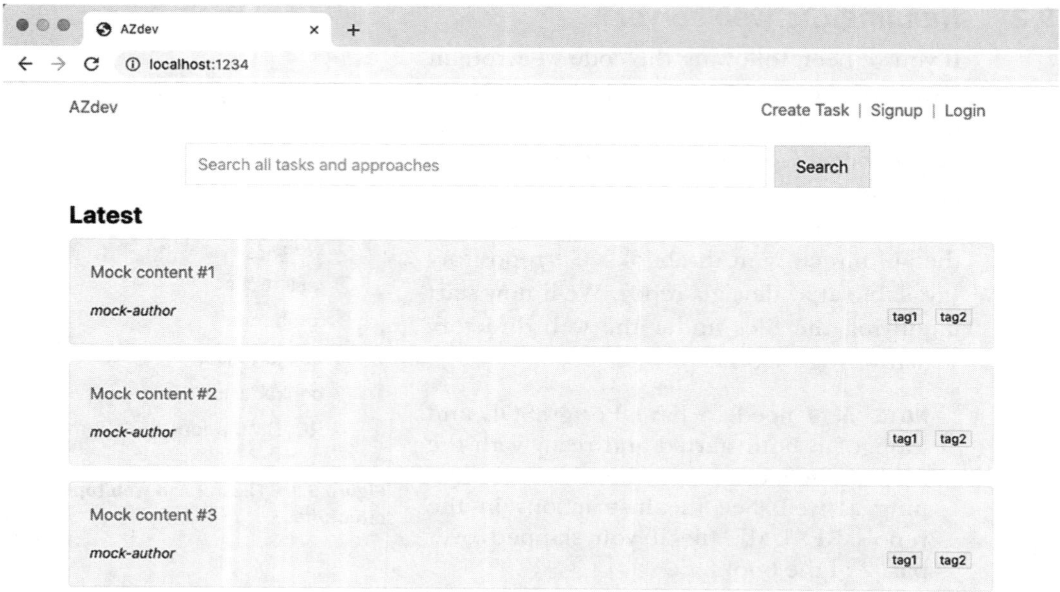

**Figure 9.2   Project's main page with mock data**

web/src/components/index.js. You can think of these components as the virtual pages of the app.

> **WARNING** The starting point for this chapter's code will have a lot of ESLint errors because I left many unused variables in the template, and ESLint is configured to complain about that. We'll use these variables when we need them. There should be no ESLint errors when we are finished with this chapter.

A React component is a basic JavaScript function that can optionally take arguments (known as *props* in React). It can have custom logic (like fetching data from an API), and it always returns a virtual DOM node. React takes care of mounting that virtual node in the right place and updates it (efficiently) when it needs to be updated. You can assume that the declarative state of that component will always be reflected in the browser. You just need to invoke JavaScript functions (which I have documented for you in the code) to get the DOM updated.

The state of this project's UI is managed with a simple global context object. In React, a context object is

**Figure 9.3   The web/src directory**

global to the app that defines it, and every component in the tree can read it and modify it. The context object is defined in web/src/store.js. The two main things that are managed in the global context are the current component information (what component to render and what props to pass to it) and the current information of the logged-in user (if any). A few functions are defined on the context object and imported into the components that need them. For example, the useLocalAppState function can be used to read values from the app state, and the setLocalAppState function can be used to update the app state. These functions are defined on the context object because they need to access and modify the global app state.

---

### Module bundlers

All JavaScript code in this project gets bundled using Parcel. Parcel is a simple module bundler that can also compile special things like React's JSX extension, modern JavaScript features, and even TypeScript. We're using Parcel's default configuration, which has hot module reloading configured out of the box. This will auto-refresh your browser session when you make changes to the code (and save them). Try that by changing the content of the mockTasks array in web/src/components/Home.js, and note that the browser auto-refreshes.

A couple of other popular module bundlers are Webpack and Rollup. Webpack, being the first, is more widely used. I've picked Parcel for this project for its simplicity and excellent default configurations. The official AZdev open source repository (az.dev/contribute) uses Webpack.

---

We will be modifying almost every component file (under web/src/components) and the context object (in web/src/store.js), but you don't need to create any new files in the project to follow this chapter. All the components are ready except where they require data reads and writes. You also don't need to modify any of the components' output (their returned JSX nodes). All the HTML work has been done, but it's rendered with empty or mock data. We will modify the places in the code where these data variables are defined. In places where we need to make modifications, I have added notes in code comments (labeled "GIA NOTES"; see figure 9.4).

You also don't need to modify any styling code or add any CSS classes to the HTML managed by React. The CSS is all wired and ready (in web/src/index.css), but it's certainly not the best. I only made a few general style tweaks to make things look decent. The styles were based on the Tailwind CSS framework, but I extracted them out and made the project use them directly for simplicity.

> **TIP** If you have any questions about the code as it is now or the new code we will be writing, feel free to create a GitHub issue on the book's repository. You can also ask your questions in the official jsComplete help channel at jscomplete.com/help.

```
 3    import { useStore } from '../store';
 4    import Search from './Search';
 5    import TaskSummary from './TaskSummary';
 6
 7    /** GIA NOTES
 8     * Define GraphQL operations here...
 9     */
10
11  > const mockTasks = [ …
30    ];
31
32    export default function Home() {
33      const { request } = useStore();
34      const [taskList, setTaskList] = useState(null);
35
36      useEffect(() => {
37        /** GIA NOTES
38         *
39         *  1) Invoke the query to get list of latest Tasks
40         *     (You can't use `await` here but `promise.then
41         *
42         *  2) Change the setTaskList call below to use the
43         *
44         */
45
46        setTaskList(mockTasks); // TODO: Replace mockTasks w
47      }, [request]);
48
```

**Figure 9.4   GIA
book notes in code**

## 9.3   *Making Ajax requests*

To make a GraphQL request from a web application, we need to invoke an Ajax HTTP call. Remember that we made our GraphQL service available through HTTP POST requests.

Up to this point, we've been sending these POST requests through the GraphiQL editor. Under the hood, the GraphiQL editor issues Ajax calls in the background when you execute any document there.

Modern browsers have native APIs to make Ajax requests. For example, browsers today come with a built-in fetch method that can be used to invoke any type of HTTP Ajax requests. However, if you need to support older browsers, you cannot use fetch directly, but you can use a library that wraps the native API or polyfills it if it doesn't exist. One common option is cross-fetch, as it will also allow you to do data fetching from Node.js; that's something you'll need if you plan to do any server-side rendering of your web applications. We'll use it; it's already part of this project's dependencies.

Let's do a test GraphQL request. Remember the currentTime field we started with back in chapter 5? Let's make the app temporarily console.log it when it loads.

Make the following temporary code changes to the `Home` component (in web/src/ components/Home.js).

Listing 9.2 Temporary changes in web/src/components/Home.js

```
export default function Home() {
  // .-.-.

  useEffect(() => {
    request('{ currentTime }').then(({ data }) => {
      console.log(`Server time is: ${data.currentTime}`);
    });

    // .-.-.
  }, [request]);

  return (
    // .-.-.
  );
}
```

This code assumes that the already defined `request` function receives a GraphQL request text (like a query or mutation) and returns the GraphQL response object (which has `data` and `errors` attributes).

**TIP** The `useEffect` function is called a *hook function,* and it runs every time the host component is rendered. This makes the `console.log` line appear in the browser's console when the browser renders the output of the `Home` component. For more details on how React hooks work, check out jscomplete .com/react-hooks.

The `request` function's skeleton is already defined in web/src/store.js. The function has to submit the Ajax `POST` request to the GraphQL service endpoint and return the response object. It needs to include `requestText` (its first argument) and any variables as well (second argument). Here's a basic implementation.

Listing 9.3 Changes in web/src/store.js

```
export const useStoreObject = () => {
  // .-.-.

  const request = async (requestText, { variables } = {}) => {
    const gsResp = await fetch(config.GRAPHQL_SERVER_URL, {
      method: 'post',
      headers: { 'Content-Type': 'application/json' },
      body: JSON.stringify({ query: requestText, variables }),
    }).then((response) => response.json());
```

```
    return gsResp;
  };

  // ·-·-·.
};
```

If you're using the default port for the GraphQL API service, you don't need to do anything. If you used a different port, then you have to specify your new GRAPHQL_SERVER_URL in the web/src/config.js file.

The code in listing 9.3 sends an Ajax POST request to the GraphQL service endpoint. The requestText argument, which is passed as { currentTime } from the Home component (listing 9.2), is sent as the query variable, which is the default variable that represents a GraphQL request text in the server HTTP handler (graphqlHTTP) that we defined in chapter 5.

> **TIP** This implementation of the request function is a simple happy path that expects a successful response. A more practical implementation will include error handling. I'll leave the simple call here, as we're going to replace this function in the next chapter.

You should now see the server time log message in your browser console (figure 9.5).

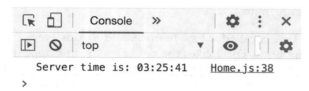

**Figure 9.5  The server time log message**

Working with all GraphQL requests is really similar to this simple request. You make an Ajax request call, supplying a query or mutation operation text (and you include the variables that the operation uses). Then you do something with the resolved data response.

There are really no special tricks to using GraphQL directly without a client. You just need to make Ajax calls and handle their responses! However, there are some special tricks to organize your GraphQL client code in a readable and maintainable way. We'll cover a few of them in this chapter.

Now that we know things are working well, remove the test request code we added in the Home component (in the useEffect function). Instead, let's figure out the official data request (to fetch a list of the latest Task records) that we have to do in that useEffect function.

## 9.4    *Performing GraphQL query requests*

The Home component is already wired to display a list of mock Task records in the UI. We now need to issue a GraphQL query that will get information from the GraphQL service about actual Task records and use the response data to replace the mock object.

The GraphQL root field we designed for this page is taskMainList. You can look at the code in web/src/components/Home.js to see what subfields must be included in this taskMainList query. The structure of the data required for this view is the same as that for the mockTasks object.

**Listing 9.4  The mockTasks object**

```
{
  id: 1,
  content: 'Mock content #1',
  author: { username: 'mock-author' },
  tags: ['tag1', 'tag2'],
}
```

Relying on the structure of that object, here's the GraphQL query required by the HOME component.

**Listing 9.5  Query that matches the mockTasks object structure**

```
query taskMainList {
  taskMainList {
    id
    content
    author {
      username
    }
    tags
  }
}
```

This taskMainList query does not need GraphQL variables. We can use its text directly in the request function. However, it is a good practice to put the text of GraphQL operations next to the UI components that use them. Let's do that.

**Listing 9.6  Changes in web/src/components/Home.js**

```
const TASK_MAIN_LIST = `
  query taskMainList {
    taskMainList {
      id
      content
      author {
        username
      }
      tags
    }
  }
`;
// delete the mockTasks object...
```

```
export default function Home() {
  const { request } = useStore();
  const [ taskList, setTaskList ] = useState(null);

  useEffect(() => {
    request(TASK_MAIN_LIST).then(({ data }) => {
      setTaskList(data.taskMainList);
    });
  }, [request]);

  // -.-.-.
}
```

We first define the query operation text (which I named TASK_MAIN_LIST to match
what it returns). The all-uppercase naming convention is common but not required.

We then send that text to the GraphQL service (sometime in the life cycle of this
component). When a successful response is returned, it will have a data property,
which is an object that has a property for every root field in the query. We have only a
single root field in this query (taskMainList). When we have the response (in the
.then promise method), we make React aware of it (through the noted method).
React will automatically update the browser's DOM tree with the new data.

In your browser, you should see the sample data Task entries listed with their
author and tags information (figure 9.6).

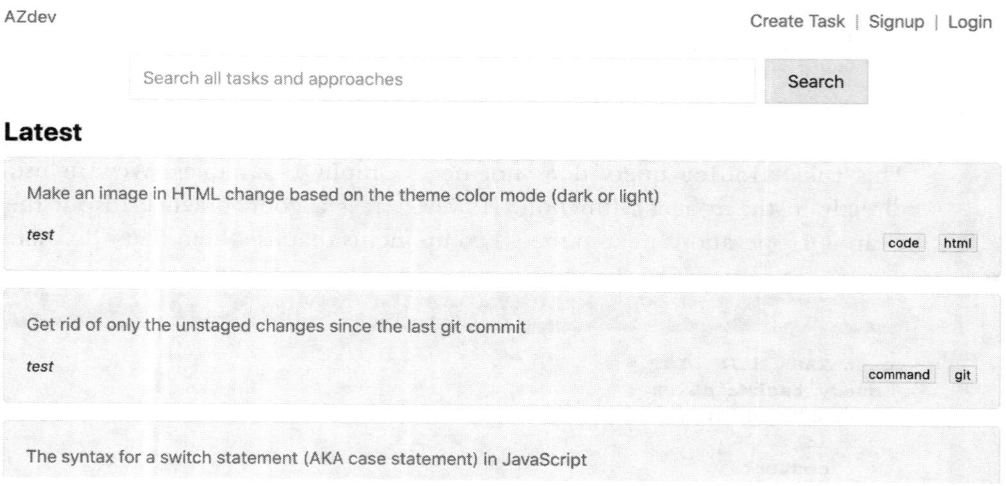

AZdev                                                    Create Task  |  Signup  |  Login

Search all tasks and approaches                                    Search

## Latest

Make an image in HTML change based on the theme color mode (dark or light)

*test*                                                              code    html

Get rid of only the unstaged changes since the last git commit

*test*                                                           command   git

The syntax for a switch statement (AKA case statement) in JavaScript

**Figure 9.6   The list of latest Task records on the home page**

## Current code
Use git checkout 9.1 to reset your local repo to the current progress in the code.

### 9.4.1 Using GraphQL fragments in UI components

The `mockTasks` object in the `Home` component helps us easily figure out what GraphQL fields are required for that component. But what if we did not have that object? Also, what if we did not have the UI component? Is it better to start with a UI component or with a GraphQL query text?

The concept that helps me wrap my thoughts around these questions is one that we briefly touched on in previous chapters, but it's now time to bring it to the fore-front. I am talking about how every UI component (view) has specific data require-ments and should be responsible for declaring those requirements. To figure out the data requirements of a view tree composed of multiple UI components, you put together the individual data requirements.

For example, the data from the `taskMainList` operation is actually used by two UI components: `Home` and `TaskSummary`. The view tree has only these two components, and each has its own data requirements. The `Home` component needs the `id` of a Task object. There is no mention of `content`, `author.username`, or `tags` in the `Home` com-ponent. These other fields come from the data requirements of the `TaskSummary` component, because that component is where they are used.

Take a look at the `TaskSummary` component (under web/src/components/ TaskSummary.js), and note the following (in bold).

**Listing 9.7 The `task.*` variables in the `TaskSummary` component**

```
export default function TaskSummary({ task, link = false }) {
  const { AppLink } = useStore();

  return (
    <div className="box box-primary">
      {link ? (
        <AppLink to="TaskPage" taskId={task.id}>
          {task.content}
        </AppLink>
      ) : (
        task.content
      )}
      <div className="box-footer">
        <div className="text-secondary">{task.author.username}</div>
        <div className="flex-end">
          {task.tags.map((tag) => (
            <span key={tag} className="box-label">
              {tag}
            </span>
          ))}
        </div>
      </div>
    </div>
  );
}
```

Do you see the direct mapping between what variables are used in this component (the bold parts) and what GraphQL fields were included in the TASK_MAIN_LIST query in listing 9.6? We don't have to rely on mock objects. We can use the component's code to directly come up with its GraphQL data requirements. In fact, instead of putting the entire taskMainList query text in the Home component, let's officially make every component declare its own data requirements. In most cases, one UI component does not care about the data requirements of its children, parents, or siblings.

This is where GraphQL fragments can play a role. We can make the TaskSummary component define a GraphQL fragment that declares that component's exact data requirements and then make the Home component use that fragment to compose the main GraphQL query that's needed to render the component (and its child component).

For example, we can define the following GraphQL fragment in the TaskSummary component.

---

**Listing 9.8    Changes in web/src/components/TaskSummary.js**

```
// ·-·-·

export const TASK_SUMMARY_FRAGMENT = `
  fragment TaskSummary on Task {
    content
    author {
      username
    }
    tags
  }
`;

export default function TaskSummary({ task, link = false }) {
  // ·-·-·
}
```

This fragment simply represents the data required to display a TaskSummary component instance.

Note that we exported this new constant so that other components can import and use it, which is what we now have to do in the Home component.

---

**Listing 9.9    Changes in web/src/components/Home.js**

```
// ·-·-·

import TaskSummary, { TASK_SUMMARY_FRAGMENT } from './TaskSummary';

const TASK_MAIN_LIST = `
  query taskMainList {
    taskMainList {
      id
```

```
        ...TaskSummary
    }
  }
  ${TASK_SUMMARY_FRAGMENT}
`;
// ......
```

Isn't this a beautiful abstraction?

Every component is responsible for its own part of a bigger data requirement. With this change, the `Home` component basically reaches out to its child (the `TaskSummary` component) and asks it, "What fields would you like me to fetch for you?"

Furthermore, with this structure, if the `TaskSummary` component is modified to require more (or fewer) fields from the API service, the `Home` component will not need any modifications.

This concept is often referred to as *colocating fragments* (or fields). Usually, the fields in a colocated fragment match the props of the colocated component. I think this is a good practice to follow, whether you use GraphQL directly (as in this example) or a GraphQL client, as we will see in the next chapter.

One trick to identify which UI components are candidates to define their own data fragments is to look at the components that are not rendered at the top level (directly by the `Root` component). For example, we cannot render a `TaskSummary` component on its own page. It's always rendered by other pages (like `Home`, `Search`, and so on). This is similar to how we cannot invoke a GraphQL fragment on its own.

What other components are not rendered on their own in this example? If these components depend on their props to render their content, chances are they should have their own data fragments.

> **TIP** A child component can define multiple fragments and can also compose the fragments using subfragments of its own children components.

> **Current code**
> Use `git checkout 9.2` to reset your local repo to the current progress in the code.

### 9.4.2 Including variables in requests

The home page has a list of the latest Task records. The user can click a Task record to see its Detail page. The navigation is already implemented, but the data requirement for the page is not. Currently, when you navigate to a Task record page, you see mocked data.

We can display this page with the partial data that we've already fetched for a Task record through the `taskMainList` request (and then fetch the rest of the required data, like the list of Approaches). A featured client for GraphQL will do that automatically. It will cache any data it fetches from the server, and it will make partial data available.

However, for our simplified example, let's just issue a full request for this page. The component for this page is TaskPage (under web/src/components/TaskPage.js).

To determine what GraphQL fields are required for this new view tree, we need to look at the TaskPage component and all its children. It has two children components: TaskSummary and Approach.

We've already implemented the fragment for TaskSummary, and we can use it as is. The data requirements for a child component do not change based on which parent component renders it.

To complete the data requirements for the TaskPage component, we first have to come up with the data requirements for the Approach component, which renders a single Approach record (with all of its detail records).

Look at web/src/components/Approach.js, and find all the variables it uses to come up with a GraphQL fragment that matches these used variables.

> **Listing 9.10   The `approach.voteCount` variables in the `Approach` component**

```
export default function Approach({ approach, isHighlighted }) {
  // ......

  const [ voteCount, setVoteCount ] = useState(approach.voteCount);

  // ......

  return (
    <div className={`box highlighted-${isHighlighted}`}>
      <div className="approach">
        <div className="vote">
          {renderVoteButton('UP')}
          {voteCount}
          {renderVoteButton('DOWN')}
        </div>
        <div className="main">
          <pre className="code">{approach.content}</pre>
          <div className="author">{approach.author.username}</div>
        </div>
      </div>
      <Errors errors={uiErrors} />
      {approach.detailList.map((detail, index) => (
        <div key={index} className="approach-detail">
          <div className="header">{detail.category}</div>
          <div>{detail.content}</div>
        </div>
      ))}
    </div>
  );
}
```

Here's the fragment I came up with for the Approach component.

**Listing 9.11   Changes in web/src/components/Approach.js**

```
// .-.-.

export const APPROACH_FRAGMENT = `
  fragment ApproachFragment on Approach {
    content
    voteCount
    author {
      username
    }
    detailList {
      content
      category
    }
  }
`;
// .-.-.
```

With fragments for both children components ready, we can now write the full data requirements for the TaskPage component. We can use the taskInfo root query field and include the approachList field in its sub-selection. This query will have to import and use the two fragments declared by the component's children.

**Listing 9.12   Changes in web/src/components/TaskPage.js**

```
// .-.-.

import Approach, { APPROACH_FRAGMENT } from './Approach';
import TaskSummary, { TASK_SUMMARY_FRAGMENT } from './TaskSummary';

const TASK_INFO = `
  query taskInfo($taskId: ID!) {
    taskInfo(id: $taskId) {
      id
      ...TaskSummary
      approachList {
        id
        ...ApproachFragment
      }
    }
  }
  ${TASK_SUMMARY_FRAGMENT}
  ${APPROACH_FRAGMENT}
`;
// .-.-.
```

This query requires the use of a GraphQL variable ($taskId). We can issue the data request where noted in the component's code and pass the taskId variable as part of the second argument to the request function.

**Listing 9.13    Changes in web/src/components/TaskPage.js**

```
// delete the mockTaskInfo object...

export default function TaskPage({ taskId }) {
  // .-.--.

  useEffect(() => {
    if (!taskInfo) {
      request(TASK_INFO, { variables: { taskId } }).then(
        ({ data }) => {
          setTaskInfo(data.taskInfo);
        },
      );
    }
  }, [taskId, taskInfo, request]);

  // .-.--.
}
```

That's it. When you navigate to a Task page now, all the data for the Task record, its list of Approach records, and the Detail list for each Approach should be fetched (with one GraphQL request) and displayed properly in the UI (figure 9.7).

So far, we've implemented read-only query operations. Let's now take a look at how to invoke mutation requests. Spoiler alert: it's not that different.

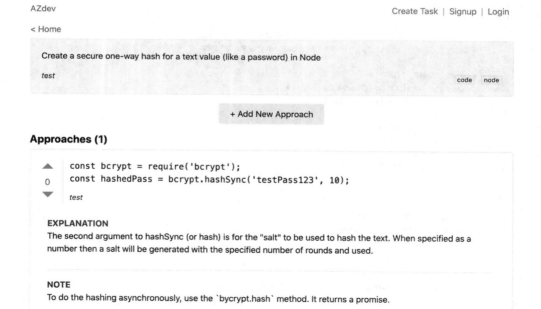

**Figure 9.7    The page for a full Task record**

> **Current code**
> Use `git checkout 9.3` to reset your local repo to the current progress in the code.

## 9.5 Performing GraphQL mutation requests

A GraphQL mutation is usually invoked as part of an `onSubmit` event in an HTML form. The mutation input is generally read from the HTML form elements (text input, select value, check box, and so on).

We have five basic forms in this project: login, signup, create Task, add an Approach to a Task, and search all Tasks and Approaches. Each of these forms will invoke a single mutation.

Sometimes mutations are invoked with a simple `onClick` event without any input elements in a form. An example is the vote-on-Approach feature.

Some mutations can be invoked publicly without the scope of a logged-in user account. Examples include the mutations to create a new user account and log in an existing user account. We also kept the vote-on-Approach mutation public.

Some mutations require the scope of a logged-in user account. For example, only logged-in users can create Task/Approach records.

Some mutations can be invoked publicly, but they behave differently if invoked with the scope of a logged-in user. An example is the search mutation, which includes private Task records that belong to the user who is making the search. It will only include public records when invoked without an authenticated user scope.

Let's start with the `userLogin` and `userCreate` mutations. They can be invoked without including any authentication headers, and they both return an active `auth-Token` value that can be used with the other mutations.

### 9.5.1 The login/signup forms

You can get to the login/signup forms using the links in the top-right corner of the home page. The components used for these pages are as follows:

- The `Login` component is under web/src/components/Login.js.
- The `Signup` component is under web/src/components/Signup.js.

These components display simple HTML forms with submit buttons. Our task is to implement their `onSubmit` event handlers. These handlers are pretty much the same in both components. They have to read the mutations' input object from the form elements, submit the mutation request, and then store the user record on the global state of the app so that they can navigate to other pages and submit other mutations.

Here's the mutation operation that can be used to log in a user using their username/password. Put this in the `Login` component.

**Listing 9.14    Changes in web/src/components/Login.js**

```
// .-.-.
const USER_LOGIN = `
  mutation userLogin($input: AuthInput!) {
    userLogin(input: $input) {
      errors {
        message
      }
      user {
        id
        username
      }
      authToken
    }
  }
`;
// .-.-.
```

Here's the mutation operation that can be used to create a new user account. Put it in the `Signup` component.

**Listing 9.15    Changes in web/src/components/Signup.js**

```
// .-.-.
const USER_CREATE = `
  mutation userCreate($input: UserInput!) {
    userCreate(input: $input) {
      errors {
        message
      }
      user {
        id
        username
      }
      authToken
    }
  }
`;
// .-.-.
```

We've seen and tested these mutations directly in GraphiQL before, but now we will invoke them in submit handlers within components. In the `Login` component, we invoke the request function using the `USER_LOGIN` mutation after capturing its input from the form elements. Here's one way to do that.

**Listing 9.16    Changes in web/src/components/Login.js**

```
// .-.-.

export default function Login() {
  // .-.-.
```

```
const handleLogin = async (event) => {
  event.preventDefault();
  const input = event.target.elements;
  const { data } = await request(USER_LOGIN, {
    variables: {
      input: {
        username: input.username.value,
        password: input.password.value,
      },
    },
  });
  const { errors, user, authToken } = data.userLogin;
  if (errors.length > 0) {
    return setUIErrors(errors);
  }
  user.authToken = authToken;
  window.localStorage.setItem('azdev:user', JSON.stringify(user));
  setLocalAppState({ user, component: { name: 'Home' } });
};

// .-.--.

}
```

**The input data is read with a DOM API call. The state of this form is not controlled with React.**

**Checks for the existence of any user errors after the mutation, and sets these errors for the UI to display somewhere. This part of the code will display the "Invalid username or password" error message when you test the form with invalid credentials.**

Test the Login form with invalid credentials. You should see the "Invalid username or password" message (figure 9.8).

To test the Login form with valid credentials, use the test account in the sample data script (test/123456). You should be redirected to the home page, and the navigation bar should now display the user's username (figure 9.9).

To invoke the userCreate mutation, we have to read the values of firstName, lastName, username, and password. The form also has a confirmPassword field, but the GraphQL API we implemented for this mutation does not support it. This is an example of a validation check that we can do before allowing a GraphQL mutation operation to go through.

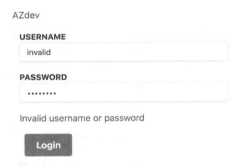

**Figure 9.8 `UserError` example for this mutation**

Create Task | test | **Logout**

**Figure 9.9 Navbar link for a logged-in user**

### Challenge
Try to implement the userCreate mutation in the Signup component on your own first. The code is very similar to what we did in the Login component.

## Persisting user sessions

The code as of now will persist the user session with `localStorage`. This is a simple example of the persistent caching of an element from the local app state. This is different from caching API data (which we're not doing yet in this example). An example of API data caching would be to not fetch the `taskMainList` array again when you navigate away from the home page and then navigate back to it. In the next chapter, we will see how a GraphQL client library seamlessly performs API data caching when it can.

There is more to persisting user sessions than using a simple `localStorage` record, but that is beyond the scope of the book. You can check out the official AZdev project (at az.dev/contribute) to see how we do session persistence for the project.

Here's how I implemented the mutation call.

#### Listing 9.17   Changes in web/src/components/Signup.js

```
// ·-·-·-.

export default function Signup() {
  // ·-·-·-.

  const handleSignup = async (event) => {
    event.preventDefault();
    const input = event.target.elements;
    if (input.password.value !== input.confirmPassword.value) {
      return setUIErrors([{ message: 'Password mismatch' }]);
    }
    const { data } =
      await request(USER_CREATE, {
        variables: {
          input: {
            firstName: input.firstName.value,
            lastName: input.lastName.value,
            username: input.username.value,
            password: input.password.value,
          },
        },
      });
    const { errors, user, authToken } = data.userCreate;
    if (errors.length > 0) {
      return setUIErrors(errors);
    }
    user.authToken = authToken;
    window.localStorage.setItem('azdev:user', JSON.stringify(user));
    setLocalAppState({ user, component: { name: 'Home' } });
  };
  // ·-·-·-.
}
```

You can test the signup form now. You should be able to create a new user account, and you should be logged in after you do.

### 9.5.2 *Handling generic server errors*

The happy paths for login/signup are working, but we should also test edge cases. Here's an edge case for you to think about. Right now, if you try to create a user record using a username that already exists in the `azdev.users` table, the UI will fail to display an error message and instead log a 500 Internal Server Error in the console (figure 9.10). Why is this happening, and how can it be fixed?

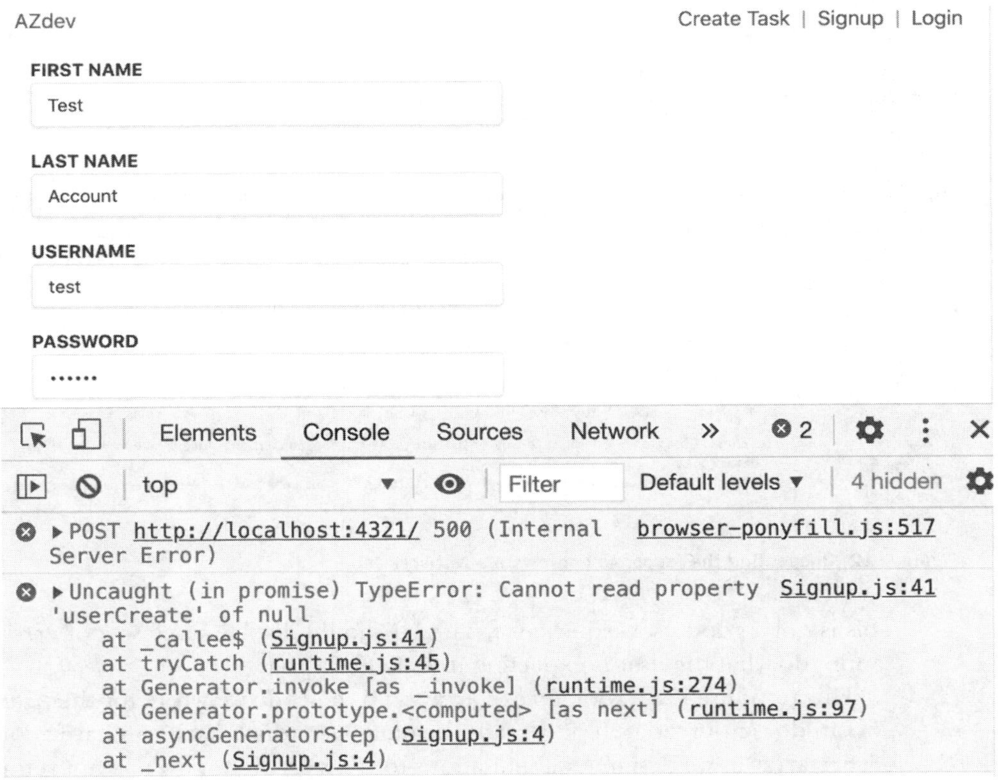

**Figure 9.10   Unhandled error in the server response**

The database's unique constraint on the `username` column is blocking this operation. It's making the `pg` driver throw an error in the code. We can actually see the error in the server logs (thanks to the `customFormatErrorFn` function we added earlier; see figure 9.11). You can also see the error in the Network tab in your dev tools if you inspect the server response for that network request (figure 9.12).

```
GraphQL Error {
  message: 'duplicate key value violates unique constraint "users_username_key"',
  locations: [ { line: 3, column: 5 } ],
  stack: [
    'error: duplicate key value violates unique constraint "users_username_key"',
    '    at Parser.parseErrorMessage (/Users/samer/graphql-in-action/node_modules/pg-protocol/dist/parser.js:278:15)',
    '    at Parser.handlePacket (/Users/samer/graphql-in-action/node_modules/pg-protocol/dist/parser.js:126:29)',
    '    at Parser.parse (/Users/samer/graphql-in-action/node_modules/pg-protocol/dist/parser.js:39:38)',
    '    at Socket.<anonymous> (/Users/samer/graphql-in-action/node_modules/pg-protocol/dist/index.js:8:42)',
    '    at Socket.emit (events.js:315:20)',
    '    at Socket.EventEmitter.emit (domain.js:483:12)',
    '    at addChunk (_stream_readable.js:295:12)',
    '    at readableAddChunk (_stream_readable.js:271:9)',
    '    at Socket.Readable.push (_stream_readable.js:212:10)',
    '    at TCP.onStreamRead (internal/stream_base_commons.js:186:23)'
  ],
  path: [ 'userCreate' ]
}
POST / 500 48.078 ms - 1004
```

Figure 9.11    Server logs

Figure 9.12    Inspecting the response in browser's Network tab

This is not a good user experience. The UI should display some sort of error when it cannot do what the user is expecting it to. Let's fix that.

This response has a root `errors` array, and the code we wrote for the `Signup` component does not read it. It only reads the data part, which itself can have another user `errors` array as we designed all mutations to. This error, however, is not returned as a user error; it's returned as a root error.

We can fix the API's `mutators` method to return the error as a user error, and that will fix the problem (since we're already accounting for the user `errors` array in the code). However, this is just one of many root errors that might happen. Let's make sure this form will display an error in all cases.

Since we already have an `errors` variable in the code, let's rename the root errors array `rootErrors`. All we need to do is check for its existence and update the UI if it's there.

**Listing 9.18   Changes in web/src/components/Signup.js**

```
// .-.-.

export default function Signup() {
  // .-.-.

  const handleSignup = async (event) => {
    // .-.-.
    const { data, errors: rootErrors } =
      await request(USER_CREATE, {
        variables: {
          input: {
            firstName: input.firstName.value,
            lastName: input.lastName.value,
            username: input.username.value,
            password: input.password.value,
          },
        },
      });
    if (rootErrors) {
      return setUIErrors(rootErrors);
    }
    const { errors, user, authToken } = data.userCreate;
    if (errors.length > 0) {
      return setUIErrors(errors);
    }
    // .-.-.
  };
```

**NOTE**   Make this same change in the Login component.

With this change, if you try to submit the same data for this mutation, you should see the error in the UI (figure 9.13). That's better. Remember that the error will be replaced by a generic error in production so we don't leak implementation details (figure 9.14).

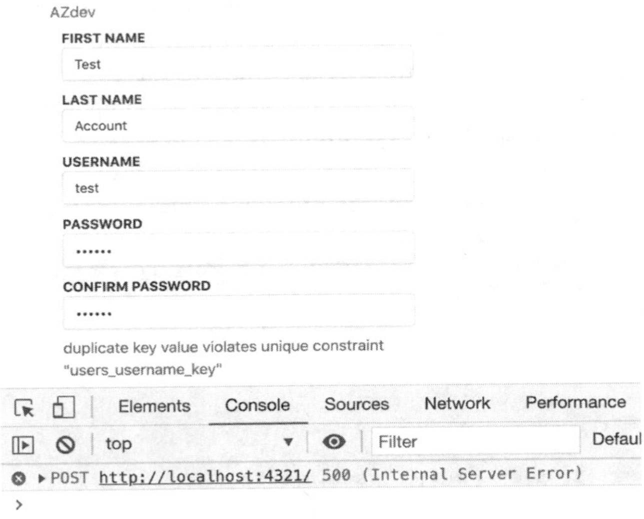

**Figure 9.13   Showing development root errors in the UI**

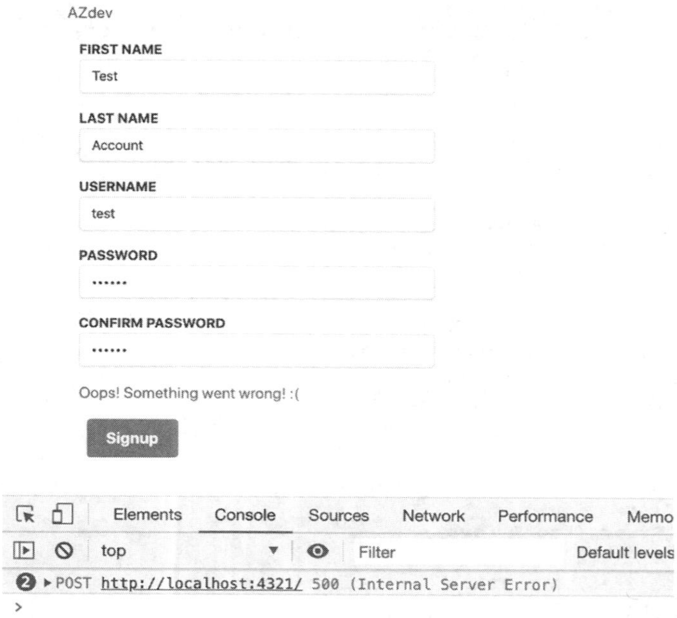

AZdev

**FIRST NAME**

Test

**LAST NAME**

Account

**USERNAME**

test

**PASSWORD**

......

**CONFIRM PASSWORD**

......

Oops! Something went wrong! :(

Signup

| Elements | Console | Sources | Network | Performance | Memo |

top ▾ | 👁 | Filter | Default levels

▶ POST http://localhost:4321/ 500 (Internal Server Error)

>

**Figure 9.14   Showing generic root errors in the UI**

Note that I kept the error local to this component instead of handling it on a global level (for example, in the `request` function) because that makes for a better user experience. We will have to handle server root errors every time we send any GraphQL request! We'll do so in the next chapter as we're learning about how a GraphQL client simplifies these challenges.

Now that we can handle unexpected root errors, we can improve this particular case and give the user a better error message when they attempt to use a username that's already used. Take a look at the mutator function for this operation. It's the `userCreate` function in api/src/db/pg-api.js. The method has no error handling when the `pgQuery` promise fails, which is what's happening in this case.

We can modify this method to not throw an error, either by doing a SQL read first to verify or by capturing the error of the SQL insert (in a `try/catch` statement), and return a normal user error if the thrown error is caused by the database `users_username_key` unique constraint. Maybe do something like the following.

**Listing 9.19   Example: handling database errors in mutators**

```
userCreate: async ({ input }) => {
  // .....

  if (payload.errors.length === 0) {
    const authToken = randomString();
    try {
      const pgResp = await pgQuery(sqls.userInsert, {
```

```
      $1: input.username.toLowerCase(),
      $2: input.password,
      $3: input.firstName,
      $4: input.lastName,
      $5: authToken,
    });
    if (pgResp.rows[0]) {
      payload.user = pgResp.rows[0];
      payload.authToken = authToken;
    }
  } catch (err) {
    console.error(err);
    // Check the err object and either:
    // - Push a custom error message to payload
    // - Throw the err object again }
  }

  return payload;
},
```

I'll leave this part for you to experiment with. Think of other database-level errors that might happen in all the other mutations!

**Current code**

Use `git checkout 9.4` to reset your local repo to the current progress in the code.

## 9.5.3 *Authenticating GraphQL requests*

In the handler logic for both the login and signup forms, the returned `authToken` value is made part of the current user state object (listings 9.17 and 9.18). That's the value we now need to include in other mutation requests (and some query requests as well).

We can simply include that `authToken` value (if one exists) as part of *any* GraphQL request we send to the API service and let the API service determine whether to use it or ignore it. To do that, we have to modify the `request` function and include the `AuthorizationBearer` token. For the `fetch` function, this is done through the headers property that's part of the third argument.

**Listing 9.20  Changes in web/src/store.js**

```
const request = async (requestText, { variables } = {}) => {
  const headers = state.user
    ? { Authorization: 'Bearer ' + state.user.authToken }
    : {};
  const gsResp = await fetch(config.GRAPHQL_SERVER_URL, {
    method: 'post',
    headers: { ...headers, 'Content-Type': 'application/json' },
    body: JSON.stringify({ query: requestText, variables }),
```

```
    }).then((response) => response.json());

  return gsResp;
};
```

Now, when a user is logged in, all GraphQL requests will include their current auth-Token value, and they can invoke the mutations that depend on it. You can verify that by inspecting the headers of any XHR request in the Network tab in your dev tools (figure 9.15).

▼ **Request Headers**      view source

  **accept:** */*

  **Accept-Encoding:** gzip, deflate, br

  **Accept-Language:** en-US,en;q=0.9

  **authorization:** Bearer 4ca6ab66661a460e627b0f551b5d331d6f404dcb341!

  **Connection:** keep-alive

  **Content-Length:** 267

  **content-type:** application/json

  **Host:** localhost:4321

**Figure 9.15   The** `authToken` **is sent with every network request to the API.**

### 9.5.4   *The Create Task form*

Now that users can log in and their authToken value is included in the headers of all GraphQL operations, we can have users create a new Task record. The HTML form to do so can be reached by clicking the Create Task link in the top-right corner (figure 9.16).

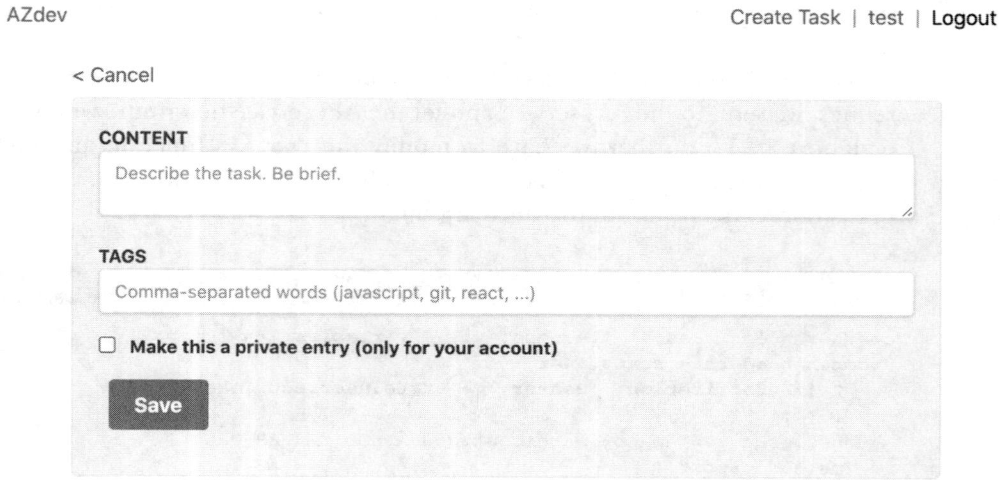

AZdev                                        Create Task | test | **Logout**

< Cancel

**CONTENT**

Describe the task. Be brief.

**TAGS**

Comma-separated words (javascript, git, react, ...)

☐ **Make this a private entry (only for your account)**

**Save**

**Figure 9.16   The Create Task form**

The component that renders this HTML form is under web/src/components/
NewTask.js. The form has three elements: the content box, the tags text box, and the
public/private check box.

These three input elements match the `TaskInput` type structure that can be used
with the `taskCreate` mutation field. However, we have to send the `tags` input value as
an array of strings rather than one string. We can use a `.split(',')` call on the input
text value to do so.

When a Task object is created successfully, we can use the commented out `set-
LocalAppState` call to navigate the user to the page of that newly created Task object.

Here's the implementation I came up with for this component.

**Listing 9.21  Changes in web/src/components/NewTask.js**

```
// .-.-.
const TASK_CREATE = `
  mutation taskCreate($input: TaskInput!) {
    taskCreate(input: $input) {
      errors {
        message
      }
      task {
        id
      }
    }
  }
`;

export default function NewTask() {
  // .-.-.

  const handleNewTaskSubmit = async (event) => {
    event.preventDefault();
    const input = event.target.elements;
    const { data, errors: rootErrors } = await request(TASK_CREATE, {
      variables: {
        input: {
          content: input.content.value,
          tags: input.tags.value.split(','),
          isPrivate: input.private.checked,
        },
      },
    });
    if (rootErrors) {
      return setUIErrors(rootErrors);
    }
    const { errors, task } = data.taskCreate;
    if (errors.length > 0) {
      return setUIErrors(errors);
    }
    setLocalAppState({
      component: { name: 'TaskPage', props: { taskId: task.id } },
```

```
      });
    };

    // ------

}
```

As a logged-in user, you should now be able to create your own Task records.

Before we implement the next mutation, let me tell you about a good chance to optimize the UI that handles this mutation. Right now, the code makes one GraphQL mutation request to create a Task object. It then navigates the user to the Task page and makes another GraphQL query request to read the data for that new Task object. You can verify that in the Networks tab in your browser's dev tools.

However, we can skip the second request (to fetch the data in the Task page) because that same data can be read in full as part of the mutation request. To do that, we have to make the taskCreate mutation ask for all the data required to render the TaskPage view.

This means the TaskPage component should declare its full data requirements as a fragment (even though it's a top-level component).

In the TaskPage component, refactor the TASK_INFO query to use a fragment and export that fragment for others to use it. Let's name the fragment FullTaskData.

---

**Listing 9.22   Changes in web/src/components/TaskPage.js**

```
// ------
export const FULL_TASK_FRAGMENT = `
  fragment FullTaskData on Task {
    id
    ...TaskSummary
    approachList {
      id
      ...ApproachFragment
    }
  }
  ${TASK_SUMMARY_FRAGMENT}
  ${APPROACH_FRAGMENT}
`;

const TASK_INFO = `
  query taskInfo($taskId: ID!) {
    taskInfo(id: $taskId) {
      ...FullTaskData
    }
  }
  ${FULL_TASK_FRAGMENT}
`;
// ------
```

Then modify the taskCreate mutation to ask for all the data required by TaskPage.

**Listing 9.23  Changes in web/src/components/NewTask.js**

```
// ......
import { FULL_TASK_FRAGMENT } from './TaskPage';

const TASK_CREATE = `
  mutation taskCreate($input: TaskInput!) {
    taskCreate(input: $input) {
      errors {
        message
      }
      task {
        id
        ...FullTaskData
      }
    }
  }
  ${FULL_TASK_FRAGMENT}
`;
// ......
```

To optimize the UI of the TaskPage component to not do the extra fetch, we have to change that component to accept an optional data object (instead of just an ID), check for it before the TASK_INFO query, and only perform that request if the object does not exist. This is a React-only change, so I'll skip it here. It's a good practice to always fetch all the data the UI would need to handle the creation of any object, even if the UI discards it at first (and fetches it again). As we transition into a more featured client for GraphQL requests, caching and optimizing requests will be managed for us by that client.

### Current code

Use `git checkout 9.5` to reset your local repo to the current progress in the code.

#### 9.5.5  *The Create Approach form*

Next up, let's implement the mutation to add an Approach record to an existing Task record. You need to be logged in first to access the UI form for this feature. While looking at a Task page, click the Add New Approach button. You should see the Create Approach form (figure 9.17).

One challenge I prepared for this form is the Details category selector. Remember that an Approach Detail can be a Note, an Explanation, or a Warning; but I did not hardcode these values in the HTML form (the HTML select element is empty in figure 9.17).

What if the GraphQL service adds a new category (or removes one) in the future? Is there a way to future-proof this HTML form?

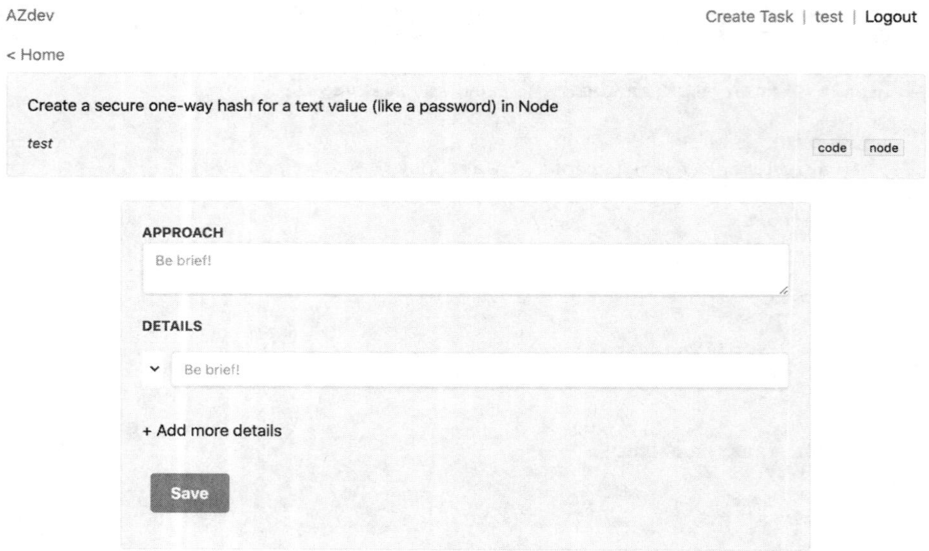

**Figure 9.17   The Create Approach form**

Yes! This is where you're going to appreciate GraphQL's introspective queries. We can ask the GraphQL service what values it supports in the `ApproachDetailCategory` type using the `__type` introspective field.

---

**Listing 9.24   Changes in web/src/components/NewApproach.js**

```
// -----
const DETAIL_CATEGORIES = `
  query getDetailCategories {
    detailCategories: __type(name: "ApproachDetailCategory") {
      enumValues {
        name
      }
    }
  }
`;
// -----
```

Then, we can use the response to build the HTML form. The React UI code to do that is already implemented, but we have to make the request for this introspective query somewhere. For example, we can make it every time this form is rendered. That's what I prepared in the code. Here's how to do it.

---

**Listing 9.25   Changes in web/src/components/NewApproach.js**

```
// -----

export default function NewApproach({ taskId, onSuccess }) {
  // -----
```

```
useEffect(() => {
  if (detailCategories.length === 0) {
    request(DETAIL_CATEGORIES).then(({ data }) => {
      setDetailCategories(data.detailCategories.enumValues);
    });
  }
}, [detailCategories, request]);

// .-.-.

}
```

This should make the values supported by the server appear in the HTML form (figure 9.18).

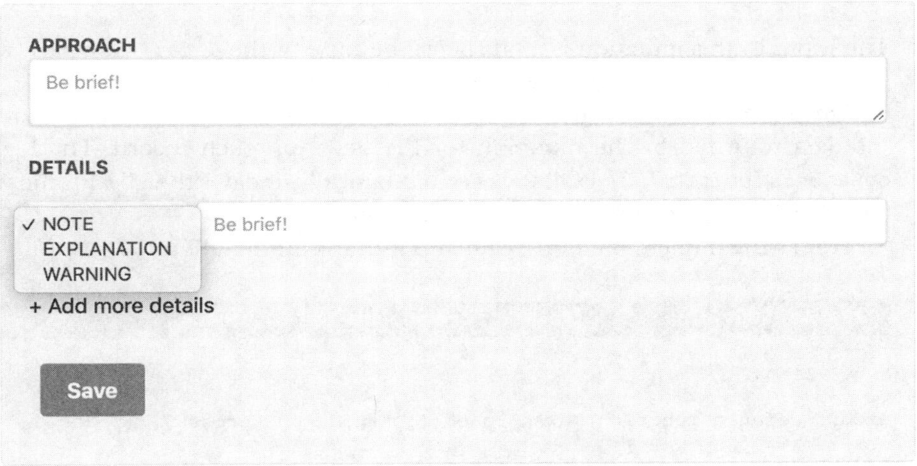

**Figure 9.18   The detail categories from the API response**

> **TIP**   This type of request should be cached and not invoked every time a user renders the HTML form. These categories will not change that frequently. I would even cache this particular request server-side.

Now that the HTML form is ready, let's figure out how to make the approachCreate mutation work with it. That mutation takes a taskId variable and an ApproachInput object. In its returned data, we can ask for the details of the newly created Approach record. The exact fields that we have to include in the output of this mutation are what the UI requires to render an Approach record. We've already created a fragment in the Approach component to represent these fields. We can just reuse it here.

**Listing 9.26   Changes in web/src/components/NewApproach.js**

```
// .-.-.

import { APPROACH_FRAGMENT } from './Approach';
```

```
// .-.--.
const APPROACH_CREATE = `
  mutation approachCreate($taskId: ID!, $input: ApproachInput!) {
    approachCreate(taskId: $taskId, input: $input) {
      errors {
        message
      }
      approach {
        id
        ...ApproachFragment
      }
    }
  }
  ${APPROACH_FRAGMENT}
`;
// .-.--.
```

The input to this mutation is a bit special because of the detailList part, which has to be an array of objects (where each represents one detail record).

Once the mutation is successful, we can call the noted onSuccess method, passing the data returned by the mutation for the new Approach record. The logic of the onSuccess function here is all React, but it basically updates the UI with the newly created Approach record (and highlights it as well).

Here's the implementation I came up with for this handler.

**Listing 9.27  Changes in web/src/components/NewApproach.js**

```
// .-.--.

export default function NewApproach({ taskId, onSuccess }) {
  // .-.--.

  const handleNewApproachSubmit = async (event) => {
    event.preventDefault();
    setUIErrors([]);
    const input = event.target.elements;
    const detailList = detailRows.map((detailId) => ({
      category: input[`detail-category-${detailId}`].value,
      content: input[`detail-content-${detailId}`].value,
    }));
    const { data, errors: rootErrors } = await request(
      APPROACH_CREATE,
      {
        variables: {
          taskId,
          input: {
            content: input.content.value,
            detailList,
          },
        },
```

```
    },
  );
  if (rootErrors) {
    return setUIErrors(rootErrors);
  }
  const { errors, approach } = data.approachCreate;
  if (errors.length > 0) {
    return setUIErrors(errors);
  }
  onSuccess(approach);
};

// ......

}
```

You can test adding a new Approach entry to a Task entry. The new Approach should appear on top with a slight background highlight (figure 9.19).

Figure 9.19　UI for a newly created Approach

> **Current code**
> Use `git checkout 9.6` to reset your local repo to the current progress in the code.

### 9.5.6    *Voting on an Approach*

The vote count for each Approach is displayed between two arrows. Users should be able to click these arrows to up-vote or down-vote an Approach record.

The API service schema provides the approachVote mutation for this feature. It expects an approachId field and an input object that has an up Boolean property.

The code for this feature is in the Approach component under web/src/components/ Approach.js. There is a handleVote function that's wired to deal with this mutation. It receives a direction argument whose value is either UP or DOWN.

The mutation should return the updated Approach record We can read the new voteCount from that record so that we can update the state of this component to make it show the new vote count.

By now, you have many similar examples of how to define a GraphQL operation for a component and how to invoke it, deal with its errors (if any), and deal with its success response to update the UI. Give this one a try on your own first.

Here's the implementation I came up with for this component.

**Listing 9.28    Changes in web/src/components/Approach.js**

```
// -------
const APPROACH_VOTE = `
  mutation approachVote($approachId: ID!, $up: Boolean!) {
    approachVote(approachId: $approachId, input: { up: $up }) {
      errors {
        message
      }
      updatedApproach: approach {
        id
        voteCount
      }
    }
  }
`;

export default function Approach({ approach, isHighlighted }) {
  // -------

  const handleVote = (direction) => async (event) => {
    event.preventDefault();
    const { data, errors: rootErrors } = await request(
      APPROACH_VOTE,
      {
        variables: {
          approachId: approach.id,
          up: direction === 'UP',
        },
      },
    );
    if (rootErrors) {
      return setUIErrors(rootErrors);
    }
```

```
    const { errors, updatedApproach } = data.approachVote;
    if (errors.length > 0) {
      return setUIErrors(errors);
    }
    setVoteCount(updatedApproach.voteCount);
  };

  // -·-·-·

}
```

With this change, you can test the voting arrows. Note that voting is unrestricted in the API service. A user can vote as many times as they want on any Approach. Practically, a vote operation like this should be restricted. That would be a fun exercise for you to go through end to end. It requires changes to both the API code and the UI code.

I think this is a good set of examples to demonstrate how to invoke GraphQL mutation requests. You can experiment with a lot more on your own. But before we conclude, we still have two more query requests to implement: the user's Task-list feature and the search feature.

> **Current code**
>
> Use `git checkout 9.7` to reset your local repo to the current progress in the code.

## 9.6 *Performing query requests scoped for a user*

As a logged-in user, you can click your username link in the top-right corner to navigate to a page that should list all the Task records you have created (including private ones). This page is similar to the home page, but the GraphQL query it requires is different. This one has to use the me root field and ask for the `taskList` field under it. It can reuse the `TaskSummary` fragment just as the home page did.

Try to do this on your own as well. The component that you have to change is `MyTasks` under web/src/components/MyTasks.js. Here's how I implemented it.

**Listing 9.29  Changes in web/src/components/MyTasks.js**

```
// -·-·-·

import TaskSummary, { TASK_SUMMARY_FRAGMENT } from './TaskSummary';

const MY_TASK_LIST = `
  query myTaskList {
    me {
      taskList {
        id
        ...TaskSummary
      }
    }
  }
```

```
  ${TASK_SUMMARY_FRAGMENT}
`;

export default function MyTasks() {
  // ·-·-·

  useEffect(() => {
    request(MY_TASK_LIST).then(({ data }) => {
      setMyTaskList(data.me.taskList);
    });
  }, [request]);

  // ·-·-·
}
```

We don't need to do anything special for this query because we're already sending the current user's `authToken` value with every GraphQL request. The server uses that value to authenticate the request and return the data for the user who is making it. Log in with test/123456, and click the username link in the navigation bar to test the user's Task-list feature (figure 9.20).

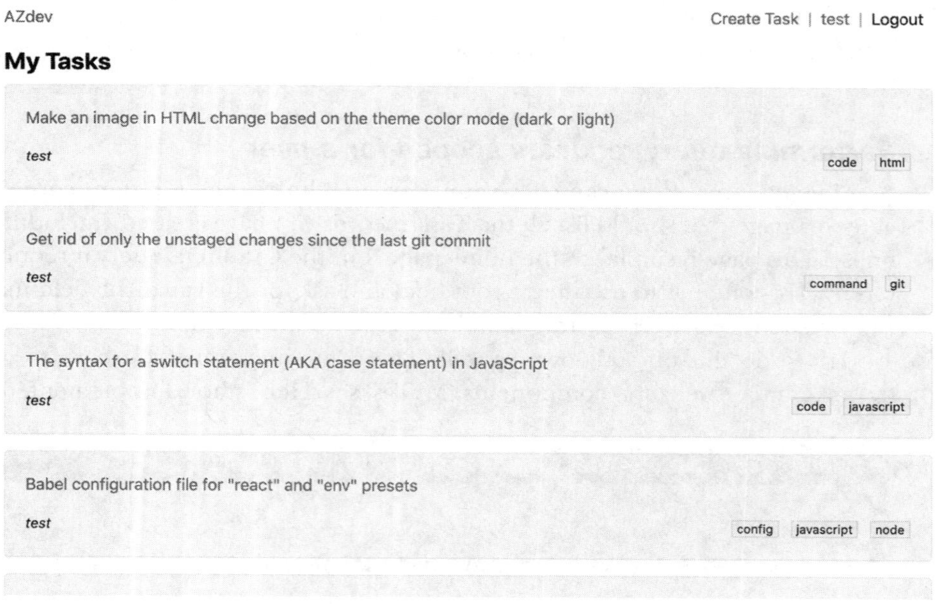

AZdev                                                    Create Task | test | **Logout**

## My Tasks

Make an image in HTML change based on the theme color mode (dark or light)

*test*                                                              code    html

Get rid of only the unstaged changes since the last git commit

*test*                                                          command    git

The syntax for a switch statement (AKA case statement) in JavaScript

*test*                                                          code    javascript

Babel configuration file for "react" and "env" presets

*test*                                                    config    javascript    node

**Figure 9.20   The page for the user's own Task records**

### Current code
Use `git checkout 9.8` to reset your local repo to the current progress in the code.

### 9.6.1 *The Search form*

The search feature is probably the most important feature in the AZdev application. It will be heavily used because it's the entry point for all Task records.

It's also special because it should work with or without a user session. Without a user session, the API we implemented will exclude all private Task records. By including an authToken, the API will include the private Task records owned by an authenticated user. This is why I kept this feature for last so that we can test these two branches from the UI.

The root GraphQL field that we can use is search. We'll alias it as searchResults. It expects a term string as its only argument. That string is what we need to read from the search input text box. However, the UI is designed such that the state of the component changes when a user clicks the Search button, and the search-term value can be read from the local app state. That part is already implemented in the code.

Another special thing about the search query is how it represents two API object types. Search results can include both Task and Approach records. The UI is implemented to display these types differently (based on a .type attribute). Look at the JSX in web/src/components/Search.js to analyze what fields this search query requires (by looking at used variables):

```
<h2>Search Results</h2>
<div className="y-spaced">
  {searchResults.length === 0 && (
    <div className="box box-primary">No results</div>
  )}
  {searchResults.map((item, index) => (
    <div key={index} className="box box-primary">
      <AppLink
        to="TaskPage"
        taskId={
          item.type === 'Approach' ? item.task.id : item.id
        }
      >
        <span className="search-label">{item.type}</span>{' '}
        {item.content.substr(0, 250)}
      </AppLink>
      <div className="search-sub-line">
        {item.type === 'Task'
          ? `Approaches: ${item.approachCount}`
          : `Task: ${item.task.content.substr(0, 250)}`}
      </div>
    </div>
  ))}
</div>
```

The bold parts on each search item tell us that we need the following fields: type, id, content, approachCount (if it's a Task), and task.content and task.id (if it's an Approach). We made the search root field an interface implemented by both Task and Approach models. This means the __typename introspective field will hold the value of Task or Approach. We'll have to alias that as type since that's what the UI is using.

The content field can be read directly under the search field because it is common in both types. However, both the approachCount and task fields will have to be included conditionally using inline fragments. Here's the query I came up with after this analysis.

**Listing 9.30  Changes in web/src/components/Search.js**

```
// .-.-.
const SEARCH_RESULTS = `
  query searchResults($searchTerm: String!) {
    searchResults: search(term: $searchTerm) {
      type: __typename
      id
      content
      ... on Task {
        approachCount
      }
      ... on Approach {
        task {
          id
          content
        }
      }
    }
  }
`;
// .-.-.
```

Here is how I invoked the searchResults query.

**Listing 9.31  Changes in web/src/components/Search.js**

```
// .-.-.

export default function Search({ searchTerm = null }) {
  // .-.-.

  useEffect(() => {
    if (searchTerm) {
      request(SEARCH_RESULTS, { variables: { searchTerm } }).then(
        ({ data }) => {
          setSearchResults(data.searchResults);
        },
      );
    }
  }, [searchTerm, request]);

  // .-.-.
}
```

You can test the Search form now. Make sure it works for both Task and Approach content. Also test the public/private feature. If you create a private Task entry, it should only be included in search results when you're logged in. The sample data has a private entry owned by the "test" user. Test searching for "babel" as a guest and as the "test" sample data user (figures 9.21 and 9.22).

AZdev     Create Task | Signup | Login

babel     Search

**Search Results**

No results

< Home

**Figure 9.21   A guest searching for a private Task**

AZdev     Create Task | test | **Logout**

babel     Search

**Search Results**

**Task**    Babel configuration file for "react" and "env" presets
Approaches: 1

< Home

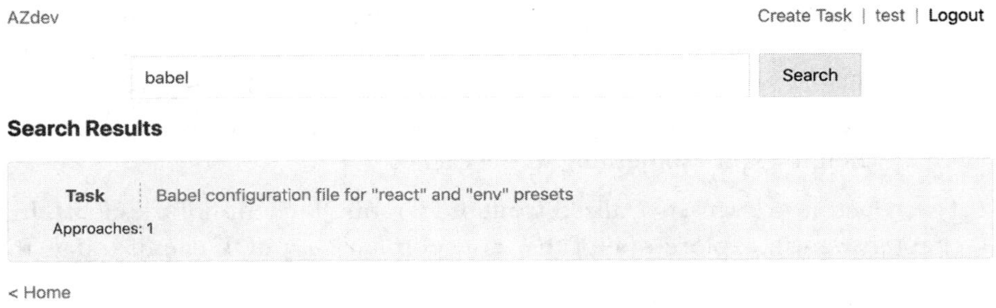

**Figure 9.22   An owner searching for a private Task**

---

**Current code**

Use `git checkout 9.9` to reset your local repo to the current progress in the code.

---

## 9.7   Next up

We have skipped many complexities in this chapter. While some simple applications will not need to worry about such complexities, most will. You should be aware of them in all cases. For example, what if the API service takes too long to reply? What if it's down? What if it returns partial data with errors?

In each of these situations, the UI should behave in a user-friendly way. It might need to retry a request, display a global error message, or display a warning to tell the user that a request is taking longer than usual.

The complexities are on both ends of this stack. The browser has many limitations. What if it cannot allocate more memory? What if it has a limited network or CPU power? There is a lot we can do to make this application a bit more usable on slow and restricted devices. Just as we used `DataLoader` to cache and batch SQL operations, we can use a specialized GraphQL client library to cache and batch GraphQL operations.

Here are a few generic considerations when deciding whether to use a client library like Apollo or Relay. These libraries greatly simplify things like the following:

- *Performance*—For example, caching responses and batching multiple network requests into one. Also, displaying a big list of records using pagination, to avoid overwhelming the app memory.
- *Efficiency*—For example, asking servers for only the new data required by a view and then merging new data with old data; or asking servers for only the data used in the visible window and asking for the rest of the data as the user scrolls up or down.
- *Dealing with failure*—For example, employing standard error-handling for failing requests and a standard retry strategy.
- *Responsiveness*—For example, showing expected data changes optimistically while waiting on a confirmation from the server. Then, possibly performing a rollback on those optimistic changes if the server fails to persist the data.
- *Cache management*—For example, deciding what to cache, where to cache it, and when to expire something in the cache.

These factors are why specialized frontend GraphQL client libraries exist. In the next chapter, we will explore one of the most popular GraphQL clients today: the Apollo Client.

## Summary

- To use a GraphQL operation in a frontend web application, you need to make Ajax calls. These calls usually cause the UI state to change. You'll have to make them in a place where it's possible to read and update the state of the UI.
- Components can define operations and fragments. An operation can be a query, a mutation, or a subscription. A component query operation is generally used to display that component. A mutation operation is usually used within a DOM event handler (like `onSubmit` or `onClick`). A subscription operation is generally used to autoupdate a frequently changed view.
- Fragments allow components to be responsible for their own data requirements. Parent components can use these fragments to include the data required by their children components.
- Mutation operations usually require the reading of input element values. The structure of a UI form should match the structure of the mutation input type.
- GraphQL introspective queries can be used to future-proof parts of the UI that depend on dynamic values.

# Using GraphQL APIs with Apollo client

## This chapter covers

- Using Apollo Client in plain JavaScript and React
- Understanding Apollo's links and cache
- Using Apollo's hook functions for queries and mutations
- Managing local app state with Apollo
- Implementing and using GraphQL subscriptions over WebSockets

Shortly after GraphQL implementations started getting attention on GitHub, another class of GraphQL libraries began to attract notice as well: client libraries.

GraphQL client libraries are designed to manage communications between frontend applications and backend GraphQL services. A client library abstracts the tasks of asking a GraphQL service for data, instructing it to do mutations, and making its data responses available to the view layer of a frontend application.

Just as a GraphQL service can be thought of as an agent that does all the communication with your databases, a GraphQL client can be thought of as an agent that does all the communication with your GraphQL services.

Many GraphQL client libraries also have server components to enrich the server experience and support common frontend application requirements like caching, paginating through lists, and using real-time data.

Some GraphQL clients are designed to work with React exclusively. The most popular one in that category is Relay (relay.dev), which is primarily a Facebook project influenced by how Facebook uses GraphQL. Relay is the first client framework for GraphQL, and it shaped the evolution of the GraphQL language at Facebook.

Other GraphQL clients are designed for multiple view libraries with a primary focus on React. The most popular one in that category is Apollo Client (apollographql.com), which is part of a stack of GraphQL tools managed by Meteor Development Group.

There is also AWS Amplify (aws.amazon.com/amplify) by Amazon. It is a complete development platform that covers the entire development workflow of frontend applications.

These are just some of the top JavaScript projects that include a GraphQL client, but there are many more clients in JavaScript and many other languages. Check out az.dev/graphql-clients for a full list of all GraphQL client libraries.

GraphQL clients offer similar features with varying levels of complexity and customization. To explore an example of how to use a GraphQL client library with a GraphQL API, we will use Apollo Client simply because it's the most popular client that supports multiple view libraries.

**TIP**   If you're interested in learning how to use Relay.js, check out the material at jscomplete.com/relay.

---

**Current code**

Use `git checkout 10.0` to reset your local repo to the current progress in the code. If you need to stash any local changes, use `git add . && git stash`. Remember to run `npm install` to install any missing dependencies.

---

## 10.1   Using Apollo Client with JavaScript

Apollo Client can be used with React, Vue, Angular, and many others. It can also be used with plain JavaScript. Let's start with an example of how to do that first; then we will see how to use it in the AZdev React project.

The first step to work with Apollo Client is to add it to the project dependencies. It's hosted under the npm package `@apollo/client`.

**Listing 10.1  Command: installing the Apollo client package**

```
$ npm install @apollo/client
```

**TIP**  All the code examples in this chapter are designed to work with Apollo Client version 3, the latest version as of this writing. If, by the time you're reading this book, a newer version of Apollo Client is out, its API will most likely be different. Check out az.dev/gia-updates to see any API updates you might need for this chapter.

### 10.1.1  *Making a query request*

Let's start by looking at how to make a simple GraphQL query request using the Apollo Client query method (which is not React-specific).

**NOTE**  Listings 10.2—10.5 are temporary examples for testing. We'll revert things back in listing 10.6.

Delete all the content in web/src/index.js, and replace it with the following.

**Listing 10.2  Example: initializing and using Apollo Client (in web/src/index.js)**

```
import {
  ApolloClient,
  HttpLink,
  InMemoryCache,
  gql,
} from '@apollo/client';

import * as config from './config';

const cache = new InMemoryCache();
const httpLink = new HttpLink({ uri: config.GRAPHQL_SERVER_URL });
const client = new ApolloClient({ cache, link: httpLink });

async function main() {
  const { data, errors } = await client.query({
    query: gql`
      query {
        numbersInRange(begin: 1, end: 100) {
          sum
        }
      }
    `,
  });

  console.log({ data, errors });
}

main();
```

This is the simplest example of using Apollo Client in plain JavaScript, but it introduces many new concepts. Let's walk through them:

- A client library like Apollo replaces any other Ajax library in your application. You don't need "fetch" to make Ajax requests directly because the client makes all the requests internally. This is the primary task of every GraphQL client: they make all the Ajax requests for you and abstract the complexities of dealing with HTTP requests and responses.

- The `ApolloClient` object is a constructor that can be used to initialize a client object per GraphQL service. An application might use multiple client instances to work with multiple GraphQL services. In this example, we have one `httpLink` object, and I initialized it using the same `config.GRAPHQL_SERVER_URL` that we've been using so far.

- In addition to the `link` attribute, Apollo Client requires the `cache` attribute. This attribute is used to specify the cache object that Apollo will use for its store. The default cache is an instance of the `InMemoryCache` object, which makes Apollo Client use the browser's memory for caching. That's what most web applications need to do. This cache flexibility allows an Apollo Client instance to be used with other types of cache. For example, if you need your application's cached data to be persisted between sessions, you can use a cache object that works on top of `window.localStorage`.

- Once you have a client object initialized and configured with a valid GraphQL service link attribute and caching strategy, you can use its API methods. The code in listing 10.2 uses the `query` method to send a GraphQL query operation and retrieve the server response for it. The `query` method takes an object whose `query` property is an object representing the GraphQL operation text to be sent.

- Instead of using a string with the Apollo Client `query` method, we wrap that string with the `gql` tag function. You can use `gql` either as a template string tag (as we did in listing 10.2) or as a normal function call with the string as its argument. The `gql` function parses a GraphQL string into an abstract syntax tree (AST). It basically converts the string into a structured object. Strings are limited. Structured objects give GraphQL clients more control over GraphQL operations and make it easier for them to offer advanced features.

If everything works fine, you should see the `console.log` message in the browser's console displaying the result of summing the numbers in the range 1–100 (figure 10.1).

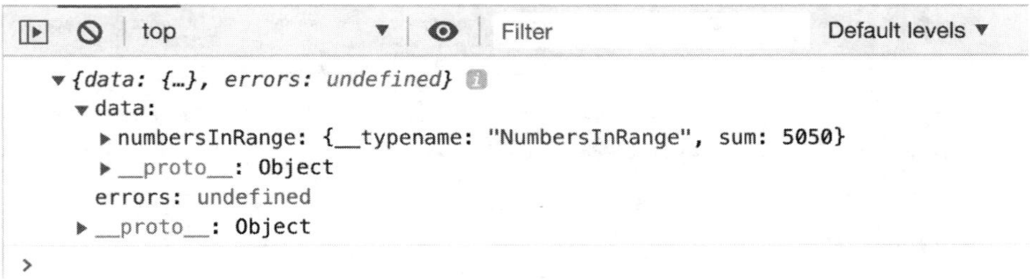

**Figure 10.1 Output of the query request**

At first glance, listing 10.2 is a lot of code to make a small request that can be done with a simple, direct Ajax call. However, this code comes with a huge win that we can see right away. Repeat the same query operation, and look at the Network tab in your browser when you refresh the session. Here's an example to demonstrate.

**Listing 10.3 Example: repeating a query with Apollo Client**

```
async function main() {
  const resp1 = await client.query({
    query: gql`
      {
        numbersInRange(begin: 1, end: 100) {
          sum
        }
      }
    `,
  });
  console.log(resp1.data);

  const resp2 = await client.query({
    query: gql`
      {
        numbersInRange(begin: 1, end: 100) {
          sum
        }
      }
    `,
  });
  console.log(resp2.data);
}
```

Figure 10.2 shows what you should see in the browser's Network tab, filtered to show only XHR requests (XMLHttpRequest). Apollo Client issued only *one* Ajax request for both query operations because the response of the first request was automatically cached (in memory), and Apollo Client figured out that there is no need to ask the server again for data that we already have.

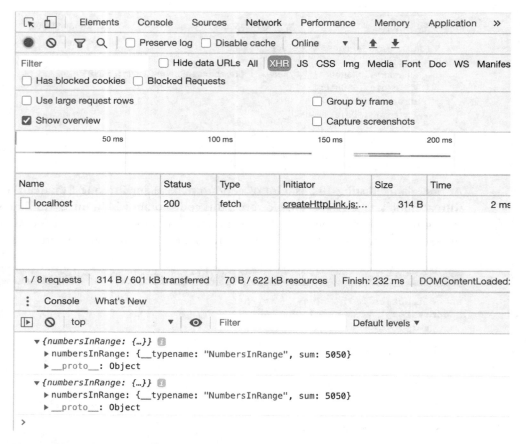

**Figure 10.2   Output of the repeated query request**

This is a simple example, but Apollo Client does a lot of heavy lifting under the hood to make the cache as useful as it can be. For example, it caches every data response in a flattened data structure so that it can use the cache of individual objects to determine what future network requests are needed, even for different queries. For example, make the following changes in web/src/index.js.

**Listing 10.4   Example: repeating a partial query**

```
async function main() {
  const resp1 = await client.query({
    query: gql`
      {
        taskMainList {
          id
          content
          tags
          createdAt
```

```
        }
      }
    `,
  });
  console.log(resp1.data);

  const resp2 = await client.query({
    query: gql`
      {
        taskMainList {
          content
        }
      }
    `,
  });
  console.log(resp2.data);
}
```

This code asks to send two different query operations to the server. However, because the second one is a subset of the first, Apollo Client will not go to the server a second time (as shown in figure 10.3).

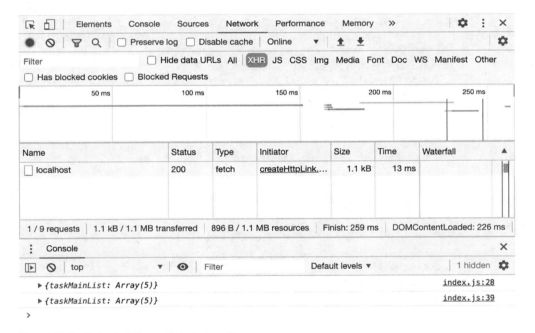

**Figure 10.3  Output of the partial query code**

While this is impressive, wait until you see the other features offered by Apollo Client (caching and more). Let me give you another example, but this time with a mutation operation.

### 10.1.2  *Making a mutation request*

To make a mutation request with Apollo Client, you use the .mutate method (instead of .query) and supply an object with a mutation property. If the operation to be sent uses variables, you can supply a variables property to specify their values.

The following is an example of sending the mutation operation to vote on Approach 2. I've also included a query to fetch the voteCount field for Approach 2 (which is under Task 2) before and after the mutation to verify that it worked.

---

**Listing 10.5   Example: sending a mutation request**

```
async function main() {
  const resp1 = await client.query({
    query: gql`
      query taskInfo {
        taskInfo(id: "2") {
          approachList {
            id
            voteCount
          }
        }
      }
    `,
  });
  console.log(resp1.data);

  const resp2 = await client.mutate({
    mutation: gql`
      mutation approachVote($approachId: ID!) {
        approachVote(approachId: $approachId, input: { up: true }) {
          approach {
            id
            voteCount
          }
        }
      }
    `,
    variables: { approachId: '2' },
  });
  console.log(resp2.data);

  const resp3 = await client.query({
    query: gql`
      query taskInfo {
        taskInfo(id: "2") {
          approachList {
            id
            voteCount
          }
        }
      }
    `,
  });
  console.log(resp3.data);
}
```

The first query request should show that Approach 2 has 0 votes. The second request updates that vote count to 1, and the third verifies that Approach 2 now has 1 vote.

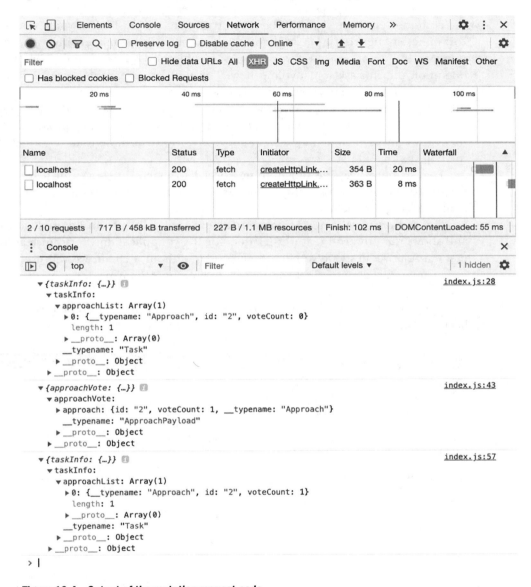

**Figure 10.4  Output of the mutation request code**

Note that Apollo Client included the introspective __typename field in all three operations, although we did not specify it (see figure 10.4). How did it do that? And, more important, why did it do that?

That's one other reason we're wrapping all operations with gql. Since the requests are represented as objects, Apollo Client can inspect these objects and easily modify them to, for example, include the __typename field.

To understand why Apollo Client did that, take a good look at your Network tab (or mine, in figure 10.4), and note that Apollo Client made only two network requests. It did not issue a network request for the third query operation because that operation did not ask for anything new. The mutation operation already informed Apollo Client that the new voteCount is 1, so it cached that number. Since it asked for the __typename as well, it can use a combination of __typename and id to uniquely identify each object it sees on a global level. It did exactly that for Approach 2. It used the Approach's globally unique ID (Approach:2) to determine that we already know the object's id and voteCount.

That's impressive. We did nothing special to make this powerful feature work. We're just issuing the same simple queries and mutations, and Apollo Client is intelligently making the cache work seamlessly for them.

The rest of this chapter demonstrates how Apollo Client can be used with React and shows the powerful features it offers for React applications. First, instead of the manual Ajax requests we've been doing so far without a client, we will use Apollo's query and mutate methods. Then we will explore how to invoke these mutations with Apollo's React-specific methods.

You can now revert all the test changes made so far in web/src/index.js and put back the original code.

---

**Listing 10.6   Code in web/src/index.js**

```
import 'regenerator-runtime/runtime';
import React from 'react';
import ReactDOM from 'react-dom';

import { useStoreObject, Provider } from './store';
import Root from './components/Root';

export default function App() {
  const store = useStoreObject();
  return (
    <Provider value={store}>
      <Root />
    </Provider>
  );
}

ReactDOM.render(<App />, document.getElementById('root'));
```

**Current code**

Use git checkout 10.1 to reset your local repo to the current progress in the code.

## 10.2  Using Apollo Client with React

To use Apollo Client with React, we first need to initialize it (just as we did in listing 10.2). A good place to do so for this application is in web/src/store.js, where we have been managing the local app state so far.

```
import React, { useState } from 'react';
import fetch from 'cross-fetch';

import * as config from './config';
import {
  ApolloClient,
  HttpLink,
  InMemoryCache,
} from '@apollo/client';

const httpLink = new HttpLink({ uri: config.GRAPHQL_SERVER_URL });
const cache = new InMemoryCache();
const client = new ApolloClient({ link: httpLink, cache });
// ·-·-·
```

### 10.2.1  Using the query and mutate methods directly

Now, instead of the fetch-based request method that is exported in the store's context object, we need to introduce two new methods: one for queries and one for mutations. To keep the changes in the app to a minimum, we will start by having the exact same function signature as the good-old request function. The new methods will just be wrappers around Apollo Client's methods.

```
// ·-·-·

export const useStoreObject = () => {
  // ·-·-·

  const query = async (query, { variables } = {}) => {
    const resp = await client.query({ query, variables });
    return resp;
  };

  const mutate = async (mutation, { variables } = {}) => {
    const resp = await client.mutate({ mutation, variables });
    return resp;
  };

  return {
    useLocalAppState,
    setLocalAppState,
```

```
      AppLink,
      query,
      mutate,
    };
  };
```

**TIP**   You can remove the request method. We no longer need that dependency.

Note that I kept these new methods within the useStoreObject function because we still need to include the authToken header, which is part of the user state object (which is managed by the store). Later in this chapter, we will see how Apollo Client can replace the entire local app state store.

Now, for every call to the old request function in all components, we have to do the following:

1  Add an import { gql } from '@apollo/client' statement.
2  Wrap the query or mutation text with gql.
3  Instead of request, destructure query or mutate out of useStore.
4  Replace the request method with query if the operation is a query or mutate if the operation is a mutation.

For example, in web/src/components/Home.js, here are the changes we have to make.

---

**Listing 10.9   Changes in web/src/components/Home.js**

```
// ..-.-.
import { gql } from '@apollo/client';

const TASK_MAIN_LIST = gql`
  query taskList {
    taskList {
      id
      ...TaskSummary
    }
  }

  ${TASK_SUMMARY_FRAGMENT}
`;

export default function Home() {
  const { query } = useStore();
  const [ taskList, setTaskList ] = useState(null);

  useEffect(() => {
    query(TASK_MAIN_LIST).then(({ data }) => {
      setTaskList(data.taskList);
    });
  }, [query]);

  if (!taskList) {
```

```
    return <div className="loading">Loading...</div>;
  }

  // .-.--.
}
```

Here's an example of how to replace the `request` call for a mutation operation. In web/src/components/Login.js, the changes to make are as follows.

```
// .-.--.
import { gql } from '@apollo/client';

const USER_LOGIN = gql`
  mutation userLogin($input: AuthInput!) {
    userLogin(input: $input) {
      errors {
        message
        field
      }
      user {
        id
        name
      }
      authToken
    }
  }
`;

export default function Login() {
  const { mutate, setLocalAppState } = useStore();
  const [ uiErrors, setUIErrors ] = useState();
  const handleLogin = async (event) => {
    event.preventDefault();
    const input = event.target.elements;
    const { data, errors: rootErrors } = await mutate(USER_LOGIN, {
      variables: {
        input: {
          username: input.username.value,
          password: input.password.value,
        },
      },
    });
    // .-.--.
  };

  // .-.--.
}
```

That's it on the simplest level. You can now test the home page and the login form. GraphQL operations will be done through Apollo Client instead of the previous fetch-based `request` method.

**NOTE**  Everything else would error out for you if you removed the old `request` method.

Go ahead and change all the other components to use `query/mutate` instead of `request`. Look for `request(` in your code editor to find all the components that need to be changed. Some operations will not work correctly because the new `query/mutate` methods do not include the current user's `authToken` yet. We'll fix that next.

The Git branch 10.2 has all these changes. All GraphQL operations are done with the new `query/mutate` methods.

---

**Current code**

Use `git checkout 10.2` to reset your local repo to the current progress in the code.

---

Did you notice that the changes we made in the components were minimal? We just wrapped operation texts with `gql` and replaced a method with another one. That's the power of having good abstractions.

What we have done so far is a basic use of Apollo Client in a React application, but it's already paying off. The home page data is now cached after the first hit. If you navigate to a Task page and then back to the home page, Apollo Client will not issue another network request for the `taskList`.

### 10.2.2  *Including authentication headers*

While caching is great, it introduces some challenges that we need to learn about. Test the search form right now. Since we're no longer including the `authToken` in all requests, the search operation will not work correctly for private Task entries. As an example, test searching for "babel" after you log in with test/123456. That user owns the sample data Task record about Babel, but the `search` field is not currently returning it. We need to include the current `authToken` value in the headers of GraphQL requests to fix that.

However, now that we're making the Ajax request through Apollo Client, we don't have direct control over what headers to send. We need to do the request through Apollo Client methods and flow. We can do Ajax requests through the `@apollo/link-context` package, which can be used to change the context of the GraphQL operations issued by Apollo Client. We just create a new `link` object and make it part of Apollo Client's link chain.

**TIP**  Apollo has a few different `link` objects that you can make part of the link chain. For example, `@apollo/link-schema` can be used to perform GraphQL operations directly on a provided schema object. That is commonly used for server-side rendering. There is also `@apollo/link-ws`, which we will use later to make Apollo Client work with WebSockets. There is even `@apollo/link-rest`, which can be used to integrate data from REST APIs to your Apollo Client's cache. See the full list of Apollo links at az.dev/apollo-links.

To make the current user's `authToken` value part of the link chain context, start by installing the new package.

---
**Listing 10.11  Command: installing the Apollo `link-context` package**

```
$ npm install @apollo/link-context
```

Then change web/src/store.js as follows to make the new link part of the chain for Apollo Client.

---
**Listing 10.12  Changes in web/src/store.js**

```
// .-.-.
import { setContext } from '@apollo/link-context';
// .-.-.

export const useStoreObject = () => {
  // .-.-.

  const AppLink = ({ children, to, ...props }) => {
    // .-.-.
  };

  const authLink = setContext((_, { headers }) => {
    return {
      headers: {
        ...headers,
        authorization: state.user
          ? `Bearer ${state.user.authToken}`
          : '',
      },
    };
  });

  client.setLink(authLink.concat(httpLink));

  // .-.-.
};
```

Note that I placed the new `authLink` in the `useStoreObject` app so that it can use JavaScript closures to access the `state.user` object (which is stored on the React context object). Now, if you search for "babel" while logged in as the "test" user, it should work.

> **TIP** If the search for "babel" does not work, try restarting your web server to clear any previous cache.

However, there is a problem. To see it in action, test this flow without refreshing the browser:

1  Log in with test/123456.
2  Search for "babel" (which should work).
3  Log out.
4  Search for "babel" again (which should not work).

You'll notice that the second public search returns the private Babel Task entry (figure 10.5). Why?

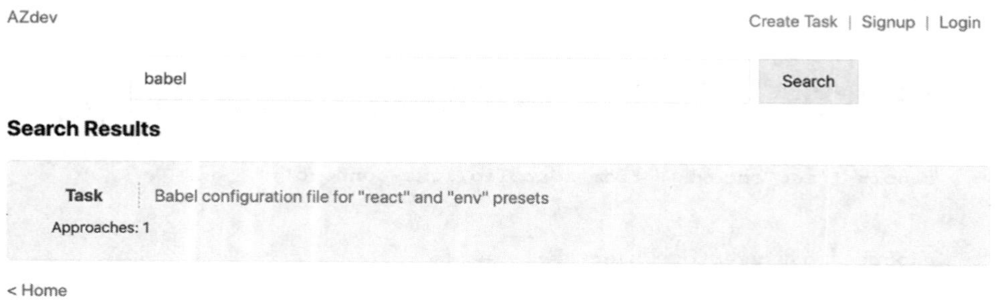

**Figure 10.5   Cache user session problem**

This is happening because of Apollo Client caching. The search for "babel" was cached when the owner was logged in, and it remained cached when the owner logged out.

This is a common challenge when dealing with caching. The application logic often needs to manually reset the cache.

**TIP** You should install the Apollo Client devtools extension (az.dev/ac-devtools). It will add an Apollo tab in your browser's dev tools where you can inspect and debug Apollo-related problems. This extension will also enable you to visualize your Apollo cache store, view active queries and variables, and test GraphQL mutations using the same network interface that's used by the Apollo Client object we configured in web/src/store.js.

Apollo Client provides many methods to work with the cache. You can reset the cache in part or in whole, and you can do that either directly after operations (for example, right after the USER_LOGIN mutation) or globally when the state of your application changes. Let's do the latter. Let's reset the entire stored cache when the user logs in or out. We can do that in the setLocalAppState context method (which is the one this code uses to make updates to the local app state).

**Listing 10.13   Changes in web/src/store.js**

```
const setLocalAppState = (newState) => {
  if (newState.component) {
    newState.component.props = newState.component.props ?? {};
  }
  setState((currentState) => {
```

```
    return { ...currentState, ...newState };
  });
  // Reset cache when users login/logout
  if (newState.user || newState.user === null) {
    client.resetStore();
  }
};
```

Now, if you test the double search flow again, it should work properly.

> **TIP**  You don't have to reset the whole store. You can reset it in parts. For example, you can clear cached data for a single query using the `cache.write-Query` method. We'll see an example of how to use that later in the chapter.

---

**Current code**

Use `git checkout 10.3` to reset your local repo to the current progress in the code.

---

### 10.2.3  *Using Apollo hook functions*

While we have a working solution to make all GraphQL communications through Apollo Client, this is not the ideal way to use it. We are simply not utilizing a big part of the power Apollo Client offers.

Apollo Client offers React hook functions to simplify the logic of view components. The two most common Apollo hook functions are `useQuery` and `useMutation`, and they are the primary way of using Apollo Client with React. In fact, if we change the code to use them, we will not need the `query`/`mutate` methods that we have so far.

To be able to use these hook functions in components, we have to wrap the components tree with a *provider* component. The provider component concept is simple: you supply a provider component with an object, and it makes that object available to all the children components in the components tree it wraps.

Inspect the code in web/src/index.js, and see how it uses a `Provider` component to make the global store available in children components. Components do not generally use the store object directly but rather methods that have access to it (through React's context). Examples of such methods in the current store are `useLocalAppState`, `setLocalAppState`, and `AppLink`.

Apollo Client's provider component works in a similar way. You make the `client` instance (which is becoming our new app state store) the provided context value. Children components can then use the hook functions (like `useQuery`) to access and modify Apollo Client's state (the cache).

React supports having multiple provider wrappers (that provide different contexts). To make the changes minimal for this first step of using Apollo hooks, let's wrap the components tree as is with the Apollo provider component.

First, let's remove the `query` and `mutate` methods from the store and expose the `client` instance object instead.

**Listing 10.14    Changes in web/src/store.js**

```
// .-.-.
export const useStoreObject = () => {
  // .-.-.

  const authLink = setContext((_, { headers }) => {
    // .-.-.
  });

  client.setLink(authLink.concat(httpLink));

  // Remove query/mutate methods

  return {
    useLocalAppState,
    setLocalAppState,
    AppLink,
    client,
  };
};
```

**NOTE**  Remember, the Apollo Client object still has to be bound to the current local app state store (to access the user state and include the current authToken value). Later in this chapter, we will see how to manage the app state through Apollo Client itself to simplify the code and use only one global context object.

Apollo exports the ApolloProvider component that can be used to make the client instance available to all children components. Here are the changes in web/src/index.js to define and use ApolloProvider.

**Listing 10.15    Changes in web/src/index.js**

```
// .-.-.
import { ApolloProvider } from '@apollo/client';

import { useStoreObject, Provider as StoreProvider } from './store';
import Root from './components/Root';

export default function App() {
  const store = useStoreObject();
  return (
    <ApolloProvider client={store.client}>
      <StoreProvider value={store}>
        <Root />
      </StoreProvider>
    </ApolloProvider>
  );
}

ReactDOM.render(<App />, document.getElementById('root'));
```

Note that I renamed the previous `Provider` component `StoreProvider` because it's no longer "the" provider. More-specific names are better.

With the `client` instance object available to all components, we can now use Apollo hooks everywhere in the components tree. Let's start with the `Home` component.

Here are the changes that I made to that component to make it use the `useQuery` hook function.

**Listing 10.16   Changes in web/src/components/Home.js**

**Invokes the query operation, and returns the**
**GraphQL response object and loading state**

```
import React from 'react';
import { gql, useQuery } from '@apollo/client';

import Search from './Search';
import TaskSummary, { TASK_SUMMARY_FRAGMENT } from './TaskSummary';
// -----

export default function Home() {
  const { loading, data } = useQuery(TASK_MAIN_LIST);

  if (loading) {
    return <div className="loading">Loading...</div>;
  }

  return (
    <div>
      <Search />
      <div>
        <h1>Latest</h1>
        {data.taskMainList.map((task) => (
          <TaskSummary key={task.id} task={task} link={true} />
        ))}
      </div>
    </div>
  );
}
```

While the query is pending, the UI can show an indicator. When the query operation is finished, React rerenders the component, and Apollo sets loading to false.

How simple and nice is that? Look at the output of `git diff` on this change to see what we're able to replace (figure 10.6).

The simple `useQuery` hook function enabled us to replace the `useState` and `useEffect` React hook functions, which were previously used to manually do the data fetching and manage the request status. This is now all done internally in Apollo Client.

The `loading` variable is a Boolean value that Apollo sets to `true` while the network data request is pending. `useQuery` also returns an `error` variable, which holds any GraphQL root errors or network errors. Your UIs should always handle both the

```
+++ b/web/src/components/Home.js
@@ -1,7 +1,6 @@
-import React, { useState, useEffect } from 'react';
-import { gql } from '@apollo/client';
+import React from 'react';
+import { gql, useQuery } from '@apollo/client';

-import { useStore } from '../store';
 import Search from './Search';
 import TaskSummary, { TASK_SUMMARY_FRAGMENT } from './TaskSummary';

@@ -17,16 +16,9 @@ const TASK_MAIN_LIST = gql`
 `;

 export default function Home() {
-  const { query } = useStore();
-  const [ taskList, setTaskList ] = useState(null);
+  const { loading, data } = useQuery(TASK_MAIN_LIST);

-  useEffect(() => {
-    query(TASK_MAIN_LIST).then(({ data }) => {
-      setTaskList(data.taskMainList);
-    });
-  }, [query]);
-
-  if (!taskList) {
+  if (loading) {
     return <div className="loading">Loading...</div>;
   }

@@ -35,7 +27,7 @@ export default function Home() {
       <Search />
       <div>
         <h1>Latest</h1>
-        {taskList.map((task) => (
+        {data.taskMainList.map((task) => (
           <TaskSummary key={task.id} task={task} link={true} />
         ))}
```

**Figure 10.6**   Output of `git diff` for src/components/Home.js

`loading` and `error` states. For example, we can add another `if` statement and render an error message when the `error` variable has a value.

**Listing 10.17   Changes in web/src/components/Home.js**

```
export default function Home() {
  const { error, loading, data } = useQuery(TASK_MAIN_LIST);

  if (error) {
    return <div className="error">{error.message}</div>
  }

  if (loading) {
    return <div className="loading">Loading...</div>;
  }

  // .....
}
```

If useQuery returns an error value, that value is an object that has a message property describing the errors.

**TIP** When it comes to handling errors in the UI, you should try to make the error branch as close as possible to the data associated with it. For example, the `if` statement I added in listing 10.17 blocks the entire home page, including the search box. The search box has nothing to do with any possible errors in the `TASK_MAIN_LIST` query. Try to fix that as an exercise.

This change in the `Home` component was straightforward because the replaced code was a common task that components do. We'll soon see examples of less common things to do with Apollo; but first, let's look at how to do a mutation with the `useMutation` hook function.

The `useMutation` hook function is similar to `useQuery`, but it does not send the operation right away. It returns a two-item tuple, where the first item is a function that sends the mutation operation when invoked. The second item is the mutation result (after the function is invoked).

Here's an example of how we can use both items in the returned tuple.

**Listing 10.18   Example: a `useMutation` call**

```
const [ loginUser, { error, loading, data } ] = useMutation(USER_LOGIN);
```

The `loginUser` function makes the network request when it's invoked, and it returns the GraphQL response object. For example, we can do the following to invoke `loginUser` and read the `data`/`errors` properties of its GraphQL response object.

**Listing 10.19   Example: invoking a mutation function**

```
const { data, errors } = await loginUser({
  variables: ······
});
```

Here are the changes I made to web/src/components/Login.js to make it send its mutation operation with the `useMutation` hook function.

**Listing 10.20   Changes in web/src/components/Login.js**

```
import React, { useState } from 'react';
import { gql, useMutation } from '@apollo/client';
// ······

export default function Login() {
  const { setLocalAppState } = useStore();
  const [ uiErrors, setUIErrors ] = useState();

  const [ loginUser, { error, loading } ] = useMutation(USER_LOGIN);   ◁─┐

  if (error) {
    return <div className="error">{error.message}</div>;
  }
```

Defines the mutation
operation but does
not invoke it

```
const handleLogin = async (event) => {
  event.preventDefault();
  const input = event.target.elements;
  const { data, errors: rootErrors } = await loginUser({
    variables: {
      input: {
        username: input.username.value,
        password: input.password.value,
      },
    },
  });
  if (rootErrors) {
    return setUIErrors(rootErrors);
  }
  const { errors, user, authToken } = data.userLogin;
  if (errors.length > 0) {
    return setUIErrors(errors);
  }
  // ·-·-·-·
};
// ·-·-·-·
}
```

Invokes the mutation operation and returns its GraphQL response object

Note that the changes are minimal here because the Login component does not have UI state after the mutation is successful (it simply gets unmounted).

---

**What to do with the loading state**

You should change your UIs to indicate that a request is pending. For query operations, this can be as simple as displaying a loading indicator where the data will appear. For mutations, you should at least disable the Submit button (to prevent making multiple operations with multiple clicks). I usually also make the button show a loading indicator in its label.

For example, in React, here's how you can disable a button and change its label based on a loading Boolean variable:

```
<button
  type="submit"
  disabled={loading}
>
  Save {loading && <i className="spinner">...</i>}
</button>
```

I'll change all the buttons in this project to reflect the loading state. You can see these changes in the final version at the book's GitHub repository.

---

It's now time for you to get comfortable with useQuery and useMutation. Convert the TaskPage component next. This component currently has three useState calls and one useEffect. Introducing the useQuery method can get rid of the useEffect call and one of the three useState calls. Give it a try. Here's what I ended up doing.

**Listing 10.21   Changes in web/src/components/TaskPage.js**

```
import React, { useState } from 'react';
import { gql, useQuery } from '@apollo/client';
// ------

export default function TaskPage({ taskId }) {
  const { AppLink } = useStore();
  // const [ taskInfo, setTaskInfo ] = useState(null);
  const [ showAddApproach, setShowAddApproach ] = useState(false);
  const [ highlightedApproachId, setHighlightedApproachId ] = useState();

  const { error, loading, data } = useQuery(TASK_INFO, {
    variables: { taskId },
  });

  if (error) {
    return <div className="error">{error.message}</div>;
  }

  if (loading) {
    return <div className="loading">Loading...</div>;
  }

  const { taskInfo } = data;

  const handleAddNewApproach = (newApproach) => {
    // setTaskInfo((pTask) => ({
    // ...pTask,
    // approachList: [newApproach, ...pTask.approachList],
    // }));
    setHighlightedApproachId(newApproach.id);
    setShowAddApproach(false);
  };

  return (
    // ------
  );
}
```

The remaining useState objects (showAddApproach and highlightedApproachId) manage state elements that are local to this component. Apollo usually is not used for this type of local component state. However, we will soon see how Apollo can help us get rid of the useStore call.

**NOTE** I commented out the part that handles appending a new Approach record to the list of Approaches under a Task object. Now that the Task object is managed in the Apollo cache, we will have to figure out what to do to append an Approach record to it. We'll talk about that in section 10.2.5.

**Current code**

Use git checkout 10.4 to reset your local repo to the current progress in the code.

**TIP** Another popular project named `react-query` (dev/react-query) also offers `useQuery`/`useMutation` methods. It offers the same concept of fetching and updating asynchronous data in React. The project can be used with any promise-based data request. You can use it with REST APIs, for example.

### 10.2.4 *Using the automatic cache*

Let's now redo the `Approach` component and replace the `mutate` method with `use-Mutation`. That component has one mutation to update the `voteCount` of an `Approach` object. This redo comes with a nice little surprise; but before I tell you about it, go ahead and try to do it on your own.

Here's what I did. Try to figure out what surprise I am talking about.

---

**Listing 10.22   Changes in web/src/components/Approach.js**

```javascript
import React, { useState } from 'react';
import { gql, useMutation } from '@apollo/client';

import Errors from './Errors';
// .-.-.

export default function Approach({ approach, isHighlighted }) {
  const [ uiErrors, setUIErrors ] = useState([]);
  const [ submitVote, { error, loading } ] = useMutation(APPROACH_VOTE);

  if (error) {
    return <div className="error">{error.message}</div>;
  }

  const handleVote = (direction) => async (event) => {
    event.preventDefault();
    const { data, errors: rootErrors } = await submitVote({
      variables: {
        approachId: approach.id,
        up: direction === 'UP',
      },
    });
    if (rootErrors) {
      return setUIErrors(rootErrors);
    }
    // Remove the setVoteCount call
  };

  const renderVoteButton = (direction) => (
    <button
      className="border-none"
      onClick={handleVote(direction)}
      disabled={loading}
    >
      {/* .-.-. */}
    </button>
  );
```

```
  return (
    <div className={`box highlighted-${isHighlighted}`}>
      <div className="approach">
        <div className="vote">
          {renderVoteButton('UP')}
          {approach.voteCount}
          {renderVoteButton('DOWN')}
        </div>

        {/* ······· */}
    </div>
  );
}
```

I am now always handling the error/loading states because Apollo makes that so easy. Note that I previously even skipped that part because it meant adding a new useState call. In addition to making the error, loading, and data states easy to use, Apollo also makes the code required to use them similar and often reusable.

The vote UI will now work through the Apollo Client hook functions. Verify that.

Did you find the surprise? I was able to get rid of the voteCount local state that was there to reflect the voting result in the UI. Yet the voting count still gets updated in the UI with this new code. How is it working without the local state? The answer is, once again, the cache!

Instead of the voteCount local state, I made the UI use approach.voteCount directly. Since the id and voteCount fields are included in the mutation data (and remember, Apollo auto-adds the __typename field as well), when this mutation's data is received, Apollo uses the unique approach:id identifier to update the identified Approach object. I didn't use the data part of this mutation in the component's code, but under the hood, Apollo Client did!

> **TIP** You can test this cache update by removing the id or voteCount field (or both of them) from the mutation result. If you do that, the vote count UI will not be updated.

Automatically updated cache is great, but often we need to manually update the cache after a mutation operation. Let's take a look at that next.

### 10.2.5 *Manually updating the cache*

The Apollo cache is not automatically updated when a mutation modifies multiple objects or when it creates or deletes objects. It only gets updated when the mutation updates a single object.

In this application, we have a mutation operation that creates a new Approach object (in the NewApproach component). Apollo will not automatically update its cache for this operation.

The code I commented out in the TaskPage component (listing 10.22) manually appends a newly created Approach object to a local state element it manages for that purpose.

Since all the Approach objects under a Task object are now managed in Apollo's cache, instead of using a state element to append a new Approach object, we have to update Apollo's cache to append a new Approach object in memory.

We can update the cache in either the NewApproach or TaskPage component. The useMutation hook function accepts an update function (as a property of its second object argument), and it invokes that function after a mutation operation is successful. That update function receives the cache object and the results object for the mutation operation. For example, here's how that update function can be used with the APPROACH_CREATE mutation.

---

**Listing 10.23   Example: using the update callback after a mutation**

```
// .-.--.
export default function NewApproach({ taskId, onSuccess }) {
  // .-.--.

  const [ createApproach, { error, loading } ] = useMutation(
    APPROACH_CREATE,
    {
      update(cache, { data: { approachCreate } }) {
        if (approachCreate.approach) {
          // Modify the cache for Task (ID: taskId)
          // and append the new approachCreate.approach record }
        },
      },
    );

  useEffect(() => {
    // .-.--.
  }, [detailCategories, query]);

  // .-.--.
}
```

---

Apollo's cache object manages data using the query operations that resolved that data. It provides methods like readQuery, writeQuery, and modify to interact with cached data. For this example, we need to use the cache.modify method. Here is an example of its basic usage.

---

**Listing 10.24   Example: the cache.modify method**

```
cache.modify({
  id: cache.identify(object),
  fields: {
    fieldName(fieldValue) {
      return newFieldValue
    },
  },
});
```

The object whose cached data you need to modify. In the current example, that is the taskInfo object in the Task component. The cache.identify method returns the Apollo global ID for the object (for example, "Task:2").

A list of functions, one for each field that needs to be modified. Each field function takes the current field value as an argument and returns the new value for that field. In the current example, that is the approachList field.

Since the cache.modify function needs to use the taskInfo object from the TaskPage component, let's redesign the handleAddNewApproach function to receive a callback function (instead of the new Approach record) and call that callback function, passing in the taskInfo object. Let's also return the newly created Approach ID value from that same callback function so that we can use it to highlight the Approach.

---

**Listing 10.25   Changes in web/src/components/TaskPage.js**

```
export default function TaskPage({ taskId }) {
  const { AppLink } = useStore();
  const [ showAddApproach, setShowAddApproach ] = useState(false);
  const [
    highlightedApproachId,
    setHighlightedApproachId,
  ] = useState();

  // .----.

  const { taskInfo } = data;

  const handleAddNewApproach = (addNewApproach) => {
    const newApproachId = addNewApproach(taskInfo);
    setHighlightedApproachId(newApproachId);
    setShowAddApproach(false);
  };

  // .----.

}
```

> **Callback method that will update the cache using the taskInfo object that's already defined**

The handleAddNewApproach function is passed to the NewApproach component as onSuccess. That is a higher-order function that receives a function as its only argument. Here's how the new onSuccess function needs to be called.

---

**Listing 10.26   Example: how to call the new onSuccess function**

```
onSuccess((taskInfo) => {
  // Do something with taskInfo
  // return the new Approach ID value
});
```

Furthermore, the NewApproach component has two GraphQL operations: a query to load the detail categories (similar to previous query examples) and a mutation to create an Approach object (which is where we need to update the cache). Here are all the changes I made to the NewApproach component to make it issue both operations and then use the update function option (in useMutation) to modify the cache and account for the newly created Approach record.

**Listing 10.27   Changes in web/src/components/NewApproach.js**

```js
import React, { useState } from 'react';
import { gql, useQuery, useMutation } from '@apollo/client';
// .-.-.

export default function NewApproach({ taskId, onSuccess }) {
  const { useLocalAppState } = useStore();
  const [ detailRows, setDetailRows ] = useState([0]);
  const [ uiErrors, setUIErrors ] = useState([]);
  const user = useLocalAppState('user');

  const { error: dcError, loading: dcLoading, data } = useQuery(
    DETAIL_CATEGORIES,
  );

  const [ createApproach, { error, loading } ] = useMutation(
    APPROACH_CREATE,
    {
      update(cache, { data: { approachCreate } }) {
        if (approachCreate.approach) {
          onSuccess((taskInfo) => {
            cache.modify({
              id: cache.identify(taskInfo),        // Gets the Apollo ID of the
              fields: {                            // taskInfo object that needs
                approachList(currentList) {        // to be updated in the cache
                  return [approachCreate.approach, ...currentList];
                },                                 // Modifies the approachList
              },                                   // field and prepends the new
            });                                    // Approach object
            return approachCreate.approach.id;
          });
        }
      },
    },
  );

  if (dcLoading) {
    return <div className="loading">Loading...</div>;
  }
  if (dcError || error) {
    return <div className="error">{(dcError || error).message}</div>;
  }
  const detailCategories = data.detailCategories.enumValues;

  // .-.-.

  const handleNewApproachSubmit = async (event) => {
    // .-.-.
    const { data, errors: rootErrors } = await createApproach({
      variables: {
        // .-.-.
      },
    });
    if (rootErrors) {
```

```
    return setUIErrors(rootErrors);
  }
  const { errors } = data.approachCreate;
  if (errors.length > 0) {
    return setUIErrors(errors);
  }
  // No data handling here. It's all done in the update function
};

// ....
}
```

**TIP** This component needs to handle the loading/error state for two GraphQL operations. That's not ideal. You should really try to have one main operation per UI component. Try to split the NewApproach component into two: one to fetch the DETAIL_CATEGORIES query and one to invoke the APPROACH_CREATE mutation.

---

**Other cache functions**

The readQuery and writeQuery functions interact with cached data that's associated with a certain query (and variable values, if any). You pass them the query (for example, TASK_INFO) and its variables, if any (for example, taskId). You can read the current cached data for that query and modify it as well. These functions are also available on the client instance object (defined in web/src/store.js).

Apollo Client also has the readFragment and writeFragment functions that work similarly but with fragments. Depending on the type of cached objects that have to be updated, working with fragments is often simpler.

---

**TIP** If you need to use the client instance object in a component, you can import the useApolloClient hook function from @apollo/client.

---

**Current code**

Use git checkout 10.5 to reset your local repo to the current progress in the code.

---

**TIP** Be careful with the cache.modify method, as the cached data in Apollo might get out of sync with what's displayed in the browser. You might be trying to modify data that is no longer in the cache! The method returns a Boolean to indicate whether the modification was successful.

### 10.2.6 *Performing operations conditionally*

Let's convert the Search component code to use Apollo hooks. There is a new challenge: the query has to be sent conditionally only when the component has a value in the searchTerm prop. How do we make that work with useQuery?

If we just replace the `query` function with a `useQuery` hook and get rid of the `useEffect` hook, the code will look like this.

Listing 10.28   Changes in web/src/components/Search.js

```
import React from 'react';
import { gql, useQuery } from '@apollo/client';
// ------.

export default function Search({ searchTerm = null }) {
  const { setLocalAppState, AppLink } = useStore();
  const { error, loading, data } = useQuery(SEARCH_RESULTS, {
    variables: { searchTerm },
  });

  if (error) {
    return <div className="error">{error.message}</div>;
  }

  const handleSearchSubmit = async (event) => {
    // ------.
  };

  return (
    <div>
      {/* ------ */}
      {data && data.searchResults && (
        <div>
          <h2>Search Results</h2>
          <div className="y-spaced">
            {data.searchResults.length === 0 && (
              <div className="box box-primary">No results</div>
            )}
            {data.searchResults.map((item, index) => (
              <div key={index} className="box box-primary">
                {/* ------ */}
              </div>
            ))}
          </div>
          <AppLink to="Home">{'<'} Home</AppLink>
        </div>
      )}
    </div>
  );
}
```

However, that will send the query operation request with a null value for `searchTerm` every time this component renders (figure 10.7). This component renders as part of the home page (to display the search form). So yeah, that will not work.

Unfortunately, we cannot put the `useQuery` call in an `if` statement. That's a React requirement for using hooks (see az.dev/rules-of-hooks).

We can solve this problem in a few different ways, which we'll explore next.

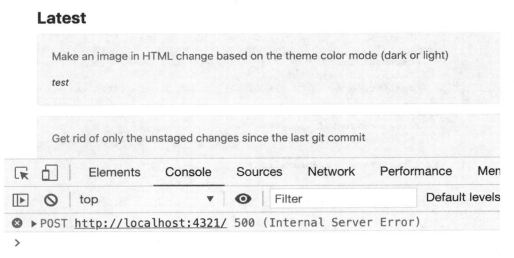

AZdev

Response not successful: Received status code 500

## Latest

Make an image in HTML change based on the theme color mode (dark or light)

*test*

Get rid of only the unstaged changes since the last git commit

| ⌖ 🔲 | Elements | Console | Sources | Network | Performance | Men |

| ▶ ⊘ | top ▼ | 👁 | Filter | Default levels |

⊗ ▶ POST http://localhost:4321/ 500 (Internal Server Error)

>

**Figure 10.7   The null `searchTerm` problem**

### USING THE SKIP OPTION

Apollo's `useQuery` method supports a `skip` Boolean option. A true `skip` value makes Apollo not send the query operation. That's exactly what we need.

---

**Listing 10.29   Example: skipping a `useQuery` operation**

```
import React from 'react';
import { gql, useQuery } from '@apollo/client';
// ·-·-·

export default function Search({ searchTerm = null }) {
  const { setLocalAppState, AppLink } = useStore();
  const { error, loading, data } = useQuery(SEARCH_RESULTS, {
    variables: { searchTerm },
    skip: !searchTerm,              ⟵——— Performs the query only
  });                                     when there is a searchTerm

  // ·-·-·
}
```

### USING A LAZY QUERY

Apollo Client has a `useLazyQuery` method that does not perform the query right away but rather gives you a function to perform the query (similar to how `useMutation` works). This means we can keep the `useEffect` hook function and invoke the lazy query function in it.

**Listing 10.30   Example: using a lazy query**

```
import React from 'react';
import { gql, useLazyQuery } from '@apollo/client';
// .-.-.

export default function Search({ searchTerm = null }) {
  const { setLocalAppState, AppLink } = useStore();
  const [
    performSearch,
      { error, loading, data },
  ] = useLazyQuery(SEARCH_RESULTS, { variables: { searchTerm } });

  useEffect(() => {
    if (searchTerm) {
      performSearch();
    }
  }, [searchTerm, performSearch]);

  if (error) {
    return <div className="error">{error.message}</div>;
  }

  // .-.-.
}
```

I like this solution a little bit better than the first one. I think it's more flexible and easier to work with. However, these solutions (and the original code) are not ideal. I designed them that way to show you the powerful features of Apollo Client; but if you find yourself needing to use a lazy query or skip a query, I would like you to first ask yourself if the problem can be fixed by reorganizing your components using the single-responsibility principle (or other clean code principles).

#### USING THE SINGLE-RESPONSIBILITY PRINCIPLE

The problem with the Search component is that it has two responsibilities. It renders a search form and search results. That violates the single-responsibility principle. A component should do only one thing.

By simply extracting the search-results part into a new conditionally rendered component, the empty-search problem goes away.

**Listing 10.31   Changes in web/src/components/Search.js**

```
function SearchResults({ searchTerm }) {
  const { AppLink } = useStore();
  const { error, loading, data } = useQuery(SEARCH_RESULTS, {
    variables: { searchTerm },
  });

  if (error) {
    return <div className="error">{error.message}</div>;
  }
```

```
    if (loading) {
      return <div className="loading">Loading...</div>;
    }

    return (
      <div>
        {data.searchResults && (
          {/* ·-·-· */} )}
      </div>
    );
}

export default function Search({ searchTerm = null }) {
  const { setLocalAppState } = useStore();

  const handleSearchSubmit = async (event) => {
    event.preventDefault();
    const term = event.target.search.value;
    setLocalAppState({
      component: { name: 'Search', props: { searchTerm: term } },
    });
  };

  return (
    <div>
      <div className="main-container">
        <form method="post" onSubmit={handleSearchSubmit}>
          {/* ·-·-· */}
        </form>
      </div>
      {searchTerm && <SearchResults searchTerm={searchTerm} />}
    </div>
  );
}
```

Because the new `SearchResults` component is rendered only when there is a `search-Term`, we can use the `useQuery` function to fetch its data. To put this solution in other words, we simply made the condition whether to render a component instead of whether to make a query request.

> **TIP** I kept the split simple in this example, but I would go so far as using three components here: one for the search form, one for the search results, and one for the search page (which renders the other two).

As an exercise, convert the rest of the components to use Apollo hook functions everywhere, and test all your changes. You need to change the `Signup`, `MyTasks`, and `New-Task` components. Compare your changes with Git branch 10.6 in the repo, which has the code after I made all the conversions.

**Current code**

Use `git checkout 10.6` to reset your local repo to the current progress in the code.

**Challenge**

Test the signup form for the duplicate username address again. Apollo Client's default error policy treats the GraphQL root errors array as network errors (and ignores any partial data). It just throws the error. You can change that behavior by specifying an `errorPolicy` string value in the operation options object (the second argument of hook functions). If you specify `errorPolicy` as `"all"`, Apollo Client will keep the GraphQL root errors array as is for your UI to handle. You can access it with `error.graphQLErrors`.

You'll also have to remove the generic `error` object `if` statement and move the handling of it to the `Errors` component.

## 10.3   *Managing local app state*

One of my favorite Apollo Client features is how it can be used to manage the local app state of an application. The word *local* here does not mean local to a single component. It's a label for the state data that is not associated with remote data.

We have already been using Apollo to manage the app state. The difference about the local app state we are going to implement in this section is that it will not be associated with a server (remote) query. Instead, it will be associated with a local query, as we will see soon.

In the AZdev application, we have two local app state elements: the current `user` and `component` objects. The entire context object in web/src/store.js is there to manage these two elements. Let's see how Apollo Client can help us get rid of that context object.

> **TIP**   The current local app state in the app is managed with a `useState` call in web/src/store.js. The new state will be managed externally to the React application. When the state is managed externally, React components that need to use that state have to subscribe to it (to be notified when the external state is changed). The `useQuery` method is a form of subscribing since it will cause a React component function to render when the Apollo cache store has any new data for that query.

The local app state management in Apollo uses the `writeQuery` method to put local app state element values in the cache. However, `writeQuery` needs a query, and the local app state has no such query. In Apollo, we just make up a fake query for it.

You can come up with any GraphQL query (regardless of the server schema) and tell Apollo that you'd like to use that query only on the client side. You can do that for a whole query or part of an existing query. You put the @client directive on any field in a query to tell Apollo that it's a client-only field that does not need to be fetched from the server.

So, let's do that for the user and component local state elements. Here's the query I made up for them. Put this in web/src/store.js.

```
import {
  ApolloClient,
  HttpLink,
  InMemoryCache,
  gql,
} from '@apollo/client';
// ...
export const LOCAL_APP_STATE = gql`
  query localAppState {
    component @client {        ◁──┐  Note the @client directive,
      name                         │  which tells Apollo that this
      props                        │  query is client-only and should
    }                              │  not be sent to the server.
    user @client {            ◁──┘
      username
      authToken
    }
  }
`;
```

Because all the fields in this query have the @client directive, Apollo will not send this entire query to the server. When we use the query in the app, Apollo will read it directly from the cache.

Note that I matched the structure the app uses for these elements in their made-up local app state query. This will keep the changes in the app to a minimum.

> **TIP** I like to keep local queries separate from the normal, remote queries. However, you can mix client-only fields with normal fields, and Apollo will split your mixed query, manage the local part locally, and send the remote part to the server.

Now we can use Apollo to read and update the query. For example, in places where we previously used state.user in the store, we can now read it from the cache.

Listing 10.33    Example: readQuery replacing the state object

```
const { user } = cache.readQuery({ query: LOCAL_APP_STATE });
```

To update the user/component objects, instead of the current setState calls in the store, we can do the following.

**Listing 10.34   Example: `writeQuery` replacing the `setState` calls**

```
cache.writeQuery({
  query: LOCAL_APP_STATE,
  data: { ...currentState, ...newState },
})
```

Since the local app state will be managed entirely with the `client` instance object, that object is now the new store of the application. We don't need the `useStoreObject` function (or its `useStore` hook). We can just define all functions as top-level exports and import them directly in components. This includes the `authLink` function, which we previously put inside `useStoreObject` so that it can access the current user `authToken`.

To make things a bit more interesting, let's keep the code in all React components as is and try to replace React's context-based local app state management with Apollo Client local app state management. This means we can only change the starting-point file (web/src/index.js) and the store file (web/src/store.js).

Let's begin with the `Provider` components. We can get rid of the `StoreProvider` context; we don't need it anymore. Let's also move the client initialization code to the project starting file and leave only local app state management in web/src/store.js. This way, the local app state methods can be extracted and used across different projects and with different client instances (instead of relying on the same scope client instance).

Here's the first step in converting the code in web/src/index.js.

**Listing 10.35   New code in web/src/index.js**

```
import 'regenerator-runtime/runtime';
import React from 'react';
import ReactDOM from 'react-dom';
import {
  ApolloProvider,
  ApolloClient,
  HttpLink,
  InMemoryCache,
} from '@apollo/client';
import { setContext } from '@apollo/link-context';

import * as config from './config';
import Root from './components/Root';

const httpLink = new HttpLink({ uri: config.GRAPHQL_SERVER_URL });     Move these lines out of
const cache = new InMemoryCache();                                     web/src/store.js (as is).
const client = new ApolloClient({ link: httpLink, cache });

export default function App() {
  return (
    <ApolloProvider client={client}>
      <Root />          ◄──────── No more nested providers!
    </ApolloProvider>
```

```
  );
}

ReactDOM.render(<App />, document.getElementById('root'));
```

I didn't do anything new here yet. I just moved a few things around and got rid of the `StoreProvider` and `useStore` calls. The interesting part is how to define the `authLink` function that causes the headers to include the `authToken` of a logged-in user.

The `authLink` function previously accessed the `state.user` object directly. Now it can read that state out of the Apollo cache.

---

**Listing 10.36  Changes in web/src/index.js**

```
// .-.--.
const authLink = setContext((_, { headers }) => {        ◁──┐  Move
  const { user } = client.readQuery({ query: LOCAL_APP_STATE });    authLink out of
  return {                                                          web/src/store.js.
    headers: {
      ...headers,
      authorization: user ? `Bearer ${user.authToken}` : '',
    },
  };
});

const client = new ApolloClient({
  link: authLink.concat(httpLink),
  cache,
});
// .-.--.
```

Note that we no longer need to use the `setLink` method since the `authLink` function no longer depends on another function scope. We can define the Apollo client object directly with the link chain.

The last change we need to make in this file is to initialize the local app state. That was previously done in `useStoreObject`, but now we can use a `writeQuery` call.

---

**Listing 10.37  Changes in web/src/index.js**

```
// .-.--.
import { LOCAL_APP_STATE } from './store';    ◁──┐  New client-only query
// .-.--.                                            defined in listing 10.32

const client = new ApolloClient({
  link: authLink.concat(httpLink),
  cache,
});                                          ┌── Move initialLocalAppState out
const initialLocalAppState = {           ◁──┘   of web/src/store.js (as is).
  component: { name: 'Home', props: {} },
  user: JSON.parse(window.localStorage.getItem('azdev:user')),
};
```

```
client.writeQuery({
  query: LOCAL_APP_STATE,
  data: initialLocalAppState,
});
```
> New way to update
> the local app state

```
export default function App() {
  // .-.-.
}
```

Now, what remains to be changed in web/src/store.js are the three functions that work with the local app state: useLocalAppState, setLocalAppState, and the AppLink component. We'll keep these three functions in a useStore function so that we don't need to make any changes in the React components.

Let's go through these three functions one at a time, starting with useLocal-AppState. Here is its new implementation.

**Listing 10.38    Changes in web/src/store.js**

```
// .-.-.
import { useQuery, gql } from '@apollo/client';
// .-.-.
export const useStore = () => {
  // .-.-.

  const useLocalAppState = (...stateMapper) => {
    const { data } = useQuery(LOCAL_APP_STATE);      ◁──  This line is what
    if (stateMapper.length === 1) {                       fundamentally changed
      return data[stateMapper[0]];                        in this function.
    }
    return stateMapper.map((element) => data[element]);
  };

  // .-.-.
};
```

We just read the LOCAL_APP_STATE data with the useQuery hook function. That query's data becomes the local app state.

The setLocalAppState method is a bit more complicated. It needs to read and write to the cache and reset it when the user logs in or out, but without losing the new local app state (which now needs to go on that cache).

Here's one way to implement that.

**Listing 10.39    Changes in web/src/store.js**

```
// .-.-.
import { useApolloClient, useQuery, gql } from '@apollo/client';
// .-.-.
export const useStore = () => {
  // Delete the useState line
  const client = useApolloClient();
```

```
// -----

const setLocalAppState = (newState) => {
  if (newState.component) {
    newState.component.props = newState.component.props ?? {};
  }
  const currentState = client.readQuery({
    query: LOCAL_APP_STATE,
  });
  const updateState = () => {
    client.writeQuery({
      query: LOCAL_APP_STATE,
      data: { ...currentState, ...newState },
    });
  };
  if (newState.user || newState.user === null) {
    client.onResetStore(updateState);
    client.resetStore();
  } else {
    updateState();
  }
};

const AppLink = ({ children, to, ...props }) => {
  // -----
};

return {
  useLocalAppState,
  setLocalAppState,
  AppLink,
};
};
// Delete the React Context lines
```

**Reads local app state from the Apollo cache directly with readQuery**

**Updates the local app state in the Apollo cache directly with writeQuery**

**The resetStore call removes all local app state data. We need to update the local app state query when that happens. onResetStore enables us to define a callback function to be invoked after the store is reset.**

**The AppLink implementation is the same.**

That's it. All the UIs work exactly the same with these changes, but now we do all the local app state management through the Apollo Client. This is simpler than what we had before. We no longer manage a context object or any custom hooks to access it.

**TIP** I use the readQuery method where I need to read the data just once (and not subscribe to it). However, in React components, the useQuery hook function should be used to read the local app state. With useQuery, components will be rerendered when the local app state changes. This is why I made the useLocalAppState function use the useQuery hook function; because of that, components that use this function will be rerendered when the local app state changes.

I hope this little example demonstrated how powerful Apollo local app state management is, but we have barely scratched the surface. There is a lot more.

For bigger local state trees, you can write custom resolvers for your local app state elements. You can also define local mutations and use them with the useMutation methods instead of doing direct writes. Another thing you get with custom resolvers is data type validation (because you define the types for arguments and input). Check out jscomplete.com/apollo for more examples of the powerful features of Apollo Client.

> **Current code**
> Use `git checkout 10.7` to reset your local repo to the current progress in the code.

## 10.4 *Implementing and using GraphQL subscriptions*

I saved the best for last! Let's take a look at how to define and use GraphQL subscriptions.

Subscriptions are extremely useful when you need your UIs to autoupdate. For example, while looking at the list of Tasks on the home page, we planned to notify the user when new Task records are available—just like the way Twitter notifies you when there are new tweets on your timeline.

### 10.4.1 *Polling and refetching*

To implement such a feature, you have two options:

- Make your app continuously ask the server about the list of Tasks.
- Make your app tell the server that it is interested in new Tasks and would like to be notified when they are created.

The second option is what GraphQL subscriptions can help you do. The first option is known as *continuous polling*, and sometimes it is good enough: if the object you're autoupdating is small and you don't need real-time updates, polling is an option to consider.

Apollo makes continuous polling easy. You add just one option to the `useQuery` second argument to make it repeatedly poll data. For example, we can update the list of Task records on the home page every five seconds using the following simple change.

> **Listing 10.40    Example: using `pollInterval`**

```
export default function Home() {
  const { error, loading, data } = useQuery(TASK_MAIN_LIST, {
    pollInterval: 5000,
  });

  // ......
}
```

That's it! Now the list will be autoupdated every five seconds.

**TIP** Test this by opening two browsers and creating a Task record in one while looking at the home page in the other.

In some cases, you can do the refetching manually instead of automatically in a polling loop. If you want Apollo to fetch the query again on demand (for example, when the user clicks a Refresh button), you can use the `refetch` function, which Apollo makes available to all `useQuery` results. Here's an example.

**Listing 10.41 Example: refetching a query on demand**

```
export default function Home() {
  const { error, loading, refetch, data } = useQuery(TASK_MAIN_LIST);

  // ·—·—·

  return (
    <div>
      <Search />
      <div>
        <h1>Latest</h1>
        <button onClick={() => refetch()}>Refresh</button>
        {/* ·—·—· */}
      </div>
    </div>
  );
}
```

This code makes Apollo fetch the same query again when the user clicks the Refresh button.

These options inefficiently fetch the entire list of the latest Task records. GraphQL subscriptions are a much more efficient option for getting new data from an API server. Undo all the polling/refetching changes, and let's autoupdate this list with a subscription operation.

---

**The fetchPolicy option**

If you want Apollo to ignore the cache and always fetch the query when the component rerenders, you can change the `fetchPolicy` option like this:

```
export default function Home() {
  const { error, loading, data } = useQuery(TASK_MAIN_LIST, {
    fetchPolicy: 'network-only',
  });

  // ·—·—·

}
```

### 10.4.2 *Implementing subscriptions*

In chapter 4, we planned two subscription operations for the AZdev API: the `task-MainListChanged` subscription to notify the user that new Task records are available and the `voteChanged` subscription to autoupdate vote counts on the Task page. However, before we start implementing them, we need to revise the API server and make it support WebSockets.

GraphQL subscriptions for web apps are usually done over the WebSockets communication protocol. A WebSocket provides a full-duplex communication channel (over a single TCP connection). The server opens the socket, and the browser connects to it and keeps the connection active. Servers can then use that active connection to push new data to the browser on demand.

The Express-based GraphQL server that we have used so far has no support for WebSockets. We need to run a new server (on a different port) for all subscription operations. There are many options for web servers that support a WebSocket transport layer designed for GraphQL subscriptions, but the most popular is Apollo Server (az.dev/apollo-server).

> **TIP** Apollo Server has many cool features, and it can completely replace our current Express-based server. Let's first see how to use its WebSocket support. When we're finished with the subscription example, we will get rid of the Express-based server and use Apollo Server as our main GraphQL API server.

Start by installing the `apollo-server` package.

---

**Listing 10.42   Command: installing the Apollo Server package**

```
$ npm install apollo-server
```

Then make the following changes to api/src/server.js to create an Apollo server instance that works with our schema.

---

**Listing 10.43   Changes in api/src/server.js**

```
import { ApolloServer } from 'apollo-server';
// .-.-.

async function main() {
  // .-.-.

  server.listen(config.port, () => {
    console.log(`API server is running on port ${config.port}`);
  });

  const serverWS = new ApolloServer({ schema });

  serverWS.listen({ port: 4000 }).then(({ subscriptionsUrl }) => {
    console.log(`Subscriptions URL: ${subscriptionsUrl}`);
```

```
    });
};

main();
```

This will run a web-socket server on port 4000.

> **NOTE** Keep the Express-based server running on port 4321 for now. It is still the main web server for the API service.

The implementation of subscription operations relies on the Pub/Sub pattern (short for Publish/Subscribe). Pub/Sub is a simple messaging pattern designed to decouple data events from services that are interested in them. You can label any change to data in your code with an event label. For example, when a new Task record is created, we can have the code publish an event; and when a vote count on any Approach record is changed, we can have the code publish another event.

Apollo server has a built-in `PubSub` implementation that we can use to do exactly that. Since the Pub/Sub operations will happen in multiple places, let's create a new file under api/src/pubsub.js to prepare a `PubSub` instance for any part of the API server code to use.

**Listing 10.44   New file: api/src/pubsub.js**

```
import { PubSub } from 'apollo-server';

const pubsub = new PubSub();

export { pubsub };
```

Now, let's publish events in the mutations related to the subscriptions we're implementing. We can use a `pubsub.publish` call to do that. We can include data as part of any published event, and that data can be used to make the subscription resolvers aware of the new mutation data.

We need to publish two events: one in the `taskCreate` mutation field to be used by the `taskMainListChanged` subscription, and one in the `approachVote` mutation field to be used by the `voteChanged` subscription. Here are the changes in api/src/schema/mutations.js to publish these events.

**Listing 10.45   Changes in api/src/schema/mutations.js**

```
import { pubsub } from '../pubsub';
// -------
const MutationType = new GraphQLObjectType({
  name: 'Mutation',
  fields: () => ({
    // -------
    taskCreate: {
      type: TaskPayload,
```

```
        args: {
          input: { type: new GraphQLNonNull(TaskInput) },
        },
        resolve: async (
          source,
          { input },
          { mutators, currentUser },
        ) => {
          const { errors, task } = await mutators.taskCreate({
            input,
            currentUser,
          });
          if (errors.length === 0 && !task.isPrivate) {
            pubsub.publish(`TASK_MAIN_LIST_CHANGED`, {
              newTask: task,
            });
          }
          return { errors, task };
        },
      },

      // .-.--.

      approachVote: {
        // .-.--.
        resolve: async (
          source,
          { approachId, input },
          { mutators },
        ) => {
          const { errors, approach } = await mutators.approachVote({
            approachId,
            input,
          });
          if (errors.length === 0) {
            pubsub.publish(`VOTE_CHANGED_${approach.taskId}`, {
              updatedApproach: approach,
            });
          }
          return { errors, approach };
        },
      },
    }),
  });
```

This is a general event, but it is published only if the Task object is not "private."

**Event payload. You can put any kind of data in here.**

Example of a dynamic event label. It can be used with a subscription operation that depends on a variable. The voteChanged subscription depends on the taskId variable. It's not a general subscription like taskMainListChanged.

You can give your event labels any names you want. I like to make them match the subscription operations they serve.

**TIP**  You should put your event labels in variables and use the variables in the code instead of using strings directly. Code editors will be more helpful when you use that approach. For example, they will alert you if you use an incorrect variable name, but they cannot alert you if you use an incorrect string value. See AZdev's official repo (az.dev/contribute) for examples of this practice.

Any part of the API server code can subscribe to the events being published and, for example, send their payload data over a WebSocket. That's exactly what a field under the Subscription type can now do.

Let's first look at the taskMainListChanged subscription. Here's one way to define it.

##### Listing 10.46   New file: api/src/schema/subscriptions.js

```
import { GraphQLNonNull, GraphQLObjectType } from 'graphql';

import { pubsub } from '../pubsub';
import Task from './types/task';

const SubscriptionType = new GraphQLObjectType({
  name: 'Subscription',
  fields: () => ({
    taskMainListChanged: {
      type: new GraphQLNonNull(Task),
      resolve: async (source) => {
        return source.newTask;         ⟵─── Event to subscribe to
      },
      subscribe: async () => {
        return pubsub.asyncIterator(['TASK_MAIN_LIST_CHANGED']);   ⟵───┐
      },                                                               │
    },                                          The source argument here will
  }),                                           have the event's payload data.
});

export default SubscriptionType;
```

To make this new subscription field available in the schema, we have to make it part of the GraphQLSchema object we defined in api/src/schema/index.js.

##### Listing 10.47   Changes in api/src/schema/index.js

```
// ------
import SubscriptionType from './subscriptions';

export const schema = new GraphQLSchema({
  query: QueryType,
  mutation: MutationType,
  subscription: SubscriptionType,
});

console.log(printSchema(schema));
```

We can now test the taskMainListChanged subscription field. However, to do that, we need a consumer that also supports WebSockets. You send the subscription operation to establish the connection and then send a mutation operation to trigger the event and see the data reported back by the WebSocket.

An Apollo server instance will make the GraphQL Playground editor available at /graphql by default (in the development environment). GraphQL Playground is a GraphiQL-based editor that supports WebSockets and has many more cool features.

To test the `taskMainListChanged` mutation, open the GraphQL Playground editor at http://localhost:4000/graphql and run the following operation.

---

**Listing 10.48    The `taskMainListChanged` subscription**

```
subscription {
  taskMainListChanged {
    id
    content
  }
}
```

You'll notice that no data is returned initially. Instead, the GraphQL Playground displays a "Listening" message reflecting the status of this subscription field resolver function, which is listening for any Pub/Sub events (figure 10.8).

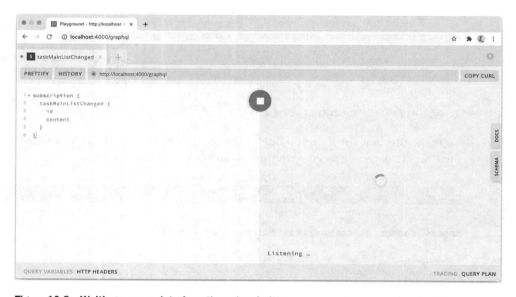

**Figure 10.8    Waiting on new data from the subscription**

**TIP**    The GraphQL playground has a default dark theme. I changed it to light for the screenshots.

To trigger a Pub/Sub event publish action, open the UI app in a different browser session, log in, and create a test public Task record. The GraphQL Playground should instantly show the new Task object you create in the subscription's data response (and it will continue listening after that). Each time you create a new public Task record, it will appear in the response data (figure 10.9).

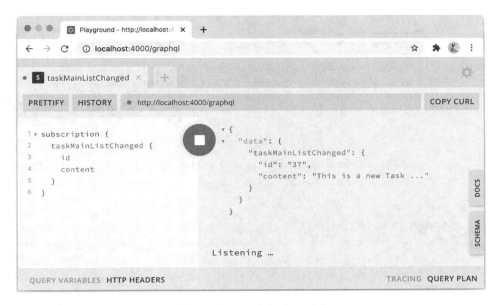

**Figure 10.9  New data from the subscription appearing in real time**

How about you try to implement the `voteChanged` subscription field on your own first? We've already added the `publish` event for it. You just need to make changes in api/src/schema/subscriptions.js. The only difference in this subscription field is that it receives a `taskId` argument, so it only subscribes to the events published for one Task object. Here's how I implemented it.

**Listing 10.49  Changes in api/src/schema/subscriptions.js**

```
import {
  GraphQLNonNull,
  GraphQLObjectType,
  GraphQLID,
} from 'graphql';

import { pubsub } from '../pubsub';
import Task from './types/task';
import Approach from './types/approach';

const SubscriptionType = new GraphQLObjectType({
  name: 'Subscription',
  fields: () => ({
    taskMainListChanged: {
      // .....
    },
    voteChanged: {
      type: new GraphQLNonNull(Approach),
      args: {
        taskId: { type: new GraphQLNonNull(GraphQLID) },
```

> **This subscription has a taskId argument.**

```
    },
    resolve: async (source) => {          ┌─ Reads the updatedApproach object
      return source.updatedApproach;   ◄──┘   from the event's payload data
    },
    subscribe: async (source, { taskId }) => {
      return pubsub.asyncIterator([`VOTE_CHANGED_${taskId}`]);   ◄─┐
    },
  },                                         Only subscribes to the VOTE_CHANGED
  }),                                        events related to the taskId argument value
});
```

Make sure this subscription works as well in the GraphQL Playground (while voting on Approaches under a Task).

> **Current code**
> Use `git checkout 10.8` to reset your local repo to the current progress in the code.

### 10.4.3 *Apollo Server*

WebSocket support is just one of the many features the `apollo-server` package has to offer. Apollo Server can actually replace many of the packages we're using server-side. It can replace GraphQL.js itself, and it supports implementing your GraphQL schema using only the SDL text (and not using objects). And as mentioned earlier, it can replace our entire Express-based server setup (everything related to Express).

> **TIP** If you're interested in learning about implementing a GraphQL service using strings instead of objects, you can find an article I wrote on that topic at az.dev/schema-first.

To replace Express with Apollo, we have to move things around a bit. We have to define the `context` property as a function. Apollo makes the `req` object available in the argument of that function. This means we can define our loaders and mutators (which depend on the `req` object) right in that context function.

Here's the new web/src/server.js file after I removed everything related to Express.js (and `express-graphql`) and modified `ApolloServer` to work with our context object.

**Listing 10.50   New code in web/src/server.js**

```
import DataLoader from 'dataloader';
import { ApolloServer } from 'apollo-server';

import { schema } from './schema';
import pgApiWrapper from './db/pg-api';
import mongoApiWrapper from './db/mongo-api';

import * as config from './config';
```

```
async function main() {
  const pgApi = await pgApiWrapper();
  const mongoApi = await mongoApiWrapper();

  const server = new ApolloServer({
    schema,
    formatError: (err) => {
      const errorReport = {
        message: err.message,
        locations: err.locations,
        stack: err.stack ? err.stack.split('\n') : [],
        path: err.path,
      };
      console.error('GraphQL Error', errorReport);
      return config.isDev
        ? errorReport
        : { message: 'Oops! Something went wrong! :(' };
    },
    context: async ({ req }) => {
      const authToken =
        req && req.headers && req.headers.authorization
          ? req.headers.authorization.slice(7) // "Bearer "
          : null;
      const currentUser = await pgApi.userFromAuthToken(authToken);
      if (authToken && !currentUser) {
        throw Error('Invalid access token');
      }
      const loaders = {
        // ......
      };
      const mutators = {
        ...pgApi.mutators,
        ...mongoApi.mutators,
      };

      return { loaders, mutators, currentUser };
    },
  });

  server
    .listen({ port: config.port })
    .then(({ url, subscriptionsUrl }) => {
      console.log(`Server URL: ${url}`);
      console.log(`Subscriptions URL: ${subscriptionsUrl}`);
    });
}

main();
```

**The loaders implementation is the same.**

This is a lot simpler. All the code related to accepting data in the request, parsing it, and then executing the GraphQL schema against that request has been deleted. That functionality is now done internally in Apollo Server.

Note that I got rid of the 4000 port and used the default config port (which is 4321). The new URLs are as follows:

```
Server URL: http://localhost:4321/
Subscriptions URL: ws://localhost:4321/graphql
```

**Current code**

Use `git checkout 10.9` to reset your local repo to the current progress in the code.

### 10.4.4   *Using subscriptions in UIs*

With all the subscription operations ready server-side, let's now talk about how to use them in a React application with Apollo Client.

Apollo Client has a `WebSocketLink` object that can be used to do WebSocket communication in the browser. It's designed to work with GraphQL subscriptions. To initialize it, you just give it the GraphQL subscription `uri` and an `options` object.

**Listing 10.51   Example: using the @apollo/link-ws package**

```
import { WebSocketLink } from "@apollo/client/link/ws";

const wsLink = new WebSocketLink({          URL to use for subscriptions
  uri: GRAPHQL_SUBSCRIPTIONS_URL, ⟵────┘
  options: { reconnect: true }, ⟵────   The reconnect option makes the link
});                                       reconnect in case of a connection error.
```

Let's define the new `GRAPHQL_SUBSCRIPTIONS_URL` config value for this project.

**Listing 10.52   Changes in web/src/config.js**

```
export const GRAPHQL_SERVER_URL =
  process.env.GRAPHQL_SERVER_URL || 'http://localhost:4321';
export const GRAPHQL_SUBSCRIPTIONS_URL =
  process.env.GRAPHQL_SUBSCRIPTIONS_URL || `ws://localhost:4321/graphql`;
```

With a `WebSocketLink` instance, we have two main links for Apollo Client to use: one to use with regular HTTP requests (`httpLink`) and another to use for WebSocket requests (`wsLink`). However, instead of making two different client objects for them, Apollo supports a `split` function that can determine which link object to use based on what GraphQL operation is being invoked.

**Listing 10.53   Changes in web/src/index.js**

```
// .-.-.
import {
  ApolloProvider,
  ApolloClient,
  HttpLink,
```

```
    InMemoryCache,
    split,
} from '@apollo/client';
import { getMainDefinition } from '@apollo/client/utilities';
import { WebSocketLink } from "@apollo/client/link/ws";
// ......
const wsLink = new WebSocketLink({
    uri: config.GRAPHQL_SUBSCRIPTIONS_URL,
    options: { reconnect: true },
});
const splitLink = split(
    ({ query }) => {
        const definition = getMainDefinition(query);
        return (
            definition.kind === 'OperationDefinition' &&
            definition.operation === 'subscription'
        );
    },
    wsLink,
    authLink.concat(httpLink),
);

const client = new ApolloClient({
    link: splitLink,
    cache,
});
```

The first argument for split is a function that receives the operation to be invoked. It should return either true or false.

getMainDefinition returns the AST of the first main operation (query, mutation, or subscription).

If the main operation is a subscription, this condition is true.

If the first argument to split returns true, the link in the second argument is used.

If the first argument to split returns false, the link in the third argument will be used. This is the link that's currently used for all regular HTTP requests.

The first argument for split is a function that receives the operation to be invoked. It should return either true or false.

Apollo Client will invoke this new `split` function for each GraphQL operation it needs to send over the wire. If the operation is a subscription, the `split` function tells Apollo Client to use `wsLink`. Otherwise, it tells Apollo Client to use `httpLink`. This enables us to work with only one client instance everywhere in the app.

That's all the setup work required to make Apollo Client ready for subscriptions. To make a React component use a subscription operation, we just invoke the `use-Subscription` hook function. For example, here's the code to make the vote counts on Approach objects update in real time.

**Listing 10.54   Changes in web/src/components/TaskPage.js**

```
import { gql, useQuery, useSubscription, } from '@apollo/client';
const VOTE_CHANGED = gql`
    subscription voteChanged($taskId: ID!) {
        voteChanged(taskId: $taskId) {
            id
            voteCount
        }
    }
`;
// ......

export default function TaskPage({ taskId }) {
    // ......
```

```
const { error, loading, data } = useQuery(TASK_INFO, {
  variables: { taskId },
});

useSubscription(VOTE_CHANGED, {
  variables: { taskId },
});

// ·····
}
```

That's it. You can test this with two browsers open on the same Task page and vote up/down on any Approach in one browser. The other browser will update in real time!

Under the hood, Apollo takes care of figuring out that this subscription is bringing updates related to an Approach record on this page. The useQuery results are auto-refreshed, causing the TaskPage component to rerender with the new vote.

Try to use the taskMainListChanged subscription on your own. The changes go in the Home component (web/src/components/Home.js). To keep things simple, when a new Task is fetched through the subscription, insert it at the top of the list and highlight it differently. I've put my solution in the next (and final!) Git branch.

### Current code
Use `git checkout 10.8` to reset your local repo to the current progress in the code.

## Summary

- A GraphQL client library like Apollo manages all the communications between a frontend application and its GraphQL API service. It issues data requests and makes their data responses available where needed.
- You can use Apollo Client with plain JavaScript or with view libraries like React, Vue, and Angular. For React, Apollo Client provides custom hook functions that greatly simplify the code in function components.
- Apollo has a powerful caching store that's designed to work with GraphQL's graph-like structure. The cache works automatically in common cases, but you can also manually read it and modify it. This cache, combined with other features in Apollo, can replace local app state management tools (like React's context or Redux).
- Apollo Client is flexible. It offers many methods to invoke queries on render, on demand, or conditionally. You can use different types of caching stores. You can modify request headers globally or per operation. You can skip queries and instruct Apollo not to cache them if needed. You can have it communicate with

multiple GraphQL services and use the same store for them. You can even use it to communicate with REST-based API services.

■ GraphQL subscriptions are great for incremental real-time data. To use subscription operations in web applications, a GraphQL server has to support Web-Sockets and a Pub/Sub messaging pattern. Apollo Server is an example of a GraphQL implementation that has that support. On the frontend, a client has to determine what communication channel to use based on the operation and use a WebSocket-based link for subscriptions.

# *Wrapping up*

We made it! We have a working product with a decent set of features. It's usable as is (but certainly far from perfect). I hope you realize now how easy it is to use a GraphQL API service (both with and without a featured client).

This is a wrap on the AZdev app features, but it's not a wrap on all the fun you're about to have making awesome things with GraphQL. You've got the skills. Now it's time to put them into action. Don't sit on this knowledge—practice and fail and practice again and again, until building GraphQL applications becomes something you can brag about and you have trophies to show (on GitHub).

I would love to see your GraphQL creations. If you use Twitter, please share them using the #GraphQLInAction hashtag (which I'll be monitoring). Writing this book was one of the hardest projects I've done. Please show me what it enabled you to build. Please tell me my efforts were worth it!

You're also welcome to come and brag about your work on the jsComplete slack channel at jscomplete.com/help. We have thousands of coders, and many will love to see your work, use it (if you wish to share it), give you feedback, and maybe even help you improve it.

Let me leave you with a few challenges that you can tackle on your own to improve the AZdev application. These challenges require changes on both ends of the AZdev stack. Don't cheat, but some of these challenges are implemented in the official AZdev repository at az.dev/contribute:

1 Display the `createdAt` field in the UI for both Tasks and Approaches, and implement a way for the list of Approaches to be sorted by date (newest first) in addition to the current vote-count order.

2 Support a Boolean flag on the search form to make the results include only Task records owned by the user who is searching.

3 Paginate the list of latest Task records on the home page. You'll need to modify the `taskMainList` field to accept a pointer pointing to the last-seen Task record and make its resolver get the set of Task records before/after that pointer. This pointer is usually named `after` or `before`, depending on which direction you're sorting before paginating. You can also make the field accept `first/`

last arguments to limit the response to a size of your choosing. You can read more about this Relay-based cursor pagination style at az.dev/gia-pagination.

4   Offer a "make private" or "make public" feature on a Task page when the user looking at that page is its owner.

5   On the search page, if a Task and some of its Approaches match the same search term, group them under the same entry in the search results. This can be done with only frontend changes, but it would be a lot more efficient if done server-side. The search-results page is another place where you can implement and use pagination, so be sure to implement your pagination's logic in a reusable way!

6   Offer a change-password feature for logged-in users. They have to provide their current password.

7   Restrict votes to one per user per Approach. A user can vote on an Approach only once. You will need to create a new database table for this feature.

8   Implement an optimistic update for the `taskCreate` mutation. Simulate a slow network to see how the app behaves. When a user on a slow network creates a Task record, make the UI show the newly created record right away (using the input values before the server response). You'll have to think about what UI change to make if the server fails to do the mutation.

9   Allow the owner of a Task record to edit and delete it.

10   Implement a way for a logged-in user to delete their AZdev account. We've prepared the API `userDelete` mutation field for that. You need to create the UI that will invoke that mutation. You also need to log out that user when the mutation call is successful.

Thank you so much for picking and sticking with this book. It means the world to me. I hope you got the value you expected out of it; if you have not, please do not hesitate to tell me. Tweet me @samerbuna (twitter.com/samerbuna) or leave me a review on Amazon (az.dev/gia-amazon).

# index

## A new online reading experience

liveBook, our online reading platform, adds a new dimension to your Manning books, with features that make reading, learning, and sharing easier than ever. A liveBook version of your book is included FREE with every Manning book.

This next generation book platform is more than an online reader. It's packed with unique features to upgrade and enhance your learning experience.

- Add your own notes and bookmarks
- One-click code copy
- Learn from other readers in the discussion forum
- Audio recordings and interactive exercises
- Read all your purchased Manning content in any browser, anytime, anywhere

As an added bonus, you can search every Manning book and video in liveBook—even ones you don't yet own. Open any liveBook, and you'll be able to browse the content and read anything you like.*

### Find out more at www.manning.com/livebook-program.

*Open reading is limited to 10 minutes per book daily